PRIDE AND PASSION

ROBERT BURNS 1759–1796

PRIDE AND PASSION
Robert Burns

1759–1796

BY

DeLancey Ferguson

'My great constituent elements are Pride and Passion.'
BURNS TO AGNES M'LEHOSE
DECEMBER 28, 1787

NEW YORK / RUSSELL & RUSSELL

FIRST PUBLISHED IN 1939
REISSUED, 1964, BY RUSSELL & RUSSELL
A DIVISION OF ATHENEUM PUBLISHERS, INC.
BY ARRANGEMENT WITH DELANCEY FERGUSON
L. C. CATALOG CARD NO: 64-18599
ISBN: 0-8462-0485-1
PRINTED IN THE UNITED STATES OF AMERICA

PREFACE

ALL witnesses agree that Robert Burns was a vivid and dynamic personality. All readers of his poetry concur. Yet somehow the personality which blazes in the poems and glows in the letters only smoulders in the biographies. Why is it so hard to write a dull life of, say, Byron, and so easy to write a dull one of Burns? For one thing, there are too many biographies, all following the same stereotyped outline of dividing the poet's life according to the places he lived in instead of according to the things he did and thought. Then really graphic memorabilia are scarce, especially for the formative years in Ayrshire. People keep saying that Burns was a brilliant talker, but they seldom report his talk. Finally, too many biographers have worked in the wrong mood, intent on moralizing or deprecating rather than interpreting.

This book is not a biography, if that word connotes a narrative written in straight time-sequence. It is, instead, my answer to the question, subordinated or ignored by most chronological biographers, What sort of a man was Robert Burns? I have therefore discarded time-sequence in favour of the relationships of everyday life in which Burns most clearly revealed his personality. The plan has at least the advantage of passing quickly over his almost undocumented youth, and concentrating attention upon his fully recorded manhood. The formal biography, whether it be Mrs. Carswell's romantic approach or Professor Snyder's scholarly one, suffers from the necessity of devoting more space to the scantily reported twenty-seven years in Ayrshire than to the five richly documented years in Dumfries. I have assumed that Burns's character can best be determined from the completest records. Perhaps to himself John Syme and Maria Riddell were not so important as Robert Muir and Margaret Chalmers, but the later friendships can be studied at full length; the earlier ones cannot. Hence I have given most space to the relationships in which guess-work can be kept to a minimum.

So, too, I have deliberately limited myself to the best authenticated sources—Burns's own letters and poems, and the letters and other records of his immediate contemporaries. Unsupported oral tradition I have avoided as basic material. Though I use such anecdotes now and again as secondary illustrations, it is always with a warning as to their nature. I have likewise tried to make clear the distinction between facts and the inferences I have drawn from them.

In one respect at least my preparation for writing about Burns is unique. Most editors and biographers have either been bred in the rosy mists of the Burns legend or have worked their way back to the original records through a mass of secondary printed matter. Up to a dozen years ago my knowledge of Burns and his times included little beyond such reading of major works and standard criticism as one does in preparation for the doctorate. In 1925 I undertook to edit a reprint of Burns's chief poems. Discovering in the course of that job how unsatisfactory were all editions of his correspondence, I thereupon plunged into the work of tracing and collating the original holographs. Not until after thorough immersion in these primary sources did I extend my studies to the letters and other records of Burns's contemporaries and to the Burns tradition embalmed in the biographies and standard editions. When I started I had therefore everything to learn, but nothing to unlearn, and my basic impression of the poet and his work was founded on intimate acquaintance with his own words, and not on what other people had said about him.

The large number of new documents which have turned up in recent years replaces conjecture with certainty in many once disputed episodes in Burns's career. We need no longer depend on libellous Saunders Tait for details of William Burnes's troubles at Lochlie; the chronology of the poet's Edinburgh peccadillos is fairly clear; we know why Mrs. Dunlop broke off her correspondence. The verification and completion of the texts of more than three-fourths of Burns's own letters is only a part of the fresh material. Collateral documents ranging from Elizabeth Paton's discharge of her claim against Burns to the almost complete correspondence of two of his most intimate friends are now available, and I have used them freely. I have also drawn upon other sources not fully utilized in the past. Most biographers, for instance, have contemned the so-called 'Train MS.' in Edinburgh University library. This collection of notes on Lockhart's *Life of Burns* consists mainly of anecdotes deriving ultimately from the poet's friend, John Richmond. It has been repudiated *in toto* for no better reason, seemingly, than that Richmond told a story about one Mary Campbell which does not tally with the romantic account of Highland Mary, and was mistaken in the identity of a lady who once called at Burns's lodgings in Baxter's Close. Against these two doubtful items I set the fact that the author of the notes so accurately described unpublished letters and verses which he had seen that every one of them since published can be instantly identified. I base no major conclusions on this MS., but I can see no justification for ignoring it.

I need not enumerate the volumes of biography, history, and memoirs which have contributed background materials. They are listed in all the standard bibliographies. The one great addition to the older lists is the *Journals* of James Boswell, which have furnished graphic details of Scottish life. I hasten to add, however, that Chapter I is not intended as a complete survey of eighteenth-century Scotland. Even had completeness been possible in the space at my disposal, it would have been useless to attempt to repeat what Professor H.W.Thompson

has so superbly done in *A Scottish Man of Feeling*.
Hence I have limited myself to those aspects of national life which bore directly upon Burns, as I have
also done in considering the influence of contemporary literature. The eighteenth century was not
all 'elegance', but it was the elegant authors, and not
Swift, Fielding, and Johnson, who appealed to
Burns.

Lest British readers charitably assume that I sin
through ignorance, I ought perhaps also to add that
in writing of Burns's world I have not hesitated to
equate some of its social and political aspects with
their twentieth-century American analogues. To
describe a dead world in dead terms seems a poor
way of revivifying it. My omission of footnotes is
likewise deliberate. In a score of articles in various
journals during the past decade I have presented,
and fully documented, the evidence on many controversial points. The articles evoked an almost passionate apathy; nevertheless they, and their footnotes, are there if anyone cares to look them up.
Furthermore, nearly all the source documents I
have used are now in print, despite the efforts of
Burns's self-appointed literary executors to suppress certain of them. On two points I recant some
of my earlier statements: I know now that the circumstances of Burns's quarrel with the Riddells are
not so clear as I once thought them, and Mr. Stan-
ley Cursiter of the Scottish National Gallery has
given me reason to doubt my identification of the miniature portrait belonging to Mr. Oliver R. Barrett.

Transcripts of most of the unpublished documents I have used are included in Mr. Robert T. Fitzhugh's Cornell University dissertation, 'Robert Burns as Seen by his Contemporaries' (1935). I am deeply indebted to Mr. Fitzhugh for the use of this material and of other documents he has discovered more recently, chief among them the letter in which Robert Ainslie described to Agnes M'Lehose his visit to Ellisland in October, 1790. In addition to the Train MS., above mentioned, Mr. Fitzhugh's thesis includes numerous letters by Burns's contemporaries, of which the most important are the forty-one which passed between John Syme and Alexander Cunningham from 1789 to 1797. On publication in the *Burns Chronicle* these letters were considerably expurgated, the deletions including details of the Caledonian Hunt's revelry in Dumfries and the most graphic description which has yet come to light in connection with Burns of a wet evening over the punchbowl.

Many other people have helped me in the work. My wife typed most of it in its original form, clarified doubtful points by debating them, and did her best to restrain the wilder excesses of Ph.D. diction. My colleague, Winfield H. Rogers, read the manuscript, and made many useful comments. A famous British firm gave me free permission to use one of Burns's bawdier letters, but after I published it they were taken to task by one of the literary executors above mentioned. Since they found it easier to repudiate a foreigner than to face the wrath of a compatriot, I shall not embarrass them by repeating my thanks here. I am indebted to Col. Sir John Murray, D.S.O., for use of the original MS. of Burns's journal of his Border tour. Mr. Davidson Cook, Mr. George W. Shirley, and Mr. John M'Vie have all shared their Burns discoveries with me, and Dr. A.S.W.Rosenbach, Mr. Gabriel Wells, and the late Mr. Charles Sessler renewed my obligations to them by allowing me to collate MSS. which came into their hands after my edition of the *Letters* was published. And finally, I owe a still deeper renewal of gratitude to the John Simon Guggenheim Memorial Foundation, to whose grant-in-aid this present volume owes its appearance.

DE L.F.

Western Reserve University
20 *August* 1938

CHRONOLOGY OF BURNS'S LIFE

I. AYRSHIRE

1759. *Jan.* 25. Robert Burns born at Alloway; eldest son of William Burnes (1721–1784) and his wife Agnes Broun (1732–1820). The other children were Gilbert (1760–1827), Agnes (1762–1834), Anabella (1764–1832), William (1767–1790), John (1769–1785), and Isabella (1771–1858).

1765. Robert and Gilbert sent to school to John Murdoch.

1766. William Burnes rents Mt. Oliphant farm.

1768. Murdoch gives up Alloway school. The *Titus Andronicus* incident.

1772. Robert and Gilbert attend Dalrymple parish school, week about, during summer quarter.

1773. Robert studies grammar and French with Murdoch for three weeks; writes his first song, 'Handsome Nell', for Nellie Kilpatrick.

1774. Hard times begin at Mt. Oliphant.

1775. Burns attends Hugh Rodger's school at Kirkoswald.

1777. At Whitsun William Burnes moves from Mt. Oliphant to Lochlie.

1779. Burns joins a dancing class 'in absolute defiance' of his father's commands.

1780. The Tarbolton Bachelors' Club organized.

1781. Burns courts Alison Begbie. His father's dispute

with David M'Lure, his landlord, begins. Burns joins the Freemasons, and about midsummer goes to Irvine as a flax-dresser.

1782. *Jan.* 1. The Irvine shop burnt out; soon after, Burns returns to Lochlie.

Sept. 24. William Burnes's dispute referred to arbiters.

1783. *Jan.* Burns wins a £3 prize for flax-seed.

April. Burns begins his Commonplace Book.

May 17. M'Lure gets a writ of sequestration against William Burnes.

Aug. 18. The 'Oversman' reports in Burnes's favor.

Aug. 25. Burnes makes first appeal to Court of Session.

Autumn. Robert and Gilbert secretly arrange to rent Mossgiel.

1784. *Jan.* 27. The Court of Session upholds William Burnes.

Feb. 13. Death of William Burnes. The family moves to Mossgiel.

1785. *May* 22. Birth of Elizabeth, the poet's daughter by Elizabeth Paton.

Nov. 1. Burial of John Burns, the poet's youngest brother. During this year Burns began to write his satires, composed 'The Jolly Beggars', and in Oct. finished his first Commonplace Book. He also met Jean Armour.

1786. *Jan.* (?). Burns plans migration to Jamaica.

April 3. 'Proposals' for the Kilmarnock *Poems* sent to press.

c. April 23. James Armour repudiates Burns as a son-in-law.

May 12. Supposed date of composing 'The Court of Equity'.

May 14. Supposed date of farewell to Highland Mary.

July 9. Burns's first penitential appearance in church.

July 22. Burns transfers his share in Mossgiel to Gilbert.

July 30. Burns in hiding from James Armour's writ.

July 31. The Kilmarnock *Poems* published.

c. Sept. 1. First postponement of Jamaica voyage.

Sept. 3. Jean Armour bears twins, who are christened Robert and Jean.

c. Sept. 27. Second postponement of Jamaica voyage.

Oct. 23. Burns dines at Catrine House.

End of *Oct.* Abandonment of Jamaica plans.

Nov. 27. Burns sets out for Edinburgh.

Dec. 1. Elizabeth Paton accepts Burns's settlement of her claim.

II. EDINBURGH

1786. *Nov.* 29. Burns arrives in Edinburgh.

Dec. 9. Henry Mackenzie praises the Kilmarnock *Poems* in *The Lounger*.

Dec. 14. William Creech issues subscription bills for the Edinburgh edition of the *Poems*.

1787. *Jan.* 13. The Grand Lodge of Scotland toasts Burns as 'Caledonia's Bard'.

April 21. Edinburgh *Poems* published.

April 23. Burns sells his copyright for 100 guineas.

May 5–*June* 1. Burns tours the Border.

End of *May*. VOL. I of *Scots Musical Museum* published.

June 2. Burns receives Meg Cameron's appeal.

June 8. Burns's '*éclatant* return to Mauchline'.

End of *June*. Burns tours West Highlands as far as Inverary.

July 29. Jean Armour 'in for it again'.

Aug. 2. Burns completes his autobiographical letter to Dr. John Moore.

Aug. 8. Burns returns to Edinburgh.

Aug. 15. Burns freed of Meg Cameron's writ.

Aug. 25–*Sept*. 16. Highland tour with William Nicol.

Oct. 4–20. Tour in Stirlingshire.

Oct. Death of poet's daughter, Jean.

Nov. Burns begins active work for the *Museum*.

Dec. 4. Burns meets Agnes M'Lehose.

Dec. 7. Burns dislocates his knee.

Dec. 8. The Clarinda correspondence begins.

1788. *Jan*. 4. Burns's first visit to Clarinda.

Feb. 13–14. Peak of the Clarinda correspondence: four letters in two days.

Feb. 18. Burns leaves Edinburgh.

Feb. 23. Burns returns to Mauchline; is 'disgusted' by Jean.

Feb. 27 (?) –*Mar*. 2. Burns visits Ellisland with John Tennant.

Mar. 3. Jean bears twin girls, of whom one dies on Mar. 10 and the other on Mar. 22.

c. Mar. 13. Burns returns to Edinburgh.

Mar. 18. Burns signs lease of Ellisland.

Mar. 24. Burns leaves Edinburgh.

Mar. VOL. II of *Scots Musical Museum* published.
Late *April.* Burns acknowledges Jean Armour as
his wife.
April–May. Burns receives Excise instructions at
Mauchline.

III. DUMFRIESSHIRE

1788. *June* 11. Burns settles at Ellisland.
July 14. Burns's Excise commission issued.
Nov. 5. Centenary of the 'Glorious Revolution'.
Nov. Jenny Clow bears Burns a son.
Dec. Jean joins Burns in borrowed quarters at the
Isle.
1789. *Feb.* 16. Burns goes to Edinburgh to close accounts
with Creech and to settle Jenny Clow's suit.
Feb. 28. Burns returns to Ellisland.
Summer. Burns meets Francis Grose.
Aug. 18. Francis Wallace Burns born.
Sept. 1. Burns begins duty as Excise officer.
Nov. Burns ill with 'malignant squinancy and low
fever'.
1790. *Jan.* 27. Burns's name placed on list of those eligible
for promotion as Examiners and Supervisors.
Feb. VOL. III of *Scots Musical Museum* published.
July. Burns transferred to Dumfries 3d Division.
July 24. Death of William Burns in London.
Dec. 1. MS. of 'Tam o' Shanter' sent to Grose.
1791. *Mar.* 31. Anne Park bears Burns a daughter, Eliza-
beth.
April 9. William Nicol Burns born.
April. 'Tam o' Shanter' published in Grose's

Antiquities of Scotland and in the March *Edinburgh Magazine.*

June 19–22. Burns in Ayrshire to attend Gilbert's wedding.

Aug. 25. Auction of crops at Ellisland.

Sept. 10. Formal renunciation of Ellisland lease signed.

Nov. 11. Burns moves into Dumfries.

Nov. 29–*Dec.* 11. Burns in Edinburgh. Farewell again to Agnes M'Lehose.

1792. *Feb.* Burns promoted to Dumfries Port Division.

Feb. 29. Capture of schooner *Rosamond.*

April 10. Burns made honorary member of Royal Company of Archers, Edinburgh.

April 19. Sale of the *Rosamond's* carronades.

Aug. VOL. IV of *Scots Musical Museum* published.

Sept. 16. Burns begins work for Thomson's *Select Collection.*

Nov. 13. Burns subscribes for Edinburgh *Gazetteer.*

Nov. 21. Birth of Elizabeth Riddell Burns.

Mid-*Dec.* Burns's last visit to Dunlop House.

Dec. 31. Inquiry into Burns's loyalty.

1793. *Jan.* 5. Burns defends himself to Graham of Fintry.

Feb. 1. France declares war against England.

Feb. Second Edinburgh edition of *Poems* published.

March. Burns asks, and receives, burgess privileges in the Dumfries schools.

May 19. Burns moves to house in Mill Vennel.

June. First number of Thomson's *Select Collection* published.

c. July 30–*Aug.* 2. First Galloway tour with Syme.

Aug. The Edinburgh sedition trials.

c. Aug. 30. 'Bannockburn' sent to Thomson.

c. Dec. 31. Beginning of the Riddell quarrel.

1794. *Jan.* 12. Final breach with Maria Riddell.

April 21. Death of Robert Riddell.

c. May 1. Burns declines a post on *Morning Chronicle*, London.

c. June 25–28. Second Galloway tour with Syme.

Aug. 12. Birth of James Glencairn Burns.

c. Dec. 22. Burns appointed Acting Supervisor at Dumfries.

1795. *Jan.* 12. Burns posts the letter which estranged Mrs. Dunlop.

Jan. 31. Burns joins in organizing the Dumfries Volunteers.

Feb. Reconciliation with Maria Riddell.

April. The Reid miniature painted. Alexander Findlater resumes his duties as Supervisor at Dumfries.

Sept. Death of Elizabeth Riddell Burns.

Dec.–Jan. Burns ill with rheumatic fever.

1796. *Mar.* 12–14. Food riots in Dumfries.

July 3–16. Burns at the Brow Well.

July 18. Burns writes his last letter.

July 21. Death of Burns.

July 25. Funeral of Burns, and birth of his son Maxwell.

Dec. VOL. v of *Scots Musical Museum* published.

CONTENTS

PRIDE AND PASSION
ROBERT BURNS 1759–1796

PRIDE AND PASSION

I

SCOTLAND

A Scot in the eighteenth century was a poor relation, subject to the slights and scorns of more prosperous kinfolk, and reared amid poverty, theology,
and filth. When Robert Burns was born, on January 25, 1759, his native land was almost at the nadir
of its independent existence. Proud and warlike and
desperately poor, Scotland had been still an essentially feudal nation when King James VI was called
from amid the bickerings of his jealous nobles and
intransigent clergy to become James I of England.
The permanent removal of the court to London left
the country more than ever the prey of contention
among its nobles and fanaticism among its ecclesias-
tics; governed by a parliament without authority;
torn at intervals by rebellion and civil strife; denied
commercial parity with England, and cut off from
the old-time free intercourse with France.

The Act of Union of 1707, by admitting Scotland to commercial privileges formerly restricted to
England, started the country on the road to material prosperity, but promised to destroy the last ves-
tiges of national pride. It was 'the end of an old
song'. Thenceforward the affairs of Scotland were
entrusted to a handful of representatives at Westminster, too small, in those days of patronage and

pocket-boroughs, to have enabled even a Scottish
Parnell, had there been one, to sway the balance of
power. Scotland was no longer Scotland; it was
North Britain. And when the House of Hanover
succeeded to the English throne, the last vestige of
Scottish influence in the government seemed to
have vanished. Ruled no longer by the Stuarts—her
own kings, even though absentee—but by 'an insolent, beef-witted race of foreigners', Scotland turned
more and more to the things of the flesh. The last
flicker of the ancient loyalties in the '45 shed only
light enough to reveal their death. The Lowlands,
though they could not stomach the double treason
of a man like Murray of Broughton, acquiesced in
the brutal destruction of the Highland clans. Most
of the comfortable merchants and landed gentry
had viewed the uprising with an apprehension even
livelier than that felt by the German court four
hundred miles away; when the Highlands were
crushed they rejoiced in their own increased security, and showed their loyalty to the reigning House
by christening their daughters Charlotte and Wil-
helmina, and their new streets and squares Hanover
and Brunswick and George.

By the middle of the century Scottish affairs had
settled into an order which might alter in degree,
but would not alter in kind, for two generations at
least. Politically, the country was little more than a
conquered province. Economically it was beginning
to emerge from age-old poverty, but the new prosperity of the lucky few was widening the gap be-

tween them and the poor and still further depressing the latter. Religiously it was awakening from the nightmare of Calvinism which had paralysed free thought and free action for two centuries. Intellectually its literary life was being overwhelmed by the fashions and standards of England, and its educated citizens were suffering from an inferiority complex of national scope.

When Warren Hastings was impeached, Burns was angry because it was done in the name of the Commons of England and not of Great Britain. Had he expressed his opinion in public, instead of in a private letter, it would have roused little sympathy among his more influential countrymen. Most would have dismissed it as the rant of a fanatic; a few would have held it downright treason. There was no money in being a Scottish patriot. As in England, all things political went by favour. The only difference was that in Scotland they went by favour of one man—the Duke of Argyll, the Earl of Bute, or Henry Dundas, as the case might be. All power concentrated at last in the hands of the national boss. He 'suggested' the choice of the sixteen Scottish peers who were to represent their country in the House of Lords; he controlled the election of the forty-five members of the Commons; his word was law as to all appointive offices. Fifteen members of the Commons were chosen by the burgh councils —self-perpetuating groups which in 'the taciturn regularity of ancient affairs' allowed no outsider to intrude on their privileges and their graft. The other thirty were chosen by the counties, and in all Scotland there were fewer than three thousand qualified electors, every man of whom was ticketed as to party allegiance and family connection. Most of them also had their prices plainly marked on their tickets. Of course the price need be nothing so crude as cash. Every job, from a cadetship with the East India Company to the governorship of a province, was obtainable by influence, and by influence only; hence there were plenty of ways of swaying a man's vote, especially if he had a rising family of hungry younger sons, without soiling his fingers with gold.

Everyone played the game, and took the rules for granted. Why wait for merited promotion, if you could get it quicker by pulling wires? The only man Sir Walter Scott ever deliberately cut was the one who publicly criticized him for securing his brother's appointment to a post which he knew was soon to be abolished—with a pension for the ousted incumbent. It was a comfortable system for those on the inside. As for the others, they were expected to do their duty in that state of life to which it had pleased God to call them.

But it was not merely in political jobs that the influential classes were doing well for themselves. The Act of Union had admitted Scottish merchants to the privileges of the colonial trade formerly open only to the English. Throughout the eighteenth century the south of Scotland experienced a whole series of industrial and real estate booms. Though by twentieth-century standards of bankruptcy the booms were small and local, they had all the familiar characteristics. Glasgow and its neighbourhood, for instance, when once it had recovered from the losses of the crazy Darien Expedition—as wild a speculation as the later Mississippi Bubble in France and the South Sea madness in England—throve soberly on its steadily increasing commerce with the West Indies and the American Colonies. The passer-by today, between the Trongate and the Broomie-law, may read in Union Street and George Square how mercantile Scotland felt towards the loss of its parliament, and find Jamaica and Virginia Streets underscoring the reason; further west, St. Vincent Street, Nile Street, Pitt Street, and Wellington Street show the direction of Glaswegian sympathies in the long struggle with Napoleon. And since commerce is by definition two-sided the ships which brought back American cotton and tobacco and sugar took out Scottish linens and woolens and shoes from steadily growing centres of manufacture.

On the east coast, Edinburgh was not merely expanding; it was on the way to transforming itself. Unable by its location to share directly in the overseas trade, it throve on the legal business which grew out of that trade, on the increasing demand for education which benefited both the university and the printers and booksellers, and on the invested profits of Scotsmen who had made money in the East or West Indies and who settled in the capital when they retired. Until after the '45 the city was still packed along the ridge from Holyrood to the

Castle, its population crowded into the tall tene-
ments which shut out the low northern sun from the
narrow wynds. Its first expansion was to the south, in
a development, near the present site of the University, on which Burns's father and uncle found work
when they struck out for themselves in 1750. To the
north of the Old Town all was then open country.
At the foot of the Castle Rock, where the railway
tracks now run, the marshy Nor Loch still received
whatever of the city's garbage did not remain in the
streets. Burns was four years old when the real
growth of the modern city began with the building
of the North Bridge to connect the Old Town with
the ridge which parallelled it to northward. Each
year thereafter saw new houses or new squares
added, but as late as 1800 the New Town still con-
sisted only of Princes, George, and Queen Streets
from St. Andrew Square to Charlotte Square.

Until after Burns's death the whole area, despite
the Georgian dignity and charm of its houses, retained many of the features of a new and raw development. In particular, the valley was half choked by
the hideous Mound formed of the earth excavated
in grading the New Town. The laying out of the
Princes Street Gardens and the crowning of the
Mound with the Scottish National Gallery were
still far in the future—there was even talk of a row
of buildings on the south side of Princes Street which
would have blinded one of the finest city vistas in
the world, and have made the Gardens forever impossible. By 1786, when Burns first saw Edinburgh,

wealth and fashion had already deserted the Old
Town, and middle-class respectability was beginning to follow, but the business life of the city still
centred in the shops and taverns which lined the
High Street, crammed the narrow Luckenbooths
which congested traffic beside disfigured St. Giles's,
and overflowed into all the adjacent courts and
closes. Professional men transacted their business
in taverns in preference to their crowded living-
quarters; all Edinburgh was accustomed to gather at
midday in the neighbourhood of the Cross to arrange business and social appointments.

Sanitation did not exist. Water for cooking and
such exiguous washing as was done was carried by
porters from the public wells to the various flats in
the tall 'lands'; the day's filth of the household was
collected in a tub on the landing of the stairs and at
bedtime the barefoot maid-servants emptied it out
of the windows—theoretically to be gathered up by
the scavengers; actually, too often, to lie where it
fell until a rain washed it away. Even the hardy nos-
trils of Londoners quailed before the marshalled
stenches of Edinburgh, and travelling Scotsmen
gauged the smells of foreign cities like Lisbon by
their nasal memories of home. That children should
die like flies was inevitable; the marvel is that any
survived. Deficiency diseases were as rife as filth
diseases. Rickets was taken for granted—a simile,
humorous in intent but ghastly in effect in one of
Scott's letters, gives a glimpse of nurse-maids in
Princes Street trying to compel unhappy rachitic

children to walk. Human life has always been Scotland's cheapest commodity. That a high degree of social and intellectual culture should flourish amid this filth is merely another proof of human capacity for ignoring what it is too indolent to correct.

Outside the cities, as well as in them, Scottish life was beginning to change. Primitive agriculture in the northern kingdom, like the sanitation of Edinburgh, seemed almost to be an effort to demonstrate just how badly a thing could be done. The poorest sorts of oats and barley, the scrubbiest of cattle, were raised by the worst methods. The unfenced fields were divided by a system of ridges and ditches which managed to combine the maximum of soil wastage with the minimum of drainage. The 'infield', as this dyked portion of the farm was called, was cultivated with ploughs so crude and awkward that they required four horses and two men to handle them. The 'outfield', or pasture, was never cultivated or manured; overrun with moss and weeds it yielded even in summer only a scanty and unwholesome pasturage, with little if any surplus to carry the cattle through the winter. All excess stock was slaughtered in the fall, and for six months of the year the people who could afford meat at all had to subsist like seamen on salt beef and smoked mutton hams. The wretched beasts which were kept through the winter were fed mainly on straw, and frequently by spring were so weak and emaciated that they had to be carried to the pasture.

The owners of the cattle lived in a style which an

Iroquois would have thought primitive. Gilbert
Burns resented the statement that his famous
brother was born in a hovel. The Alloway cottage,
he declared, was better than the houses then occupied by many substantial farmers. So it was. It had
a chimney, whereas in many a cottage and farmhouse, long after Burns's youth—Keats saw plenty
of them in Ayrshire in 1818—such of the smoke as
did not enter the eyes and lungs of the tenants escaped through the door. But even with a chimney
the average farmhouse or labourer's cottage, with its
walls of stone or rammed clay, its earthen floor and
thatched roof, and with the fire seldom built up except for cooking, had a winter chill and dampness
that bred tuberculosis in the young and rheumatism in the old. As at Alloway, the stable was usually under the same roof, and its reek mingled with
the dampness and the smell of unwashed humanity.
An English proverb in the seventeenth century asserted that the Scots had neither bellows, warming-
pans, nor houses of office; and that the proverb
still held in the eighteenth is proved alike by experiences of Johnson and Boswell in gentlemen's
homes in the Highlands and by episodes in the
chapbooks of Dugal Graham which reveal the same
use of the fireplace as Shakespeare records of the inn
at Rochester. Outside the door was the midden-dub
or glaur-hole, manure-heap of man and beast alike,
often so surrounded with stagnant water that the
'rather pretty' girl whom Keats saw standing at a
cow-house door in the Highlands, 'fac'd all up to

the ankles in dirt', would in the Lowlands a generation earlier have been a sight too commonplace to
excite remark. When the seepage from the midden-
dub reached the water-supply the cycle of filth and
typhoid was complete. Dead animals which could
not be eaten were usually dumped into the nearest
stream, so that if the water-supply was not contaminated in one way, it was pretty sure to be in another. But unless the animal were a horse, it had to
be very dead indeed not to be eaten. Sheep that had
died by accident or disease had a special name—
'braxies'—and were the perquisite of the shep-
herds; the flesh of diseased cattle was sometimes the
only meat farm servants tasted; in Edinburgh young
Henry Mackenzie once observed two bakers of
cheap 'mutton pies' suspiciously engaged by night
about the carcass of a horse on the bank at the back
of the Castle.

Within doors all domestic equipment was on the
same primitive scale as the housing. At meal-times
the pot containing the thick oatmeal porridge which
was the staple food was placed in the centre of the
table, and each member of the family—servants included—fell to work with his own spoon. Barley for
broth was prepared on the knocking-stone, counter-
part of the Mexican *metate*. Pewter dishes were a
luxury, and crockery ones almost unknown. Wooden
trenchers were frequently used even by the clergy,
and were the regular thing in farmhouses; the milk
was kept in wooden vessels so permeated with dirt
and bacteria that it soured in a few hours. The en-

tire family lived and ate and slept in two rooms, with
sometimes a windowless loft above as additional
sleeping-quarters for the servants or some of the
older children. Every cottage had at least one box-
bed built into the wall. When the occupants retired
and closed the sliding wooden doors they enjoyed a
practically airless seclusion amid their own effluvia.
The rest of the family slept on rough cots, or even
straw pallets on the floor. The popular saying, 'The
clartier [dirtier] the cosier', was not satire; it was
just a matter-of-fact summary of rural living conditions.

In dwellings like these, where a large family was
often augmented by several servants, privacy was as
impossible as in an army barrack. Any conversation
too intimate to be shouted above the uproar of the
children into the ears of a mixed audience had to be
conducted elsewhere than in the house—in the
fields, if the weather permitted; in the stable otherwise. Even so, of course, all the circumstances leading up to the conversation were known to a large
and intensely interested group. Hence the young
people, making a virtue of publicity, took their
cronies into their confidence and employed them to
arrange their trysts. Thus if James Smith beckoned
Jean Armour or Betsy Miller away from her giggling
family it was fairly certain that he was making an
appointment for Rob Mossgiel and not for himself;
if Burns waited on Jenny Surgeoner it was in John
Richmond's interests and not in his own. It was difficult to surprise, and impossible to shock by any of

the normal processes of nature, a people who lived in such conditions. No one had to explain 'the facts of life' to the children of that world; they witnessed them daily. It would almost seem that a belief in original virtue, rather than original sin, was requisite to explain why the moral status of the peasantry was often so much less squalid than their physical surroundings.

As the century advanced, however, closer intercourse with England roused ambitious landlords to attempt improvements. Trees were planted on the hillsides and about the naked houses; the 'infields' were levelled and enclosed. Yet nine-tenths of the fences in Ayrshire were not built until after 1766, and as late as 1800 two-thirds of Fife was still fenceless. Rotation of crops, better cultivation, artificial grasses, more productive types of grain, were all experimented with. Potatoes and turnips, regarded as garden luxuries in the early part of the century, began to be grown on a large scale for human food and stock feed respectively. John Wesley in 1780 noted that vegetables had become as plentiful in Scotland as in England, though on his first visit, in 1762, he had found none at all, even on noblemen's tables. Carts were introduced for farm work, to take the place of the 'creels' or panniers, in which manure had formerly been borne on horseback to the fields, and of the rough sledges on which the sheaves had been hauled from harvest field to stackyard. The wide use of carts, however, had in many districts to await the improvement of the roads; in some in-

stances, when landlords first offered wheeled ve-
hicles as gifts to their tenants, they were refused because it seemed impossible to drag them through
the mud.

Some few of the improving landlords were ac-
tuated by disinterested zeal to better living-condi-
tions; their stubborn and superstitious peasants
were helped against their will. Many more landlords
were motivated by simple greed to improve their
rent-rolls. By breaking up small holdings occupied
on short-term leases, and throwing several together,
they made more profitable farms which were rented
for long terms. The consequent evictions, however, produced an over-supply of would-be tenants
whose desperate need for land resulted in competi-
tive bidding from those willing to take a gambling
chance on getting from the soil more than it really
had to give. If they succeeded, it was too often at
the expense of the health and strength of themselves, their children, and their servants.

Nevertheless, so far as the improvements in
methods increased the productivity of the farms, the
new developments were economically sound. But
the nation's increasing foreign trade operated to in-
flate land values. Merchants who had made money
in the Indies wished to retire, and the prestige of
setting up as landed gentry combined with the lack
of sound corporate investments to bid up the value
of land in the more attractive parts of the kingdom
to levels where a fair return on the investment was
possible only by rack-renting the tenants. Burns

himself, and his father before him, were victims of
this over-capitalization. They had to pay for mar-
ginal lands at rates which would have been fair
rentals for the best. And of course speculation in
land brought with it speculative banking. In Burns's
youth many of the Ayrshire gentry were crippled or
ruined outright by the failure of the Douglas and
Heron Bank, which, organized on a lavish scale,
quickly got into trouble through excessive loans on
real estate. The ruined gentry retired to the Continent, or to lodgings in Edinburgh, and their estates
were taken over by nabobs home from the Indies.

All this drama of political corruption and of social
and economic change was played against the background of the old religious life of Scotland. Though
the intellectual life of the country had never been
squalid like its physical life, it had at the beginning
of the eighteenth century become torpid. From the
time of John Knox until after the Act of Union the
real government of Scotland, like that of colonial
Massachusetts, was a theocracy. The King and the
powers of the state were far off from the life of the
average peasant or tradesman, but the Kirk watched
all his goings out and comings in. Not only did it
administer matters which in other times and other
nations have been regarded as spiritual concerns,
but it also largely took the place of magistrates and
police. Critics of puritanism who have chosen colonial New England as their dire example have made a
mistake. They should have chosen Scotland. Whatever the theory of church government in New Eng-

land may have been, in practice the man at odds
with the establishment suffered few real hardships
beyond the loss of his vote and a moderate amount
of discriminatory taxation—provided he had the
discretion to mind his business and keep his mouth
shut. But in seventeenth-century Scotland estrangement from the church might mean exile from the
kingdom, under penalty of practical starvation if the
rebel tried to stick it out at home. Except that it
lacked the power to relax its heretics to the secular
arm for mutilation or death, the Scottish hierarchy
was own brother to the Spanish Inquisition.

In every parish the Kirk Session was supposed to
maintain a snooping committee to investigate the
conduct of the laity. The reckless parishioner who
desecrated the Sabbath by cooking a hot meal, by
puttering in his garden, or even by taking a walk,
was haled before the Session for discipline, and could
be reinstated in the communion only by confession
of his sin and payment of a fine. For more serious
offences the penalties were proportionately heavier,
unless one were wealthy or powerful enough to cow
the inquisitors. Burns had painfully intimate knowledge of the cutty stool, or mourners' bench, whereon
those guilty of fornication or other deadly sin had
thrice to appear before the congregation while the
minister rebuked them at length and with specific
detail. Girls sometimes committed suicide or mur-
dered their children to escape the public shame, and
the effect of the ordeal on those who submitted was
more likely to be hardening than chastening. Many

another youth besides Burns inwardly resolved
thenceforth to live up to the reputation thus fastened
upon him.

The Kirk frowned upon, and tried to suppress,
such secular amusements as music and dancing. In
spite of the ban, the custom of 'penny weddings',
whereby impecunious young couples in the rural districts sought, by giving what was in effect a subscription ball, to raise money enough to set them up in
housekeeping, still persisted; but even these gather-
ings had a slightly furtive quality, and in the stricter
homes all such things were taboo. The moral results
of the policy of repression were almost wholly bad.
The older men, in default of other relaxation, devoted themselves to drink; the younger, to the pleasures that give its point to Burns's simile, 'as busy as
an Edinburgh bawd on a Sunday evening'.

Probably none but a native Scot can understand
the finer points of Scottish theology. Fortunately,
however, such understanding is not needed for a
general grasp of church affairs in the eighteenth century. Primitive Calvinism shares with Marxism the
distinction of being the most completely determin-
istic philosophy ever widely accepted in the western
world. All men were held to be equally sinful and
equally deserving of eternal damnation. 'Adam as
the federal representative of the human race had determined its fate once and for all by violating that
unfortunate covenant which he and the Deity had
contracted with regard to the forbidden fruit. A
vicarious sacrifice had indeed been offered; but the

power to avail themselves of this expiation was to be communicated to only a few of the minority to whom it had been made known; and these were to be saved to show that God was merciful, as the rest were to be damned to show that He was just.' [1] This was the creed of which Oliver Wendell Holmes said that any decent person really holding it ought to go mad out of mere self-respect. And like every other rigid system it had the effect of stultifying its sincerest adherents. The most patriotic of historians are compelled to recognize the general intellectual torpor of Scottish theological and philosophical writing in the seventeenth and early eighteenth centuries. The thinking of the clergy had been finished for them by John Calvin and John Knox; all that remained for them to do was to expound. No first-rate mind can subdue itself to the mere unquestioning exposition of other men's views without losing its edge, and few of the parish clergy in Scotland had started with first-rate minds. Their preaching was commonly a dreary reiteration of the doctrine of the Four-Fold State of Man—first, Innocence or Primitive Integrity, next Nature or Entire Depravation, then Grace or Begun Recovery, and finally Consummate Happiness or Misery—brightened only by sadistic imaginings of the details of eternal torment. As if these doctrinal limitations were not sufficiently deadening, custom required that one of the minister's two discourses each Sunday should be preached from his 'ordinary' text—which meant

1 W.L.Mathieson: *Scotland and the Union* (Glasgow, 1905), p.225.

that he was expected to take the same text week after week and torture it into new applications of doctrine. If his invention failed under the strain, and he changed his 'ordinary' too often, zealous parishioners were likely to complain to the Presbytery. Add to these handicaps the fact that few ministers had money enough to buy books, even had they wished for books, and one begins to realize why Scottish manses two hundred years ago contributed no such leaders of national thought as were even then emerging from English rectories.

Nevertheless the tides of changing ideas stirred even the strongholds of Calvinism. Before the seventeenth century ended Michael Wigglesworth in Massachusetts had found himself compelled slightly to modify the doctrine of infant damnation in the direction of human decency; in Scotland the 'common sense' doctrines of the Deists penetrated during the eighteenth century even among those who abhorred the name of Deism. From 1729 until his death in 1746 Francis Hutcheson, as professor of Moral Philosophy in Glasgow University, expounded to steadily growing classes his theory of the 'moral sense'—an allegedly innate human capacity for distinguishing right from wrong. This concept of innate virtue as opposed to the idea of original sin rapidly gained ground among the laity and the younger clergy of the cities, despite bitter hostility on the part of the conservatives. Preaching began to stress conduct rather than the will of a cruel and capricious god as the way of salvation. A healthier and more prosperous nation was in fact rebelling against a harsh and depressing philosophy, and the clergy were following the lead of their congregations. By the third quarter of the century the liberal faction, the Moderates or New Lights, were in almost undisputed control in the metropolitan districts, though the fundamentalists, or Old Lights, still flourished in the smaller towns and in the rural parishes. The more rigorous extremes of kirk discipline began to relax. Though in 1757 John Home was compelled to resign his pulpit to escape the consequence of having written *The Tragedy of Douglas*— to witness the early performances of which a few of his more daring clerical brethren disguised themselves in the garments of the laity—the ban on the theatre gradually sank into desuetude. Even while the Edinburgh playhouse was still unlicensed, and dramas had to be advertised as concerts of music between the parts of which the play of the evening would be presented gratis, it became possible for ministers to attend the performances openly.

But the warfare of New Lights versus Old was not conducted wholly in the realm of ideas. The fact that the more influential laity were early converts to the new doctrines brought into the struggle politics in its most worldly form. In parishes where the local magnates exercised the right of presenting the minister, New Light candidates had the preference. Hence it was the New Lights' interest to uphold the right of patronage against the congregation's democratic claim to elect its own minister. The supporters of patronage triumphed in the election of William Robertson as Moderator of the General Assembly in 1763; the result made the church almost as much a part of the spoils system as the government was, and gave its leadership into the hands of supple ecclesiastical politicians. In consequence the spread of New Light doctrine went hand in hand with a steady decline in the moral influence of the clergy, while schisms and secessions sapped the organization. Because the Kirk was morally as well as intellectually bankrupt the laughter of Burns's satires shook it to its foundations. To the church of John Knox such ridicule would have meant no more than a mosquito means to an elephant. Burns's Edinburgh friends were right in maintaining that the conduct and doctrines which he attacked would have disappeared in another generation without his aid; what neither they nor he could foresee was that in 1843 it would be the Old Light clergy who would restore moral leadership to the ministry by daring to give up their livings for conscience' sake.

Behind the New Light doctrines expounded by Hutcheson and his followers lay of course the ideas of such English Deists as Locke and Shaftesbury. Strong convictions on philosophical and theological questions were going out of fashion; like Franklin in America the New Light Scots had persuaded themselves that enlightened self-interest, sweet reasonableness and common sense, were attainable goals for mankind at large, and could be trusted to solve problems of morals and economics alike. And this English influence in the field of theology and philosophy was typical of the entire range of literary expression in Scotland. The national inferiority complex showed itself most plainly of all in the realm of words.

Historically the Scottish language is to English what Provençal is to French and Catalan to Spanish—an ancient and independent local dialect which had developed its own literature at least as early as had the more central region which afterwards took the lead. The speech of Lowland Scotland was the direct descendant of that Northumbrian dialect of Old English which Bede and Caedmon spoke. Throughout the Middle Ages and the early Renaissance Scotland maintained amid her poverty as rich a literary tradition as England did. In fact, from the death of Chaucer until the beginning of the Elizabethan era the student of British literature must look north of the Tweed to find, in the writings of King James I, Robert Henryson, Gawain Douglas and William Dunbar, anything worthy the name of poetry. The decay of Scots as a literary language was started by the Reformation and finished by the Union. By introducing the Geneva version of the English Bible the Reformation made Southern English the language of the church, in idiom if not in pronunciation. The accession of James VI to the English throne made Southern English also the language of the court. King James himself wrote in Scots; his subject, William Drummond of Hawthornden, wrote in English. Drummond's example was followed by all the prose writers and most of the poets of Scotland from his day to ours. After the Union even the poets who used Scots did so consciously and not because such expression was wholly spontaneous.

Of these poets, Allan Ramsay, whose productive period covers roughly the three decades from 1711 to 1740, was the most popular. And Scots poetry, as practised by Ramsay and by his friend and contemporary William Hamilton of Gilbertfield, tended more and more to what Samuel Johnson would have described as the easy and vulgar, and therefore the disgusting. Their work exhibits humour, and something of the conversational quality of the familiar essay, but dignity and deep poetic emotion are notably absent. Moreover, the dialect in which they wrote tended more and more to become a synthetic and standardized language, embodying words and idioms common to a large section of southern Scotland but without firm roots in any one region. The Aberdeenshire dialect used by Alexander Ross in his *Helenore* is almost the last fresh transcription of the speech of a definite section of the country. Written Scots was rapidly becoming what nineteenth-century English and American authors made other dialects—a semi-literary vernacular employed for humorous effect or for an affectation of colloquial ease. Even Burns himself at times gave artificial Scottish flavour to his verse by using English idioms in Scottish spelling. Since the end of the eighteenth century no writer of Scots verse has succeeded in introducing any new elements. At its best, such writing sounds like imitations of Burns; at its worst, like imitations of his imitators.

But when Burns came before the public even this conventionalized literary Scots seemed on the point of extinction. Though Ramsay's *Tea-Table Miscellany*—which included many purely English verses—was still popular as a song-book, the rest of his work was neglected. Hamilton of Gilbertfield's recension of Blind Harry's *History of Sir William Wallace* was no more than a story-book for children. The unhappy Robert Fergusson, starved and neglected, had ended his life in a madhouse, and fashionable Edinburgh, glancing askance at his satirical verses, said it served him right. Ramsay was a crude homespun figure of the generation in which Thomson by writing *The Seasons* had given his countrymen a poem which they could show to Englishmen without blushing; 'The Daft Days' and the rest of Fergusson's work was little better than a national disgrace when set beside the beauties of James Beattie's *Minstrel*. Nevertheless there still underlay the new fashions a literary tradition which most of the anglicizing gentry scorned or ignored. An oral Scottish literature was still alive, though it was soon to perish when its lovers smothered it by writing it down. Percy's *Reliques of Ancient English Poetry*, which first gave highbrow sanction to the popular ballads of Scotland and northern England, were not published until Burns was six years old, and even Percy only scratched the surface of this rich deposit. Throughout the century scores of ballads still circulated by oral tradition which had never been recorded in writing, and in these the genuine spirit of the Scottish language flourished without concession to fashionable English.

Even more important than the ballads for the training of a poet like Burns were the folk-songs. The Scots had always been a musical people, and despite the opposition of the stricter clergy traditional songs or airs for almost every human occasion were known to everyone, high or low. The tradition, moreover, was still very much alive. Scottish song gave the nation its revenge for the military humiliations of the '45. The taunting lilt of 'Hey, Johnie Cope, are ye waukin yet?' could be relied on to remind English garrisons of the inglorious conduct of their fellow soldiers at Prestonpans, and all Scotland's contempt for the Hanoverian kings and their mistresses went into the ribaldry of 'The Sow's Tail to Geordie'. Even so, only a fraction of the popular songs had any political bearing. More of them were convivial; many more of them erotic. Every phase of sexual love from the crudest bawdry to idyllic beauty found some expression in verse—the latter, it must be confessed, more rarely and less effectively than the former. Yet these crude songs, interesting mainly for the surprising variety and ingenuity of their erotic symbolism, were the raw material—raw in more than one sense—from which Burns wrought such lyrics as 'My Love is like a red red rose', 'John Anderson', and 'Coming thro' the rye'. While Burns was still a lad, David Herd, a retiring antiquary in Edinburgh, began the systematic collection of this folk poetry on so large a scale and with such a complete absence of prudery that it was not until the twentieth century that the whole of his manuscript collection was printed. He had himself published in 1776 two volumes of what he considered the best work. At the same time musicians like James Oswald and Neil Gow were collecting the airs of Highlands and Lowlands alike. The singing of the old songs, with or without instrumental accompaniment, was a favourite pastime in Scottish drawing rooms, and even unliterary folk would frequently feel moved to compose new words to some well-liked melody.

Alongside this honest love of native things, whether expressed in a girl's singing at her harpsichord or in David Herd's careful recording of old words, another literature was growing up of imitation, forgery, and 'improvement'. It had become a literary convention for every composer of an imitation ballad to offer it to the public as a copy from an ancient manuscript. Though a few of these imitations, like the 'Hardyknute' of Lady Elizabeth Wardlaw, were close enough to the spirit of folk literature to deceive even experts, the mass of them were so mawkish and verbose as to bring the term 'Scottish poetry' to the verge of contempt. Primacy in these qualities, as in popularity, belonged to James Macpherson's alleged translations of the poems of Ossian—a work passionately defended by the Scots because it depicted their savage ancestors

as a trifle more chivalrous and vastly more sentimental than Bayard or Sidney, admired on the Continent because it supported the current delusion
about the nobility of man in a state of nature, and
cherished by Napoleon Bonaparte as one of the
simple pleasures which appeal to the enterprising
burglar in his hours of relaxation.

But the harm done to traditional literature by
imitations and forgeries was trivial compared with
that inflicted by some of those people who professed
to admire it. In the latter part of the eighteenth century the teaching of music in Edinburgh had passed
largely into the hands of foreigners. Names like
Domenico Corri, Pietro Urbani, and Theodor
Schetki are as prevalent on title-pages as their
owners were on the concert stage, and under this
Italianate influence many traditional melodies were
'harmonized' and 'improved' until all their native
vigour was lost in empty flourishes. And as with the
music, so with the words. 'Correct' and sentimental-
ized lyrics were substituted for the sturdy old words,
remained in use long enough to push the latter into
oblivion, and then, their novelty gone, themselves
sank into disuse and dragged the music with them.

This effort to refine the national heritage of music
was merely one phase of the whole sense of provincial inferiority which afflicted Scotland. Italian
music and English literature, speech, and manners,
were the ideals towards which genteel Scots strained.
National pride in James Thomson and John Home
exulted more in the fact that they wrote English

acceptable in England than in their use of Scottish materials. Even the devastating scepticism of David Hume was forgiven him because he had almost purified his language of Scotticisms. When Johnson ridiculed Hume's English Boswell writhed in agony, and was correspondingly elated when the dictator praised Blair's sermons and was moved to tears by Beattie's *Minstrel*.

When Thomas Sheridan came to Edinburgh in 1761 to give a course of lectures on elocution, 'he was patronized by the professors in the College, by several of the clergy, by the most eminent among the gentlemen at the bar, by the judges of the Court of Session, and by all who at that time were the leaders of public taste'.

Thenceforward, 'correct pronunciation and elegant reading' were reckoned 'indispensable acquirements for people of fashion and for public speakers'. In other words, these people of fashion, like Francis Jeffrey on his return from Oxford, gave up the broad Scots in return for the narrow English. In the very year of the Kilmarnock *Poems*, Sir John Sinclair of Ulbster, one of the most public-spirited Scots of his generation, brought out a two-hundred-page volume of *Observations on the Scottish Dialect*. His purpose was not to preserve but to destroy his native speech. His book is a comprehensive index expurgatorius of all the words, phrases, and idioms a Scotsman must avoid—many of them today a part of the standard speech of the United States, and even of England. Thus, 'best man' is a Scotticism for

'bride's man'; 'hairdresser' is to be preferred to
'barber'; 'sore eyes' is a vulgarism; 'whisky' should
be called 'usquebae' or 'aquavitae'. 'Heather' and
'peat' and 'bracken' are condemned along with
'mittens' and 'kindling'; it betrays provincial origin
to ask if a friend is in, or if he has gone out walking.
'It is, indeed, astonishing,' says Sir John, 'how uncouth, and often how unintelligible, Scotch words
and phrases are to an inhabitant of London, and
how much it exposes such as make use of them, to
the derision of those with whom they happen to
have any communication or intercourse.' However,
he adds, a Scot should choose carefully even from
the speech of London. 'Cockney phrases a Scotchman is very apt to get into when he makes his first
appearance in London. And when he can easily and
fluently bring out, *this here thing*, and *that there thing*,
for *this* or *that thing*; *I knode*, for *I knew*; *on it*, for *of it*,
as, *I heard on it*; *grass*, for *asparagus*; *your'n* and *his'n*,
for *yours* and *his*, he fancies himself a complete Eng-
lishman.'

The anglicizing mania extended even to people's
names. David Malloch, when he crossed the Border,
changed his name to Mallet; John Murray the publisher was originally M'Murray, as his predecessor,
Millan, had been Macmillan; William Almack, the
proprietor of the famous assembly-rooms in London,
had started life as M'Caul. One of Burns's own
friends, James M'Candlish, dropped the prefix when
he entered Glasgow University, and became simply
Candlish. Even today, in spite of Burns, the angliciz-

ing process continues: the visitor in Ayr, for instance, will find the street-signs pointing him to the 'New Bridge' and the 'Old Bridge'.

By 1780 Scotland could afford to smile at Johnson's dictum that her northern lights were only farthing candles. In literature at least she could face English competition on equal terms. James Thomson had become a classic; Adam Smith and Hume and Robertson had demonstrated that the north could more than hold its own with the south in history and philosophy; Mackenzie's lachrymose *Man of Feeling* disputed with *The Vicar of Wakefield* the claim to be the most popular short novel of the century. In Edinburgh a *Scots Magazine* was emulating the methods and materials of the English *Gentleman's Magazine*, though when Mackenzie and his friends tried, first in *The Mirror* and later in *The Lounger*, to produce a Scottish *Spectator* they found the city not metropolitan enough to support such an enterprise. Many people took anything sharp in the way of satire as a personal attack, but namby-pamby was not read, and so between poverty of material and poverty of support the journals' straw-fire flickered and went out.

But while the poor relations of England were thus looking forward hopefully to the day when their speech and writing should no longer betray their provincial origin, the social life of the country changed more slowly. The gentry added silks and laces to their clothing, and tea and other luxuries to their tables, but felt no special urgency for greater cleanliness. George Dempster, fresh from a visit to Brussels in 1756, was shocked to find that a baronet's son of his acquaintance had been calling on a lady of title 'in a valet de chamber's frock and an unpowdered brown greezy head'. Even at the beginning of the nineteenth century the inhabitants of a Highland mansion, though they had got beyond the point where they were satisfied to give themselves 'a "good wash" on Sundays, and make that do for the week', found their domestic routine upset by a guest who not only insisted on a daily bath but refused to go to the river to take it. Servants in the better houses were provided with shoes and stockings, but the general standards of neatness were still so low as to make the cleanliness of Holland a constant source of wonder to the visiting Scot.

But the aping of English manners had not yet undermined the traditional Scottish democracy of intercourse. Though the barriers which divided gentleman from commoner were fully as strong in Scotland as they were in England, they were not so visible. If many of the gentry lacked wealth, they did not lack pedigree, and a plebeian could rarely hope to cross the boundary that excluded him from social equality. Nobles married with nobles, and lairds with lairds. Yet until the end of the century the sons of nobles, lairds, and ploughmen commonly began their education together in the village school, where boy-fashion they took each other at face-value without regard to rank. The result was an almost total absence among the lower classes of that servility which was bred into their compeers in England. Only as more and more of the sons of gentlemen were sent to English public schools did the old system decay, and some of the gentry begin to compensate for the inferiority they had been made to feel in the presence of the English by assuming a haughty air with their humbler countrymen.

In short, all that had distinguished Scotland as a nation was on the way to oblivion. Literature, language, manners, and institutions were being anglicized as fast as a people roused to uneasy self-consciousness could manage it. In 1786 it seemed evident that when the former things passed away it would be into the darkness in which men and nations prefer to bury the ruder and more discreditable features of their early days. That the memory of the discarded heritage should be embalmed as a precious possession, and that the old world should be forever surrounded by the romantic glory of a golden sunset was due more to Robert Burns than to any other person. He made the Scots conscious of the richness of their national tradition. He could not restore it to life, but he taught his people to cherish its ruins.

II

EDUCATION

ROBERT BURNS was nearly nine years old before anything revealing his personality impressed his family enough to make them remember it. Unreliable tradition has it that he was a puny infant; slightly better evidence shows him as a nervous and temperamental child, alternating between wild high spirits and moody sullenness. Once, it is said, Robert hid in a cupboard when he and his schoolmates were frolicking. The master in restoring order struck the door a resounding blow with his tawse, and the nervous shock threw the child into such uncontrollable hysterical sobs that he had to be sent home. But the most devout worshipper would have trouble in discerning a future poet in so undifferentiated an episode. It is easier to do so in Gilbert Burns's story of what happened at Mount Oliphant one evening in 1768.

John Murdoch the schoolmaster had got a better post, and was paying a farewell visit to the parents of two of his promising pupils. As a parting gift, he brought a copy of *Titus Andronicus*. Beginning to read the play aloud, he soon came to the scene where her ravishers taunt the mutilated Lavinia. The children, in an agony of tears, implored him to read no more; whereupon their father dryly remarked that in that

case there was no use in Murdoch's leaving the
book. Robert exclaimed fiercely that if it was left, he
would burn it. Murdoch warded off the father's rebuke by commending the display of so much sensibility, though he failed, then or later, to explain why
he considered *Titus Andronicus* suitable reading for
children. *The Man of Feeling* was not yet written, but
'sensibility' was already a word of power, and
Robert Burns was already displaying the stormy
emotions which were his to the grave.

Murdoch's farewell marked the end of Burns's
elementary schooling, but the education of a boy
reared as he was cannot be appraised in terms of
mere schooling. If it could, the whole story might be
told in a few paragraphs. Burns's real education
came from his family, from what the world taught
him, and from what he taught himself. His schooling
was incidental.

The poet once had the curiosity to visit the He-
rald's Office in Edinburgh, only to discover that
'Gules, Purpure, Argent, &c., quite disowned' him
—no man of his name had ever borne coat armour.
The nearest he could come to it was 'Burn'. Inquiry
into his ancestry is fruitless, because nothing in his
ancestry explains Burns, any more than the dull line
of squires into which he was born can explain Shelley, or a London livery-stable Keats. Burns's family
produced no genius before him; it produced none
after him. It is enough to record that William
Burnes, the poet's father, came of peasant stock
from the eastern Lowlands of Scotland. The poet

cherished the belief that some of his forebears had been out in the 'Fifteen in the train of George Keith, tenth Earl Marischal, but documentary proof is lacking. The poet's grandfather, Robert Burnes, farmed, apparently with indifferent success, in Kincardineshire, first on the farm of Kinmonth, in Glenbervie, and later at Clochnahill, Dunnottar. Robert Burnes's second farming venture having failed in 1747, his son William (born 1721) set out in the following year with his younger brother, Robert, to seek work.

William Burnes had had some training as a gardener, and found his first employment in Edinburgh. By 1750, however, he was in Ayrshire, where, after brief service on two other estates, he finally entered the service of Provost William Fergusson, laird of Doonholm in Alloway parish. These frequent moves were not wholly the result of unsettled labour conditions. Pride and self-assertiveness handicap the man doomed to subordination, and these traits William Burnes possessed in full measure. 'Stubborn, ungainly Integrity', said Burns of his father, 'and headlong, ungovernable Irascibility are disqualifying circumstances'. William Burnes needed to be his own master, and in 1757 managed to 'feu' (lease in perpetuity) seven acres of land a few hundred yards north of the ruined old Kirk of Alloway.

Besides longing for a farm of his own, William Burnes wanted a wife and a home. Seven acres of market-garden, supplemented by continued part-time employment at Doonholm, made marriage possible. With his own hands he raised the rammed-clay walls of a cottage on his land—a cottage which his younger son declared, with more emphasis than the timid Gilbert usually permitted himself, to be 'such as no family of the same rank, in the present improved style of living, would think themselves ill lodged in'. From without, the whitewashed walls and thatched roof of the 'clay biggin' were picturesque enough; within, it was damp, dark, and narrow, and smelly withal, for the byre and stable were under the same roof of rat-infested thatch. But such rural Scots as lived to grow up in those days were inured to dampness, smells, and vermin, and it was probably with unmixed pride that William Burnes and his wife set up housekeeping in December, 1757.

The bridegroom was 'advanced in life'; he was in fact almost as old when he married as his famous son was when he died. His red-haired bride, twelve years his junior, was Agnes Broun of Kirkoswald. The daughter of a small farmer, she had been accustomed from childhood to the life of toil which marriage intensified. Her girlhood as housekeeper for her widowed father and manager of his younger children had given plenty of domestic training, but formal education was too great a luxury for girls; the mother of Scotland's greatest poet was never able to write her own name. She had, however, a sort of literary education more valuable for her son than savouring at first hand the dullness of Boston's *Fourfold State* could have been. Blessed with a sense of humour, a retentive memory, and a keen ear, the girl had stored her mind with a wealth of ballads, folk-songs, and country sayings which later became an integral part of her son's thought and art. The seeds of the poet's imagination and wit were his mother's; William Burnes's most conspicuous contribution to his son's character was his fierce and prickly pride.

A little more than thirteen months after his parents' marriage, on January 25, 1759, Robert Burns was born. The Scottish winter was doing its worst— 'a blast o' Janwar' win' blew handsel in on Robin'. In other words, a few days after the poet's birth a wild Atlantic gale tore out part of the clay gable of the cottage where it had settled unevenly round the stone jambs of the chimney. Mother and baby had to be carried through the storm to a neighbour's house, where they sheltered until the damage could be repaired. To Burns in later years the incident seemed an augury of his own stormy life. The world had begun to educate him to its harshness almost before he knew that he was in it. Fortunately he had a father who was determined that his children should also have an education in the more conventional sense.

Though Scotland theoretically provided a free school in every parish, the usual gap separated theory and practice. Sometimes there was no school at all; often the school was an unsanitary hovel presided over by a master who was expected to live on a salary of perhaps ten or fifteen pounds a year, and who therefore was constantly driven to desperate shifts to provide for himself and his family. John Wilson of Tarbolton, for instance, the victim of 'Death and Dr. Hornbook', tried to eke out his meagre earnings by starting a little grocery shop in his cottage, and in 1790 was ready to undertake the drudgery of a legal copyist in Edinburgh in order to better his condition. After the close of the century, when every parish was ordered by Act of Parliament to provide its schoolmaster with a house of at least two rooms, some lairds objected to erecting 'palaces for dominies'. And even when a parish had a decent schoolhouse and a competent teacher, bad roads and lack of conveyance often made it impossible for children from outlying farms to reach it.

When William Burnes built his cottage at Alloway the fact that there was no school nearer than Ayr would scarcely have worried him. His own book-learning was sketchy, his writing cramped and laborious, though his speech was more precise and 'better English' than that of most of his neighbours. But he was devoutly religious, and cherished the sound Presbyterian conviction that first-hand acquaintance with the Scriptures was essential to knowledge in this world and salvation in the next. By the time his eldest son was six years old the father, conscious of his own inadequacy as a teacher, arranged with half a dozen neighbours to hire a master of their own. Their choice fell on John Murdoch, a solemn and pedantic youth of eighteen, who in mentality somewhat resembled Ichabod Crane.

For wages of about sixpence a day and his board—
which meant a share of the oatmeal and kail and
part of a bed in each crowded cottage in turn—
Murdoch undertook to instruct his charges, not
without tears, in the three R's and also in such elementary music as would enable them to sing the
Psalms of David in metre at family worship.

In this latter accomplishment he found Robert
Burns, who in manhood was able to remember and
distinguish in all their subtle variations hundreds
of folk melodies, an almost hopeless pupil with a
harsh and untuneable voice. At the task of beating
into the future poet the elements of spelling, grammar, and syntax he was more successful. Instruction
in reading was based largely on a volume of extracts
compiled by another Scottish schoolmaster named
Arthur Masson—good enough literature for the
most part, but too declamatory to be really within
the grasp of a six- or seven-year-old intelligence.
Robert's first conscious realization of poetic experience came from Addison's hymn, 'How are Thy
servants blest, O Lord': he also memorized the 'Fall
of Cardinal Wolsey' and other set pieces so thoroughly that throughout his life their phrases came
unbidden from his pen. If Murdoch found difficulty
in making the children understand the poetic merits
of Hamlet's soliloquies or of long passages from
Home's *Tragedy of Douglas*, he at least convinced
some of them that poetry had meaning. One of his
favourite exercises was making them paraphrase
poetry into straight-forward prose—a device which

his most famous pupil subsequently employed in exposing bad grammar in a female admirer's verses.

Murdoch was not the man to set a poetic child's imagination on fire, and since he applied the usual schoolmasterly standard of judging the pupils according to their docility, it is hardly surprising that he found the timid and gentle Gilbert a more promising lad than his brother. In any case, Murdoch's service was too brief to have much permanent influence on Burns's mind. Before the master had completed his tenure of about two years and a half at Alloway, William Burnes had removed to Mount Oliphant farm, separated from the school by two miles of sodden road which must have made regular attendance difficult, and sometimes impossible. Yet the master retained a sort of puzzled affection for the boy whom he was too prosaic to understand, and Burns reciprocated the feeling with real respect and esteem. Murdoch, in the schoolroom and in the long evenings in what he called the argillaceous fabric or mud domicile at Alloway, had at least impressed the lesson that books had meaning and that words should be used with precision. That Burns in later life never had any difficulty in saying precisely what he meant, he probably owed at root to Murdoch's severe drill; that his style of saying it was frequently much too formal he likewise owed to the dominie and to the prose selections of Arthur Masson.

The earliest stages of book education are seldom important in shaping the maturity of the learner. They only furnish him with a few tools which he may later apply in his own way to his own ends. But with Burns the whole pressure of his formal education was all his life in direct conflict with his instinctive preferences. For John Murdoch, as for Arthur Masson, Scottish vernacular literature did not exist. Scottish writers like James Thomson and John Home, who had made reputations in England by writing in standard English, were admired to the far side of idolatry, but for Scottish youths, as for English, Pope was the model for poetry; the *Tatler* and *Spectator* for prose. Shakespeare, Milton, and Dryden were the only writers earlier than 1700 who were widely read and unreservedly admired, though the beginnings of romanticism were evoking some lip-service to Spenser. If Chaucer was read at all, it was in the modernizations and imitations of Dryden, Pope, and Prior; the Elizabethan and Caroline lyrists were safe sources for newspaper poets to steal from, as Sterne stole from Burton. By modern standards, the amount of native literature needed in order to appear well-read was limited, but its very limitation intensified its pressure. Poverty kept Burns from the influence, for good or ill, of the classics; nothing could preserve anyone, who read at all, from the influence of the neo-classics. Outside the door the rich vernacular literature of Scotland was still vigorously alive, but no schoolmaster in Burns's boyhood would have dreamed of letting it in.

This literature, indeed, was being steadily thrust further out of the cultivated world. Two years before the poet's father was born, Lady Elizabeth

Wardlaw had written the ballad fragment of 'Hardyknute' with genuine folk skill; in the next generation such interest as remained was contaminated with literary sophistication. The gentlefolk of William Burnes's generation could no longer write true ballads, but they could and did write true folk-songs, as witness Jean Elliot's 'Flowers of the Forest', Alison Cockburn's 'I've seen the smiling of Fortune beguiling', and John Skinner's 'Tullochgorum' and 'John o' Badenyon'. The gentlefolk of Robert Burns's generation had lost this power too. Burns was six years old when Percy's *Reliques* inaugurated the serious study of popular literature and let loose the spate of forgery and imitation of which Macpherson's *Ossian* was the most brilliant success. The national will to believe in Macpherson's fabrication was proof alike against the scorn of Dr. Johnson and the learning of antiquaries. To many Scots besides Burns Ossian was the 'prince of poets', to be read and admired as a patriotic duty, even if few of his vague and turgid phrases could be remembered long enough to quote. And what Macpherson did on the grand scale ballad 'editors' like John Pinkerton were doing on a small one, debasing even their genuine material with sentimental trash which blinded many readers to the merits of a really honest and accurate editor like David Herd.

But all this activity, alike of forgery and of honest collecting, never touched Burns in his formative years. In the boy's world the folk literature which David Herd was recording was still alive. It is a favourite fallacy of the half-educated to identify book-learning with education. The things which made the mind and the art of Burns did not come from John Murdoch, but from people whom Murdoch no doubt patronized in his most schoolmasterful style. Agnes Broun was illiterate, but she was not ignorant. Like most intelligent illiterates, she had cultivated her memory, storing it with the pithy sayings which sum up generations of folk experience, and with the words and music of scores of old songs and ballads. These simple rhythms, sung as she went about her work, sank into her son's mind without his knowing it. Years afterwards some chance association would recall an old line or stanza of his mother's to supply the 'starting note' for a song of his own. And her repertoire was powerfully supplemented by old Betty Davidson's, who 'had the largest collection in the county of tales and songs concerning devils, ghosts, fairies, brownies, witches, warlocks, spunkies, kelpies, elf-candles, dead-lights, wraiths, apparitions, cantraips, giants, enchanted towers, dragons and other trumpery'. To these tales, listened to with delighted shudders, he ascribed the first awakening of his imagination, even though some of them scared him so thoroughly that their effect stayed with him into manhood. No doubt many a gentleman's son heard similar stories from nurses and servants, but formal classical education effectually smothered any idea of putting them to literary use. Sir Walter Scott was almost the first child of the upper ranks to realize his folk-heritage, and probably he owed much of his freedom to do so to the interruption of his scholastic training. Ill-health saved him from formalism, as poverty saved Burns.

Burns's acquaintance with popular and traditional literature was not, however, limited to what he heard at home. The eighteenth century was the heyday of the chapbook and the broadside—forms of popular literature resulting from the spread of literacy among the middle and lower classes, which were finally swept away by the newspaper. In Burns's childhood every peddler's pack contained an assortment ranging from topical songs and reports of the death and dying words of the latest criminal to abridgements of old histories and romances. Even the poorest labourer could afford the penny or two these publications cost, and they passed from hand to hand until they were worn out. William Hamilton of Gilbertfield's modernization of Blind Harry's *History of Sir William Wallace*, which so roused Burns's boyish patriotism, may have reached the lad in chapbook form; the Life of Hannibal which he also mentions was almost certainly a chapbook; he was familiar from his earliest years with such ephemera as 'The Aberdeen Almanac' and 'Six Excellent New Songs'. But he nowhere mentions another group of writings which he assuredly read.

Only a few years before Burns was born, Dugal Graham, the hunchbacked bellman of Glasgow, began publishing a series of Scottish chapbooks. Their popularity was enormous; total sales are alleged to have run into the hundreds of thousands.

The most pretentious of Graham's works was a metrical history of the '45; the most characteristic were the humorous prose tales such as 'Jocky and Maggie's Courtship', 'The Adventures of John Cheap the Chapman', and 'The Comical Sayings of Paddy from Cork'. These chaps were made up of traditional anecdotes of a broadly comic sort, loosely strung together but supplied by Graham with the local colour of Scottish peasant life. Much of Graham's material had a long history; coarse jests which go back at least as far as Chaucer; folk-tales of unquenchable vitality, such as the one on which Synge long afterwards based *The Shadow of the Glen*; quaint figures of speech and wild exaggerations, some of which crossed the Atlantic to become the progenitors of the American 'tall story'. The peasant world as Graham depicted it was tough and crude and unlovely, but full of a coarse vitality which enlivened even the baldest passages of Graham's prose and which at its best expressed itself in pungent phrases remembered and used by Burns, probably long after he had forgotten their source. The most indecorous stanza in 'Holy Willie's Prayer' is based on a phrase from 'Jocky and Maggie's Courtship', as is a similar stanza in 'Death and Doctor Hornbook'.

But the peasant life of Scotland, however squalid its physical circumstances as Dugal Graham portrayed them, had a variety of interest unknown to the modern dweller in a city slum. When the technique of all the varied crafts necessary to rural life had to be learned by example and oral tradition, the whole process of living was an education. Almost as soon as they were able to walk the children began to take their part in the work of the farm. At the age of six or thereabouts the boys would be helping to guide the four-horse team which dragged the clumsy plough; not long afterwards they began to share in reaping, threshing, and winnowing, besides doing the innumerable and endless small chores of the farm. These tasks, with all their accompanying observations of plants and animals, of weather and seasons, were stronger influences on Burns than John Murdoch was. No poet has revealed a closer or more accurate knowledge of nature; no poet, it may be added, had less of romantic enthusiasm for pure scenery. Burns knew nature as the peasant and the savage knows it, as something on which his health and prosperity and his very life depend. Readers who are surprised that Burns spent much of his youth in sight of the noble peaks of Arran without ever mentioning them in his verse simply fail to understand the realism of the peasant's point of view. It was not the dalesmen who won a hard living from valley farms or kept their sheep on the bleak mountainsides who found the poetry in the Lake District. Had Burns been reared on Loch Lomond or at Aberfoyle it would have made no difference; he would have been too busy trying to wring a living from the soil to note the scenery. That had to wait for Sir Walter Scott, who had nothing to do but admire it. Even when he had won fame and had consciously accepted his vocation as a national poet Burns paid only lip-service to scenery as scenery. For him it was merely background for human figures, preferably female. The spots which really stirred his emotions were those with associations of history or song—Cawdor Castle, the field of Bannockburn, Elibanks and Elibraes, the Bush aboon Traquair. And the fact that so many of the folk-songs of Scotland celebrate the streams whose valleys were the only fertile spots may have fostered the love for running water repeatedly expressed in his poetry, as it certainly roused him to do for the streams of Ayrshire what his anonymous forerunners had done for the streams of the Border.

Not all the boy's education, however, was thus casual and informal. When his removal from Alloway to Mount Oliphant made it impossible for his sons to continue regular schooling William Burnes procured a few textbooks such as Guthrie's *Geographical Grammar* and Stackhouse's *History of the Bible* for their instruction. Despite the burden of farm work the father managed at times to set regular lessons to be conned at evening by the light of the kitchen fire or a tallow dip. Robert and Gilbert helped to teach their younger brothers and sisters to read and write; their own lessons included the use of a brief religious catechism which their father had himself prepared with Murdoch's help, for William Burnes was a devout man. Even in boyhood Burns, said Gilbert, was a reader when he could get books. He read whatever he could get his hands on, however dull or ponderous it might be, from theology to poetry. His own lists in his autobiography, highly selective though they are, are proof enough. His first knowledge of classical mythology, for instance, came from Andrew Tooke's *Pantheon*, an appallingly dull and didactic outline of Greek and Roman religion. He never had Keats's good fortune in discovering the Elizabethans: his Homer was Pope's and not Chapman's. But he reached manhood with a working knowledge of history and geography, a keen interest in current affairs, and an acquaintance with literature which, though spotty, was the more detailed because of its relatively narrow limits.

William Burnes's effort to educate his children at home was part of a family struggle which became one of the strongest influences in forming his son's character. The usual destiny of the children in a peasant family was to be hired out at the age of ten or twelve as farm servants. This fate, with its breaking of ties, cessation of schooling, and frequent moral danger, William Burnes was determined to avoid if possible. He was a stern father, but an affectionate one. John Murdoch remembered his wrath at a labourer's 'smutty innuendoes', and his children knew that carelessness in word or deed would be sharply rebuked. But they likewise remembered many acts of wordless affection, as when during a thunderstorm the father came to sit with his daughter Agnes because he knew she would be frightened.

When it became evident that the few acres at Alloway could not continue to support his growing family, William Burnes rented from his old employer, Provost Fergusson, the larger farm of Mount Oliphant. Gilbert Burns, who seldom used superlatives, declared that Mount Oliphant was almost the poorest land he had ever seen in cultivation. Yet for its seventy bleak and stony acres William Burnes undertook to pay £ 40 a year for the first six years of his lease, and £ 45 for the next six. It may not be too uncharitable to assume that the Provost saw in the tenancy of the stubbornly independent Burnes a chance to get a poor farm raised to a better level of cultivation. At any rate he showed his confidence in his tenant by advancing a hundred pounds towards stocking the place. Without this help the venture would probably have been impossible; nevertheless it saddled the family with an additional load of debt. The weight of the burden can be realized from the fact that in the 1770's in nearby Clydesdale twopence a dozen was a fair price for eggs, and chickens sold for sixpence a pair. Despite all handicaps, however, things went fairly well for the first half of the lease. In 1771 the family failed to take advantage of their privilege of relinquishing the farm, and accordingly were committed to another six years at an increased rental. Then began the series of disasters which ultimately killed William Burnes and permanently undermined the health of his eldest son.

Just at the onset of these dark days William Burnes, vexed at his children's bad handwriting, managed to send Robert and Gilbert, turn about, to

Dalrymple parish school for instruction in penman-
ship and grammar, that they might be better qualified to teach their brothers and sisters. By the following summer (1773), John Murdoch had returned
to Ayr and Robert was spared from the farm for
three weeks' additional tutoring. The lad clutched
at the opportunity like a famished man at food. He
was with Murdoch 'day and night, in school, at all
meals, and in all [his] walks'. At the end of the first
week, Murdoch says, 'I told him, that as he was now
pretty much master of the parts of speech, &c., I
should like to teach him something of French pronunciation; . . . and immediately we attacked the
French with great courage. Now, there was little
else to be heard but the declension of nouns, the
conjugation of verbs, &c. When walking together,
and even at meals, I was constantly telling him the
names of different objects, . . . so that he was
hourly laying in a stock of words, and sometimes
little phrases. In short, he took such pleasure in
learning, and I in teaching, that it was difficult to
say which of the two was most zealous in the business; and about the end of the second week of our
study of the French, we began to read a little of the
Adventures of Telemachus in Fénelon's own words.'
How much French Murdoch really knew is doubtful, though he later undertook to teach it in London,
and apparently secured some pupils until the Revolution filled the city with refugees who captured
the market. Burns ultimately acquired a reading
knowledge of the language, but if his riming *'respec-*

tueuse' with 'Susie' is a specimen of the pronunciation Murdoch taught he would scarcely have made himself understood in Paris.

Murdoch was this time most favourably impressed by Robert's ability, and, in his own inimitable language, regretted that at the approach of harvest 'Robert was summoned to relinquish the pleasing scenes that surrounded the grotto of Calypso, and, armed with a sickle, to seek glory by signalising himself in the fields of Ceres; and so he did, for although but about fifteen, I was told that he performed the work of a man.' Murdoch had seen no signs of the qualities which Burns afterwards declared made him as a child by no means a favourite with anybody; in his eagerness for learning he displayed only the retentive memory and the enthusiastic ardour which would have most endeared him to the pedantic master. The 'stubborn ungainly something' which later ripened into pride was filling him with smothered rebellion against his lot in life; the weeks with Murdoch opened for a moment a door through which it seemed that he might escape. He was becoming class-conscious, and was developing a hatred of stupid wealth and power which never left him. His earliest associations with the sons of the gentry had not been unpleasant, for these lads had not yet acquired 'a just sense of the immense distance between them and their ragged Playfellows'. 'My young superiours', he said, 'never insulted the clouterly appearance of my ploughboy carcass, the two extremes of which were often exposed to all the inclemencies of all the seasons.' They gave him stray volumes of books; one lad even helped him with his French. Nevertheless, he could remember in manhood how as a mere child he almost choked with rage in church one Sunday at the sight of a pretty servant-lass being compelled to leave her pew to make room for the stupid son of her employer.

About the time of his last association with Murdoch he began to have occasions for rage without going to church for them. Provost Fergusson died in 1771, and the administration of his property fell into the hands of a steward or factor. Fergusson had probably been lenient if his tenant could not make payment in full on each quarter-day, but it was the factor's business to get in the rents, and if they were not paid he wrote threatening letters to demand them. It is always difficult for a debtor to see things from the creditor's point of view; for Robert Burns it was impossible. For him the factor was a scoundrel, and his dunning letters were deliberate efforts to humiliate the unfortunates in his power. Not but what the Burnes family had reason for feeling resentful. They were doing everything that was humanly possible, and more than was wise, to meet the factor's demands. They lived very poorly, even by Scottish peasant standards; meat was almost unknown on their table; they gave up all hired help. At the age of fourteen, as Murdoch noted, Burns was doing a man's work, guiding the clumsy plough, flailing out grain by hand, and performing all the other tasks at which brute strength had to serve not

merely instead of machinery but instead of well-
made tools. His gait became the clumsy tread of the
ploughman; his young shoulders developed a permanent stoop from handling the awkward plough-
stilts. But the worst physical effect was invisible.
The adolescent boy doing a man's work on insufficient food was incurably injuring his heart. When
the lesion began to manifest itself in dizziness and
faintness Robert was not sent to a doctor. Probably
it would have made no difference if he had been, for
the trouble could scarcely have been diagnosed
without a stethoscope. Instead he used heroic measures which must have aggravated the ailment. At
one time he kept a tub of water beside his bed, and
when faintness came on him in the night he would
take a cold plunge. All his life he was plagued with
fits of depression which he described by the fashionable term, hypochondria. His heart lesion intensified the nervous instability he had shown as a child,
and thereby contributed to the perennially reckless
conduct of his manhood. In all his life, as in his
death, he continued to pay the heaviest share of the
price of his father's struggle to hold on at Mount
Oliphant.

A boy seldom realizes that he is overstraining
himself. What irked Burns at the time, far more than
'the unceasing moil of a galley-slave', was the fact
that he was almost wholly cut off from social intercourse. Burns may not have been wholly an extro-
vert, but he needed society as an outlet for his high
spirits and as a refuge from his low ones. In his ear-

lier boyhood he had found friends both among schoolfellows of his own rank and among the sons of neighbouring gentlemen. At Mount Oliphant he was cut off. Murdoch would come out on his half-holidays, 'with one or two persons more intelligent than [himself], that good William Burnes might enjoy a mental feast'. This conversation of 'solid reason, sensible remark, and a moderate seasoning of jocularity' was not what the boy needed. Robert and Gilbert 'began to talk and reason like men, much sooner than their neighbours', but this precocious maturity only made the lad more acutely conscious of his own lack of advantages. He envied the greater ease and assurance of his more fortunate fellows, and out of this envy and self-consciousness grew the aggressive manner upon which some of the gentry later remarked with disfavour.

As William Burnes's tenure at Mount Oliphant neared its end the clouds opened a little. The father had never wholly abandoned his hope of providing his eldest son with some sort of education, and in the summer of 1775 managed to send him for a few weeks to learn 'dialling and mensuration' at Kirkoswald. Superficially the venture seemed as fruitless as the earlier effort to learn French in three weeks. The master, Hugh Rodger, was as pedantic as Murdoch, but inclined to be harsh and sarcastic where Murdoch was earnest and encouraging. Though Burns acquired some practical mathematics which later proved useful in his Excise work, he found the more vivid part of his education outside the classroom.

With William Niven, a classmate of his own age, he indulged in spirited impromptu debates on such adolescent topics as 'Whether is a great general or a respectable merchant the most valuable member of society?' With a girl named Peggy Thomson he fell in love briefly, but so violently as to disorganize his work during his last days at school. Above all, he got glimpses of a sort of life very different from the seclusion of Mount Oliphant.

In the later eighteenth century smuggling rated as one of the major British industries. An excise tax of twenty shillings a gallon on spirits set an even higher premium on illicit dealing than prohibition did in the United States in the 1920's. Few of the 'best people' had any more scruples about dealing with smugglers than Americans had about dealing with bootleggers. Nor was smuggling confined to liquors. Tea, French silks and laces, and other goods on which the tariff was high were also run in in quantity. The coast near Kirkoswald was a centre for landing goods intended for the Ayrshire and Glasgow markets because it was almost the last point smuggling vessels could approach without grave risk of being trapped by the revenue cutters in the narrow waters of the Firth of Clyde. Samuel Brown, the uncle with whom Burns stayed at Kirkoswald, probably had a quiet share in the business; at any rate his nephew saw plenty of smugglers. In the taverns where these men spent the profits of their successful ventures Burns witnessed roistering of a wilder sort than market nights at Ayr exhibited. His

extremely limited means, however, make it impro-
bable that he often looked unconcernedly on a large
tavern bill, though ten years later he thought he
had. More likely the awkward youth was a spectator, as the poet was at Poosie Nansie's in 1785. A
Shakespearian delight in the salty flavour of raw
humanity was one of Burns's life-long characteristics which first found expression at Kirkoswald. In
1783 he wrote to John Murdoch, 'I seem to be one
sent into the world, to see, and observe; and I very
easily compound with the knave who tricks me of
my money, if there be anything original about him
which shews me human nature in a different light
from anything I have seen before.' His respectable
friends often deplored what seemed to them a de-
praved taste for low company, but, as his best friend
in Dumfries explained, it was not the lowness of the
company that attracted him; his companions were
of 'low ranks, but men of talent and humour'. It was
the colour of such company, its shrewdness, its reckless wit, and its unashamed gusto for life that made
Burns prefer it to the drab respectability of the
church-going bourgeoisie.

Crude humanity, however, was not the only
thing Burns studied at Kirkoswald. He encountered
some new books as well. Thomson's *Seasons* introduced him to the chief Scottish poet of the century
who had made his reputation by writing in standard
English; Shenstone's 'Elegies' and 'The Schoolmis-
tress' initiated him into the poetry of sentiment, and
the Spenserian stanza of the latter gave him the

verse-form for 'The Cotter's Saturday Night'. In reading these poets, however, he was merely extending an acquaintance already made through the specimens in Arthur Masson. His prose reading opened a different world. Novels were not to be found in the stricter Presbyterian homes, so *Pamela*, an odd volume of *Ferdinand Count Fathom*, and above all Mackenzie's *The Man of Feeling*, were a vivid experience. Nothing in his previous training had inoculated him against the virus of sentimentality; exposed to its most extreme form, he was infected for life. This, the lad no doubt said to himself, was the way persons of superior sensitivity looked upon life; very well, he could prove that his sensibility was equal to theirs. At the first opportunity he bought a copy of *The Man of Feeling* and carried it with him everywhere until he wore it out.

Had Burns known more of literature and of the world he would have been able to take Mackenzie's sentiment at the proper discount. Then the book's influence might have been good. It might gently have corrected the harshness of his peasant background, as the literature of sentiment in general ameliorated the brutality of the eighteenth-century world. As it was, the book set up a preposterous ideal which divided Burns's energies and sometimes vitiated his work. The crudities of peasant life needed softening and elevating, but sentimentalism made many of his efforts in this direction mawkish instead of humane. The poet who portrayed an old farmer's affection for a faithful mare was revealing sentiment

in the best sense of that much-abused word; the poet
who moralized over a ploughed-under weed was
pumping up emotions such as no real farmer ever
felt. Hence it is no exaggeration to say that the foundations for the weakest elements in his work, as well
as for the magnificent zest of 'The Jolly Beggars' and
'Tam o' Shanter', were laid at Kirkoswald.

Burns was probably right in saying that he came
home considerably improved. But he was also dis-
contented. Mount Oliphant seemed narrower and
drabber than ever after the colour of the smuggling
village, and he had become acutely conscious—
thanks equally to Peggy Thomson and to his tavern
companions—of his own awkwardness. This consciousness led him to his first overt act of rebellion.
In 'absolute defiance' of his father's commands, he
attended a country dancing school, to improve his
manners. William Burnes's 'Manual of Religious
Belief' indicates a willingness to mitigate some of the
sterner points of Presbyterian theology, but he was
in full agreement with the Kirk's condemnation of
worldly amusements. Gilbert Burns, as well as some
of his brother's biographers, tried to explain away
the remark about defiance, and the father may not
have pressed the point too far when he saw that
Robert's mind was made up. Undoubtedly, however, Burns was correctly describing his own feelings
at the time, and though the father sensibly accepted
the accomplished fact and later allowed his other
children to learn dancing he thenceforth regarded
his eldest son's conduct with suspicion and concern.

On leaving Kirkoswald Burns had undertaken to carry on a literary correspondence with some of his schoolfellows. He was bent on improving his powers of expression and acquiring a literary style. But the medium he selected was prose. Probably in retrospect he exaggerated the actual extent of this correspondence—it is hard to believe that 'every post' brought him as many letters as if he had been a merchant, or that he could have paid the postage if it had. The few surviving specimens are quite enough. The poet's uncle had once set out to buy one of the manuals of letter-writing which supply models for most of the imaginable contingencies of human life; he brought home instead 'a collection of letters by the Wits of Queen Ann's reign'. The exact volume has never been identified, though Burns's subsequent quotations show that it included letters of Pope, Bolingbroke, and Swift. But the eighteenth century, until Boswell taught it better, did not publish really familiar letters. Such collections as Pope helped to bring out were really composed of brief essays. Personal opinion was subdued; personal news was deleted. The 'unbridled effusions' which make the charm of familiar letters were suppressed. On such unfortunate models, almost as stiff as Elizabeth Rowe's 'Letters Moral and Entertaining' which he had found in his Masson, Burns set to work. The result was the same as when he encountered *The Man of Feeling*. A youth bred among literate people would have realized intuitively that these models showed only one side of letter-writing. Burns, with no other standards to measure them by, took them as the whole of the law and prophets, and shaped his epistolary style accordingly. His ear, attuned to the subtlest modulations of poetry, remained always deaf to the quieter graces of prose: when Dugald Stewart commended the simplicity of Franklin's writing, Burns could see nothing in it, 'when compared with the point, and antithesis, and quaintness of *Junius*.'

Those who have judged Burns adversely as a letter-writer would have still more grounds for their criticism had more letters survived like the few to William Niven and Thomas Orr. These country youths admired Burns's solemn analyses of Pride and Courage and his exhortations to be content with poverty; so, unfortunately, did the better-educated friends of his later life. The letters which he transcribed for Lady Harriet Don in 1787 and for Robert Riddell in 1791–93 belonged to the same school of prose as his earliest epistles to Niven. Burns would never have thought of making, nor his friends of asking for, transcripts of the admirable discussions of Scottish song which he sent to George Thomson, nor of his easier letters to John Ballantine and Mrs. Dunlop. No epistolary Robert Fergusson ever came into his hands to show him the way to a conversational style. When he wrote easy prose it was in spite of his models and because he had something to say which really demanded saying.

When the family at last escaped from Mount Oliphant in 1777 Burns was eighteen, the age at which

Chatterton, seven years before, had taken his own life. But Burns's self-education was a much slower process than Chatterton's. At eighteen he was still an awkward rustic, with all his intellectual and artistic powers still to find. The most positive result of the long ordeal at Mount Oliphant—apart from its injuries to his health—had been the building up of a strong sense of family loyalty. William Burnes had made every sacrifice to keep his family together, and the feeling that this was a primary obligation had been deeply impressed on his son. For the moment their prospects seemed hopeful. The father had managed to lease the larger farm of Lochlie near Tarbolton, and had again obtained from his landlord a cash advance for stock and improvements. But again Burnes was paying the penalty of his desperately independent character. For Lochlie's hundred and thirty acres of sour clay—so sour that the lease provided for two separate applications of lime at the rate of 400 bushels to an acre—its putative owner, David M'Lure, set a rental of £130. It was a ruinous bargain which broke William Burnes's spirit, helped to kill him, and gave his children some first-hand acquaintance with the chicanery of the law.

On Burns the first effect of the removal to Lochlie was social. The farm was within easy reach of Tarbolton village, where he found the companionship his nature craved. Of his friends at Mount Oliphant James Candlish's is the only name that has not perished; those of the Tarbolton cronies are enshrined

in both verse and prose. For the first couple of years
the records are almost blank. By his own testimony,
and Gilbert's, he was constantly falling tempestu-
ously in love, usually with girls of his own rank, or
below it, for 'he had always a particular jealousy of
people who were richer than himself, or who had
more consequence in life'. His imagination could
always endow any girl to whom he was attracted
with a plentiful stock of charms which bystanders
often failed to perceive. His ready pen, moreover,
was constantly at the service of his less fluent friends
who sought his aid in composing their love-letters,
and he 'felt as much pleasure at being in the secret
of half the amours in the parish, as ever did Premier
at knowing the intrigues of half the courts of
Europe.' But Gilbert's testimony corroborates his
own statement that none of these early affairs passed
the bounds of decorum. The fervours which he had
first experienced when reaping with Nellie Kilpatrick at the age of fifteen were growing stronger
and more clearly defined, but they were still
adolescent.

This adolescent Burns figures also in the proceedings of the Tarbolton Bachelors' Club, a social and
debating society which he and a few friends organized in the autumn of 1780. Its fragmentary records
show the youths arguing such windy topics as Burns
had discussed with Niven five years before, but with
a more direct application to his own walk of life.
E.g., 'Whether is the savage man or the peasant of a
civilized country, in the most happy situation?'

'Whether is a young man of the lower ranks of life likeliest to be happy who has got a good education, and his mind well informed, or he who has just the education and information of those around him?' 'Whether between friends, who have no reason to doubt each other's friendship, there should be any reserve?' Such topics point to Burns as their propounder, as do some of the Club's rules. The one which barred religious topics was doubtless in the interest of peace, but Burns's hand is evident in the tenth and last:

'Every man proper for a member of this society must have a frank, honest, open heart; above anything dirty or mean; and must be a professed lover of one or more of the female sex. No haughty, self-conceited person, who looks upon himself as superior to the rest of the club, and especially no mean-spirited, worldly mortal, whose only will is to heap up money, shall on any pretence whatever be admitted . . .'

Indecorum of language was likewise barred, and clerical biographers in discussing these rules have left the impression that the Club was a kind of Y.M.C.A. From what we know of peasant life in Scotland and of the adolescent male everywhere, it is possible that the biographers were mistaken. Whatever his conduct in 1780, Burns was soon applying the tenth rule in no platonic or idealistic sense.

Nevertheless the Club played an important part in developing his powers. Besides giving him an au-

dience for his ideas it showed him that he could
dominate his audience. Thenceforward Burns took
the lead in any social group where he was intimate;
his companions, re-echoing his wit, believed that
they shared it and even convinced him that they
did. The roster of his friends includes many wholly
commonplace people like John Richmond and
Robert Ainslie who shone only by reflected light, but
whose satellite nature Burns was quite unaware of
at the time. Moreover, the Club gave him almost his
first experience of the wine of applause, and he found
it a heady vintage.

Among the Tarbolton Bachelors was David
Sillar—not a charter member of the Club, but admitted to it early in 1781. A year younger than
Burns, Sillar, under his friend's inspiration, produced a few commonplace poems which gave Burns
the excuse for hailing him as brother poet. Sillar
had a certain gift for characterization in prose; he
described Tarbolton townfolk as 'uncontaminated
by reading, conversation, or reflection', and left the
most vivid extant picture of Burns on the threshold
of manhood. Burns was beginning to reveal the play-
boy elements in his nature—that desire above all
things to be conspicuous which he shared with such
very different geniuses as Sir Walter Scott, Charles
Dickens, Mark Twain, and Bernard Shaw. In a day
when strict Presbyterians still cropped their hair,
after the fashion which in the previous century had
earned them the name of Roundheads, Burns let
his grow long and wore it in a queue—'the only tied

hair in the parish'. When everyone else was wearing plaids of ordinary shepherd's gray, Burns sported one of dead-leaf colour. And since the uncontaminated parishioners of Tarbolton were orthodox Old Lights Burns acquired easy notoriety by setting up as a heretic.

Throughout his life Burns managed always to acquire a maximum of ill-repute with a minimum of actual transgression. It was not so much that he was conspicuously sinful as that he sinned conspicuously. Sometimes the conspicuousness was mere ill-luck. A fair portion, for instance, of the Edinburgh gossip which clung to his name may well have originated in the fact that both the servant girls with whom he had relations in the city brought legal action against him—a consequence he could scarcely have foreseen. On the other hand, his desire to startle the parish frequently bore fruit in suspicions and enmities impossible to live down. G.K.Chesterton once advised the village genius who wants to conquer something fundamentally and symbolically hostile and also very strong, not to come up to London but to stay at home and have a row with the rector. This was precisely what Burns did. The New Light doctrines which soft-pedalled such Calvinistic dogmas as predestination had already conquered Edinburgh and Glasgow and were beginning to invade the provinces. In any case Burns's saturation in the sentimentalism of Mackenzie and Sterne would have made him receptive to the New Light emphasis on Benevolence and the Moral Sense. But when the

congeniality of the new doctrines was joined with
an opportunity to startle his neighbours the combination was irresistible. He began, he says, to de-
bate theology with such heat and indiscretion as to
raise a cry of heresy which persisted in Tarbolton
and Mauchline as long as he remained there. An
anecdote, perhaps apocryphal, pictures him in the
kirkyard between services, expounding heretical
doctrines with such vigour as to elicit hisses and
cries of 'Shame!' from his auditors. At least the story
is true in spirit. Burns was determined to be conspicuous, even if it meant hisses instead of applause.

Masonic affiliations, which after his return from
Irvine supplanted the Bachelors' Club, gave him still
another chance to indulge both his social instincts
and his sympathies with liberal thought. A rural
lodge like St. James's at Tarbolton was, to be sure,
no such centre of political liberalism as were the
Masonic lodges of the Continent during the later
eighteenth century. The chief activity, in fact, of
most of the Scottish lodges seems to have been convivial, with the additional feature, lacking in the
ordinary social club, that the members were pledged
to help their fellows in sickness or distress. Nevertheless the knowledge that brother Masons in England
and abroad were disseminating ideas which challenged absolutism in government and religion must
have reached even village youths in Tarbolton. In
Scotland, moreover, the ritual which dignified the
childish thrill of membership in a secret organization
gave Freemasonry an emotional appeal which the

drab services of the Kirk and the narrow routine of every day lacked. From the time when he joined St. James's Lodge, about 1782, until after his sojourn in Edinburgh, Burns took his Masonic duties with the utmost seriousness. He helped to put the struggling and almost bankrupt lodge on its feet; from 1784 to 1787 he was its Depute Master. In Edinburgh he continued his affiliations, and perhaps the highest moment of all his early triumphal progress in the capital came at the meeting of the Grand Lodge of Scotland on January 13, 1787, when the Grand Master gave the toast, 'Caledonia, and Caledonia's Bard, brother Burns!' It is idle to conjecture if the coolness which followed his first acclaim in Edinburgh reached into Masonic circles; certainly the poet's interest in the craft waned in his later years. His letters from Ellisland and Dumfries scarcely mention it, except when he was in trouble and wanted Robert Graham to help him as a Mason as well as a friend. He duly affiliated himself with the Dumfries lodge, and became its Senior Warden, but if silence means anything the zest was gone.

The Masonic fellowship of course was male, but Burns was not forgetting his obligations as a member of the Bachelors' Club. His own statements and Gilbert's, already quoted, show a succession of passing infatuations with various girls whose names, even, are doubtful, and of whose personalities the most ardent legend-mongers can scarcely summon up a wraith. By comparison with such shadows as Anne Rankine and Mary Morison, even Nellie Kilpatrick who stirred the poet's blood for a single harvest, and Peggy Thomson, who overset his trigonometry at Kirkoswald, are three-dimensional. The one figure who half emerges from the shadows is Alison (or Ellison) Begbie. Burns met her in 1780 or 1781, but understanding of the matter is not clarified by the possibility that some of the five letters supposed to have been addressed to her may really be drafts of the love-letters he frequently wrote for his friends. Assuming them all to be Alison's, they prove mainly that Burns had not yet learned much about women. If ever farm-lass was wooed in such stilted and temperate phrases it is pretty certain that she was not in this humour won. Burns's intentions were serious; he wanted to marry Alison. Unfortunately the intentions made him serious too. He seemed afraid to commit himself in writing. A bystander is not surprised that Alison refused the man who told her that her company never gave him those giddy raptures so much talked of among lovers, and who announced that in his opinion married life was only friendship in a more exalted degree. It did surprise Burns. Indeed the shock of it led him subsequently to charge her with having jilted him, a difficult feat when his own letters prove she had never accepted him. No doubt she had merely employed the ancient technique of mild and non-committal encouragement while she was making up her mind. Burns had prided himself on his skill in letter-writing and on his address with women. To be flatly rejected the first time he made a serious proposal upset him for several months. It also completed his sentimental education. Thereafter, until he met Clarinda, he knew better than to do his courting by post.

But friendships with men and women, though they helped him momentarily to escape his blue devils, could not obscure the problem of his own and his family's future. He still lacked an aim. Conscious of more than average powers in himself, he had no purpose to which to direct them. Moreover, the years at Lochlie were bringing him for the first time to a realization of the workings of the larger economic laws. The American War was ruining the West of Scotland. Half its market for manufactured goods was closed; its exports to the West Indies were being raided by American privateers. Just before the war an over-expanded bank had failed, dragging down with it half the gentlemen in Ayrshire and leaving a trail of wreckage which was not wholly obliterated for a couple of decades. Even the wartime demand for farm produce was no help when multitudes of jobless artisans could not pay the high prices which at best would scarcely have yielded a fair return on the over-capitalized land. M'Lure, the landlord of Lochlie, was heavily mortgaged to the defunct bank. Hard pressed for cash, he tried to extort from his tenants more than was his due. William Burnes resisted, and became involved in litigation which followed him to the grave. In similar circumstances at Mount Oliphant Burns had seen merely a personal situation in which a vil-

lainous factor was demanding more rent than the
family could pay. Now he began to realize that a
man may be frugal and diligent in his business, and
yet be destroyed by forces which he did not start
and was powerless to control.

As early as 1780 Burns had experimented at
growing flax of his own on a few acres of land sub-
leased from his father; later he won a prize for his
seed. His success led him in 1781 to go to Irvine to
learn the trade of flax-dressing. Some consequences
of that venture belong in the next chapter; educa-
tionally the results, like those of so many youthful
experiences, were mainly negative. His distaste for
the work, and its ill effect on his health, left him
more aimless than before. He concluded that he was
unfit for the world of business, and where he had
formerly yearned for some chance of advancement
he now decided that he was destined to be only a
looker-on at life. All that restrained him from
complete shiftlessness was his sense of responsibility
for his family.

Intellectually, that sense was keener and more in-
sistent than ever, but now for the first time it was
in direct conflict with a storm of emotions. Burns
had come home empty-handed as the prodigal, to
find his father visibly sinking under the united effects of worry and tuberculosis. It was plain that
even if his contest with his landlord should be decided in his favour he would never be fit to undertake another farm. By the beginning of 1783 the
whole family, including William Burnes, realized

that death was at best a matter of months. M'Lure the landlord realized it too, and such scenes as had accompanied the reading of the factor's letters at Mount Oliphant were re-enacted at Lochlie with triple poignance. The children were old enough this time to understand the whole meaning of the affair; their father was a broken man, and where the factor had merely threatened legal action, M'Lure was taking it. The outcome of the case and the practical means whereby Gavin Hamilton helped the family through the crisis will be told later; its emotional impact on Burns himself, coming as it did on the heels of his own failure at business, could hardly be overstated. He saw his father's lifetime of struggle for independence ending in defeat and despair. Recollection of Mount Oliphant and Lochlie never ceased to haunt his own ventures as a farmer, and helped to damn them. Fear and hatred of one's economic position are seldom the heralds of success.

Burns's whole nature, in fact, was beginning to cry out against the life he was expected to lead. Not even the loyally accepted burden laid upon him from his father's weakening hands could hold him steady. He had come back from Irvine, as before from Kirkoswald, incapable of fitting again into the narrow pattern of the life he had lived before his departure. He had outgrown his mould. The dying father noted with concern that his son was spending longer hours with wilder companions, and displaying a new aggressiveness and assurance in his manner of speaking with women. Nevertheless the shadow of the old man's authority was still enough, when reinforced by the desperate need of securing the future of the family, to inhibit the full expression of the new tendencies. Gilbert's testimony is explicit. At Lochlie he and Robert were both allowed the usual labourer's wage of £7 a year, against which was charged the value of every piece of clothing manufactured at home. Neither there nor at Mossgiel did Robert's expenditures exceed this frugal sum. It was extravagance of emotion, of speech and conduct, not of expense, that beset the poet.

On his deathbed, on February 13, 1784, William Burnes muttered that there was one member of his family for whose future conduct he feared, and Robert, in tears, took the admonition to himself. Hardly was the family settled at Mossgiel, after some strictly legal dodging which must have increased the poet's inward distaste for the whole business, when the traits his father had dreaded began their full play. Though he entered on his responsibilities as head of the family with the best of resolutions, his heart was not in the undertaking. He read farming books, calculated crops, and attended markets, but his mind was elsewhere. According to his own account, he lost interest in the work because of two successive crop-failures, the first owing to bad seed and the second to a wet harvest. But this was an excuse, not an explanation. The real reasons lay within himself. They were his passions and his art.

His father's death had removed the last check

upon social indulgence. Always shunning the solitude which produced brooding melancholy, he had found in Mauchline a new and gayer set of cronies whose company was more congenial than that of his family in the crowded cottage at Mossgiel. More and more of his time was spent in the village taverns—not for drunkenness, but for the pleasure of sharing the hilarity of careless youths and the uninhibited wit of older 'men of talent and humour' like his neighbour John Rankine. The rigidly righteous began to frown on the young farmer whose reckless sallies were sure to provoke the wildest outbursts of laughter. And even at Mossgiel there were distractions from a sober and godly life. The household included a young servant-lass named Betty Paton, whose charms, like those of most of Burns's sweethearts, were mainly physical. Within a few months of his father's death Betty became Burns's mistress, and in May, 1785, bore his first child amid all the accompaniments of a public scandal in the parish.

Unpropitious though such beginnings were for a career as a tenant farmer, they were relatively unimportant compared with the inner compulsions arising from his discovery of his poetic vocation. Many another young farmer had sowed his wild oats and then settled down to rear a legitimate family and become an elder in the Kirk. For Burns such a future had really ceased to be possible even before he left Lochlie. In April, 1783, under the melancholy influence of his own ill-health and his father's dark prospects, he had begun to keep a commonplace book with the avowed intention of some day showing the world that a young plough-man, little indebted to scholastic education, was nevertheless capable of rime and reason. When he started the book his literary models were Shenstone, Mackenzie, and the folk-songs of his country. At some time during the next year, however, the poems of Robert Fergusson came into his hands. They roused him as Chapman's Homer roused Keats. For the first time he realized that the Scottish dialect might be something more than a dying relic of the past. He had been long acquainted with Allan Ramsay, but Ramsay belonged to the primitive age before Scottish letters had been ennobled by such geniuses as Henry Mackenzie, James Beattie, and John Home. Now he found that Fergusson, only ten years older than himself, had returned to the speech and the verse-forms of Ramsay. And Fergusson was no country boy but an educated lawyer's clerk bred in the Athens of the North. Reading these poems Burns realized their vivid descriptions and their wit—realized also that what Fergusson had done he could do as well, or better. Mauchline parish offered as many themes for homely satire as Edinburgh did.

The theme ready to hand was ecclesiastical controversy. The neighbourhood was ululating with disputes between Old Lights and New Lights, and the leaders on both sides were behaving with the lack of charity peculiar to Christians on the war-path.

Moreover, Burns's landlord and friend, Gavin Hamilton, was in the thick of it, standing trial before the Kirk Session on a charge of Sabbath-breaking. Two neighbouring Old Light ministers—John Russell of Kilmarnock and Alexander Moodie of Riccarton—chose this time for a quarrel over parish boundaries, and conducted their holy row with the heat and personal invective of a heresy-hunt. Burns improved the occasion by composing 'The Twa Herds'. Copying the poem in a disguised hand he showed it to Hamilton, remarking with studied gravity that he had no idea who the author was, but that he thought it pretty clever. Hamilton thought so too. Copies were passed from hand to hand; the New Lights, clergy as well as laity, received it with roars of applause; the Old Lights were correspondingly furious.

When Burns followed up 'The Twa Herds' with 'The Holy Fair', 'The Ordination', and 'Holy Willie's Prayer', the applause redoubled, and so did the enmity of the Old Lights. The man who challenges established institutions to their face needs to be sure of his own position. Burns's indiscretion with Betty Paton not only left him wide open to counter-attack but assured him of far more unpleasant notoriety than ordinarily accompanied such lapses in peasant Scotland. It was impossible to remain in the parish without submitting to the discipline of the Kirk. Even at its mildest the ordeal of three successive penitential appearances before Mauchline congregation would have been intensely humiliating to a man as sensitively proud as Burns. But a young bachelor's slips from grace were not usually treated very seriously except by the clergy and the Holy Willies. Had Burns been otherwise in good standing in the community he would have been able to go on much as before, but when the evidence of his breach of sexual morality was augmented by his ill-fame as a derider of the church he became, among all the more conservative members of the parish, little better than an outcast.

He may not have realized the full bitterness of the feeling against him until his repudiation by the Armours in the spring of 1786, but he realized enough. His reaction was as inevitable as the community's had been. If he was to be an outcast he would live up to his reputation. Many of his biographers since, as well as many of his neighbours at the time, have taken at face value the blatant pride in his ill-repute which marks such poems as the 'Epistle to John Rankine'. But this was not part of his real nature; he was simply brazening out his humiliation. The unco guid had decided that he was a dog with a bad name. He would show them that they had underestimated his capacity to shock them. That in the process he would make the parish too hot to hold him was a consideration not likely to occur to him in the full tide of his resentment.

But if his conflict with the Kirk had brought him humiliation it had also brought him the sense of power and the intoxication of applause. He had long known that his conversational wit and fire

could dominate a knot of cronies. Now he had
learned that he could write things which stirred
both the laughter and the deeper emotions of educated men as well as of his social equals. The hostility of the Holy Willies was even more inebriating
than the applause of Gavin Hamilton and his
friends. Men do not hate unless they fear; the measure of his success and power was the measure of the
antagonism he had aroused. The youth whose
weakness it had always been to lack an aim had
found one now. His education was complete. Intimate observation and experience of a small community had acquainted him with human nature,
and had at last roused him to realization of his own
capacities and his true vocation. His estimate of
himself and his work, he later told John Moore,
was pretty nearly as high in 1785 as it was two
years later, after all the adulation of Edinburgh.
All that he needed now was the opportunity to display his talents on a larger stage.

III

MEN

BURNS entered on his manhood at Irvine in 1781. Before his ill-starred venture as a flax-dresser he was an aimless and inarticulately rebellious youth; after it, though he was still aimless for a time, his rebellion against the narrow world of his origin was overt and vocal. Yet even under the stimulus of Irvine he was long in finding his proper speech. When he wrote the earliest of his extant letters, Burns, already a man in years, was still a boy in mind. His self-conscious disquisitions on such high-resounding themes as Pride and Courage mark him as less mature at twenty-one than Chatterton was at sixteen; he had passed the age at which Keats died before he began to say anything worth heeding. At twenty-two, his vague aspirations momentarily focussed on the idea of establishing himself in business as a necessary prelude to matrimony, he made his sole attempt at living according to the standards of a working-day world. Materially, the attempt was an abject failure; spiritually, it set him on the direct road to realizing himself.

Knowledge of the material side of the Irvine partnership is limited to what Burns himself told in his autobiographic letter, which is not wholly reliable evidence. Not that Burns intentionally coloured the facts. The safest rule in reading his letters is to take it for granted that if he said a thing about himself it was true; if he said a thing about someone else, he believed it to be true. But to his passionate temperament and 'skinless sensibility' (the phrase is his own) anyone through whom he suffered loss or humiliation became almost automatically a villain of the blackest. Hence his charges that Peacock, his Irvine partner, 'was a scoundrel of the first water, who made money by the mystery of thieving', need not be taken literally. Burns, a complete greenhorn at business, may possibly have been taken in by an unscrupulous rascal, but it is equally possible that Burns in retrospect blamed Peacock for a failure in which they were both at fault. In any case, the business side of these months influenced Burns's future only as it convinced him of his unfitness for 'the little chicaning art of bargain-making'. What really mattered were the new friends, and the new ideas of himself and his place in the world inspired by these friends and by the introspection resulting from ill-health.

Chief of the new friends was the sailor, Richard Brown, whom Burns looked up to as a junior schoolboy looks to the athletic senior. Brown was about the poet's age, but had all the worldly experience Burns lacked. He was better educated than most seamen of his day, though perhaps his story of having been patronized by a wealthy man who promised to set him up in life was only another sailor's yarn. He had at any rate abilities of a sort. An incompetent man could not have become the master of a West Indiaman while still in his twenties. But in 1781 that promotion was still to win. Brown just then was down on his luck. His ship had recently been captured by an American privateer, and he had been put ashore on the coast of Connaught with nothing but his life and the clothes he wore. Nevertheless the friendship with Burns probably began with something of patronage on Brown's part. The experienced, far-travelled, and distinctly hard-boiled sailor was interested in the awkward, stoop-shouldered country lad who in company alternated between sullen silence and—if he felt himself at ease—unusually vivid and copious speech. Obviously Brown realized that there was something in him; obviously also he took pleasure in enlightening him as to the ways of the world. Burns saw in Brown 'every noble, manly virtue' and strove to imitate him. Burns was already proud; Brown taught his pride to flow in proper channels—whatever that may mean. But Brown also was the only man the poet ever met who was a bigger fool than himself where women were concerned. The various god-desses by whom Burns's tinder heart was continu-ally lighted up still roused a hobbledehoy calf-love, as adolescent as his hero-worship of the sailor. Brown taught him that direct action might usually be counted on to bring results, and here, as Burns later admitted, the friendship did him a mischief.

Yet Brown was something more than a hard-boiled sailor initiating a green youngster. One

Sunday afternoon the pair took a walking trip to Eglinton Wood, where under the inspiring influence of a spot associated with the memory of Sir William Wallace Burns confided to his mentor that he occasionally tried to write poetry. He was already poet enough to have a copy in his pocket. Brown listened, and declared that verses of such merit ought to be sent to a magazine. It was actually this, Burns recorded long afterwards, that first gave him the idea that he might amount to something as a poet. It was one thing to have one's verses praised by a rural maiden like Nellie Kilpatrick or by one's own admiring family; it was quite another to have them endorsed by a man of the world. Unfortunately Burns failed to name the poem Brown commended. At a guess it may well have been the two somewhat bawdy stanzas beginning 'I murder hate by field or flood', Andrew Dunlop's manuscript of which was headed, 'On the great Recruiting in the year 17— during the American war'. Burns had no motive for mystifying Dunlop; hence the date of these stanzas can scarcely be later than 1781, and Brown would have been more likely to applaud such lines than the conventional religious pieces more or less contemporary with them.

The good as well as the ill of Brown's friendship belongs to the six or eight months at Irvine. If the friends met during the next four or five years, no references to their intercourse survive. When the Kilmarnock *Poems* were published, Brown received the only inscribed presentation copy on record, and in December, 1787, the two began a correspondence which lasted for a couple of years in the intervals of Brown's voyages. Their only recorded meeting, however, was in Glasgow in February, 1788, when the poet told Brown all about Jean Armour. Burns's last letter, in November, 1789, in reply to a complaint about his silence, is as cordial as ever, yet the friendship ended. According to tradition, Burns's charge about Brown's moral influence had reached the sailor, now a married man with a steadily improving position to maintain and far from eager to be reminded that he had heard the chimes at midnight. After Brown's death, the presentation copy was found hidden away in the back of an old sideboard. The sailor was not the only friend who in later years wanted to live down his associations with the poet. The descendants of John Wilson concealed for more than a century the fact that instead of resenting 'Death and Dr. Hornbook' he appealed to Burns for help when his position as schoolmaster at Tarbolton became intolerable. On the other hand, James Humphry of Mauchline continued till his dying day to boast that he was 'Burns's bletherin' bitch'.

During the same months in which Brown was stirring Burns to a new self-confidence his health was producing opposite effects. Throughout his life his diseased heart reacted unfavourably to nervous stress; the Irvine experience was the first of many. Realization of his bad bargain with Peacock combined with the unaccustomed strain of dusty indoor labour to bring on a period of 'hypochondria'—in other words, nervous depression resulting from defective heart-action. Its tangible results were such lachrymose verses as the 'Prayer in the Prospect of Death' and the letter to his father in which he announces that he is 'quite transported at the thought that ere long, perhaps very soon, I shall bid an eternal adiew to all the pains, and uneasiness, and disquietudes of this weary life; for I assure you I am heartily tired of it.' The letter is not merely morbid, it is adolescent; and Mrs. Carswell has noted that the solemn announcement that 'I am not formed for the bustle of the busy nor the flutter of the Gay' is cribbed verbatim from *The Man of Feeling*. William Burnes, however, probably regarded it as admirable proof that his son was beginning to take serious views of religion and life. In any case it represents only a passing mood of ill-health. The important fact about the Irvine days is that Burns was considering seriously his own abilities and his future position.

The partnership had at least the merit of a dramatic and even spectacular finish. A New Year's Eve celebration, whatever it may have done for Burns, brought his partner and his wife to such a state of drunkenness that they knocked over a lamp and set fire to the shop. The place was completely burned out, and after a month or two Burns returned to Lochlie poorer than he went, but with a rich store of experiences, a new outlook on life, and a mature confidence in himself which he had never before possessed. But he still lacked an aim. For another four years the pride which Brown had

taught to flow in proper channels was still to display itself mainly in obscure rebellion against his
lot in life, and in anything but obscure defiance of
the unco guid.

The situation confronting him at home would in
any event have matured him, but without Irvine
it might have been in a different way. Firmly convinced as always of his own justice and rectitude—
a conviction which he imparted with equal vigour
to his eldest son—William Burnes was closing his
long series of misfortunes in a violent contest with
his landlord, David M'Lure. The dispute had begun in a difference over their respective shares of
the expenses of liming and fencing the farm and
erecting new buildings. Pending arbitration of the
case, William Burnes had held up payment of his
rent. In September, 1782, the matter was submitted to James Grieve of Boghead and Charles
Norval of Coilsfield—chosen respectively by M'Lure
and Burnes—for adjudication. When they were unable to agree, John Hamilton of Sundrum was
chosen as 'Oversman' or referee. Not until August,
1783, did Hamilton complete his analysis of the
accounts and hand down his decision, which was
that of £ 775 claimed by M'Lure, £ 543 was offset
by credits for improvements made by Burnes, part
payments on rent, and other items. But before this
decision was rendered M'Lure, whose estates were
heavily mortgaged to the defunct Douglas and
Heron Bank, and who desperately needed cash, had
tried to force payment by entering a sequestration

on the stock and crops of Lochlie. By the time John
Hamilton reported, M'Lure was so deep in debt
that it was uncertain whether the rent belonged to
him or to his creditors. Thereupon indomitable
William Burnes carried the case to the Court of
Session at Edinburgh. His first petition being
thrown out on a technicality, he renewed it, and
at last, on January 27, 1784, less than three weeks
before his death, won his case. He had had the cash
on hand to deposit with the court, when he made
his appeal, the whole amount due; the decision ab-
solved him of further responsibility in the matter,
and summoned the various claimants to bring in
their claims for adjudication. William Burnes had
vindicated himself; his view of his obligations had
been upheld by the highest court in the land. All
that it had cost him was the last of his money and
the last of his strength. He was not an old man, but
the long struggle for livelihood, culminating in the
protracted lawsuit, made him the easier prey to
tuberculosis. His conviction of his own rightness, like
his irascibility, grew stronger as his body weakened,
and mingled with his wrath at M'Lure was anxiety,
bluntly expressed, over Robert's growing defiance
of Presbyterian decorum.

In calmer circumstances, his father's displeasure
would have weighed heavily on the poet's mind,
but now he was looking beyond it. Watching their
father's sinking health, the children were consulting
with each other about their future. The end of
Lochlie could not be long delayed: death would

evict them, because after the litigation none of the
claimants to the property was likely to give them a
renewal of the lease. Though Robert subsequently
gave Gilbert the credit of being a full partner in the
next undertaking, he probably was not. It is difficult to imagine the timid and subservient Gilbert
taking the lead in anything. Not long after returning
from Irvine Burns had made the acquaintance of a
prosperous Mauchline lawyer named Gavin Hamilton, who may have been attracted to the young
farmer by reports of his outspoken ridicule of the
Old Lights in the Kirk. Hamilton being also a
Mason, they doubtless met first in the fellowship of
square and compass. The lawyer, already in hot
water with his more orthodox neighbours, may also
have realized the potential value of Burns's wit in
the impending contests, but whatever his motives it
was Hamilton who suggested to William Burnes's
children a practical and legal way out of their
trouble.

Several years before, Hamilton had rented Mossgiel farm, about three miles from Mauchline, and
had rebuilt the cottage as a country retreat. The
plan of being gentleman farmer as well as lawyer
had palled, and Hamilton now offered to sublet
Mossgiel to Robert and Gilbert at a lower rental—
£ 90 a year for 118 acres—than they were paying at
Lochlie. The lease was quietly signed at Martinmas,
1783, it being apparent by that time that William
Burnes had not many weeks to live. Secrecy was
necessary; the Court of Session had not yet rendered

its decision, and their action, if it became known, might be unfavourably construed. Whatever small savings had not gone for legal expenses were invested in the new enterprise, and Hamilton pointed out a loop-hole through which the children might salvage something after their father's death. Robert and Gilbert were already credited with the regular wages of labourers. Let the other children also get themselves ranked as employees on the farm. Then they could enter claims for unpaid wages against their father's estate, thereby becoming preferred creditors who must be paid in full before M'Lure or his mortgagors got anything. The scheme worked. Enough was saved from the wreck to enable the family, shaken and desperately poor—when the youngest boy, John, died in November, 1785, they could not raise the few shillings to pay for the best mortcloth at his funeral—to re-establish their household at Mossgiel, intact except for its head.

The new head was Robert, and in the months that followed his father's death the full results of his Irvine lessons showed for the first time. In the two intervening years he had been too much oppressed with labour and anxiety to have time or inclination to show the new spirit in all its fullness, though he had shown enough to disturb his father. Now he was free, and the fruits of his freedom were varied and not always edifying. The earnest young debater of the Tarbolton Bachelors' Club and the self-conscious author of essay-letters gave place to Rab Mossgiel. Burns became the focus for a group of reckless youngsters, most of them younger than himself, who looked up to him much as he had looked up to Richard Brown three years before. Foremost in the group were John Richmond and James Smith, both of them full of the animal high spirits which so often disguise the basic common-placeness of young minds. Along with Burns they set out to scandalize the orthodox, and succeeded. By the end of 1785 Richmond and Smith, like Burns, had mounted the cutty-stool for fornication, and Richmond had fled from the turmoil to the comparative sanctuary of an Edinburgh lawyer's office.

These cronies are chiefly noteworthy as evidence of Burns's still uncritical mind. As with Bob Ainslie later, there was really nothing to them except youthful exuberance. Their laughter was the ready chorus for Burns's wit; his sparkle made them shine with a reflected light to which they actually contributed little. By comparison the poor poetaster, Davie Sillar of the Tarbolton Bachelors, was almost a genius. In his characterization of Tarbolton towns-folk Sillar left behind him at least one quotable phrase, which is more than any of the Mauchline group did. They cannot be charged with leading Burns astray—if any leading was needed Burns supplied it—and their biographical importance is negligible except as they gave him an outlet for confidences which might not otherwise have been recorded. When Burns went to Edinburgh he lodged with Richmond during his first winter; during the second winter Richmond was in Mauchline a good

part of the time. Burns's last extant letters to him
reveal some details about Jean Armour and her
children, but lack the enthusiasm of the ones written
in 1786. Smith left Mauchline to engage in calico-
printing at Linlithgow. Failing there, he fled to the
West Indies and died obscurely, as Burns came so
near doing. Both friendships were spent and empty
before the correspondence closed. The contrast between the mediocre abilities of the two men and the
quality of the poetry they evoked from Burns is
even more remarkable than the disparity between
the illiterate farm-lasses of Tarbolton and Mauchline and the lyrics Burns addressed to them.

By the time he was twenty-six Burns's status
among people of his own rank was firmly established. He was the unquestioned leader of the reckless young; the welcome companion of ribald and
unorthodox elders. The attitude toward him of the
staid and sober ranged from sad head-shaking to
violent denunciation. With people of rank above
his own, however, he was still uneasy. Hamilton
was probably the first man of the professional class
with whom he formed a genuine friendship. John
Mackenzie, the Mauchline surgeon who attended
William Burnes in his last illness, remembered that
on first visiting Lochlie he found Gilbert frank, modest, well-informed, and communicative, the father
revealing the remains of an able mind beneath the
cloud of illness and distress, and the mother quiet,
sagacious, and self-possessed. But Burns sat glower-
ing in a dark corner, 'distant, suspicious,' and with-

out any wish to interest or please'; scrutinizing
Mackenzie and obviously prepared to resent any
display of superiority or patronage. As the doctor
showed himself affable Burns gradually thawed.
Though the written records of the friendship are
meagre, Burns plainly liked and trusted Mackenzie,
and Mackenzie reciprocated. From the time of their
first meeting, the doctor declared, 'I took a lively
interest in Robert Burns, and, before I was acquainted with his poetical power, I perceived that he
possessed very great mental abilities, an uncommon,
fertile and lively imagination, a thorough acquaintance with many of our Scottish poets, and an enthusiastic admiration of Ramsay and Fergusson. I have
always thought that no person could have a just
idea of the extent of Burns's talents who had not an
opportunity to hear him converse. His discrimina-
tion of character was great beyond that of any person I ever knew. . . .' The surgeon introduced
Burns as a poet to his own friend and patron, Sir
John Whitefoord, who had previously known of
the young farmer only as an earnest member of
St. James's Lodge; he also gave an introduction to
Captain Andrew Erskine of Edinburgh, Boswell's
friend, and claimed to have been the first to bring
the Kilmarnock *Poems* to the attention of Hugh
Blair. It was to Mackenzie and not to Gavin Hamilton that Burns turned for very practical help in the
stormy weeks preceding his final acknowledgement
of his marriage to Jean Armour, and when Mackenzie provided Jean and her lover with quarters in his

own house he must have faced a weight of criticism from the embattled saints and gossips of the village that would have daunted many a man with a professional status to maintain.

The pride which Richard Brown had taught to flow in proper channels was becoming all the more touchy as Burns's confidence in himself increased. Sure of himself now among his equals, he was still resentfully helpless when superiors rubbed in their superiority. He had come as far as he could in his merely social capacity; what carried him the rest of the way was his poetry. Here Gavin Hamilton more or less unwittingly took the lead in introducing Burns to a new world. The Kirk Session of Mauchline, seeking to re-establish the old-time rigours of the Scottish Sabbath, had decided for once to make an example of a prominent citizen instead of an obscure one. Accordingly in the summer of 1784 Hamilton was summoned to stand trial for various ecclesiastical crimes such as absenting himself from church, habitually neglecting family worship, and causing a servant to dig new potatoes on a Sunday. On being convicted, Hamilton promptly appealed his case to the Presbytery of Ayr, and ultimately won it. How Burns intervened with 'The Twa Herds' has already been told. His authorship of that poem and its successors was soon avowed as the manuscripts passed from hand to New Light hand amid roars of Homeric laughter. People and institutions accustomed to taking themselves and being taken by others with the most intense serious-

ness are helpless in the face of mirth. Burns had
found the one weapon which the orthodox could
not withstand, though they could, and did, revenge
themselves on the author of their humiliation. The
fury generated by his satires did as much as, or
more than, the odium of his personal sins to make
Mauchline so unbearable that by 1786 Burns was
ready to flee to Jamaica.

But if his satires made the village too hot for him
they were also the direct means of enabling him to
escape both from the village and from the ranks of
the peasantry. One of the first friends to whom
Hamilton showed 'The Twa Herds' was another
lawyer, Robert Aiken of Ayr, who conducted and
won Hamilton's case before the Presbytery. Hamilton, apart from the conviviality almost inseparable from a man of his profession in eighteenth-
century Scotland, was cool and businesslike. Aiken
was emotional and enthusiastic, a good forensic
reader and speaker, and an easy prey to sentiment.
Pathos, in life or in a poem, suffused his eyes with
tears and set the buttons popping on his tight waistcoat. But, like the more famous Man of Feeling,
Henry Mackenzie, Aiken seldom in daily life permitted sentiment to overcloud common sense. Along
with his fellow townsman, John Ballantine the
banker, the lawyer soon became the poet's confidant
and chief literary adviser. 'Orator Bob' lost no opportunity of reading his young friend's verses aloud,
with such expression that Burns later declared he
had never fully appreciated his own work until he

heard Aiken read it. As the poet's troubles thickened in the early months of 1786 it was with Aiken and Ballantine that he discussed both his plans for emigration and his arrangements for publishing his poems, their decision as to what ought to be included in the Kilmarnock volume apparently being final. Though Aiken's action, as James Armour's legal adviser, in cancelling whatever 'lines' Burns had given Jean, caused a momentary chill, the lawyer soon proved that his professional conduct did not interfere with his private friendships. He obtained 145 subscriptions for the Kilmarnock *Poems*— nearly one-fourth of the entire edition. Even amid the excitement of his first dazzling fame in Edinburgh Burns recalled with a glow of affection the kindly patronage of Aiken and Ballantine, and long after he had quitted Ayrshire forever he continued from time to time to send them new poems which he thought they might like. As late as 1791 he was still gratefully remembering Ballantine's part in handing him 'up to the "Court of the Gentiles" in the temple of Fame'—a figure of speech which combined neatness and literal accuracy. It was only to the outer court—that of the bourgeoisie and minor gentry—that Aiken and Ballantine were able to conduct him.

The association with Hamilton fared worse. Poetry, except in the form of humour and satire, did not, it would seem, appeal to Hamilton as it did to Aiken, and between him and Burns was always the barrier of their business relation as landlord and tenant. Ultimately, indeed, a matter of business estranged them. In the spring of 1788, nearly two years after Gilbert Burns had become the sole lessee of Mossgiel, Hamilton apparently asked Burns to become his brother's surety. The poet, who was lending Gilbert nearly half the proceeds of the Edinburgh *Poems*, declined to commit himself any further:

'The language of refusal is to me the most difficult language on earth, and you are the man of the world, excepting One of R^t Honble designation [i.e., Lord Glencairn], to whom it gives me the greatest pain to hold such language. . . . I never wrote a letter which gave me so much pain in my life, as I know the unhappy consequences: I shall incur the displeasure of a Gentleman for whom I have the highest respect, and to whom I am deeply oblidged.'

The foreboding was justified. After that reluctant refusal, Burns's relations with his former landlord never regained their old cordiality.

In his contacts with Aiken, Ballantine, Hamilton, and certain of the New Light clergy Burns had, by the spring of 1786, taken a further step in the realization of his own capacities. He found himself quite at ease, at least in male company, among members of the professional class to whom as a lad he had looked up with awe. He was discovering, moreover, that he was not their inferior in native ability. Though he did not know it then, he had in fact reached as high a level as he was ever to maintain in Scottish society. These lesser gentry not only received him, but treated him as an equal. The higher gentry—people of estates and pedigrees—the higher professional classes, and the nobility, might receive him for a time, but always with a latent condescension. Sooner or later, even with Mrs. Dunlop, even with Robert Riddell, some incident would reveal that their feeling toward him was after all *de haut en bas*. The friends whom he kept among men of social and professional standing, from Aiken and Ballantine at the beginning of his career to Alexander Findlater and John Syme at its close, were gentlemen, were men of education, but they were not, in Burns's favourite capitalized phrase, Great People.

But in the summer and autumn of 1786 it seemed there might be no limit to Burns's social advancement. As he went about the country during August and September, collecting the subscriptions for his poems, the parish outcast of a few months earlier found himself everywhere courted and applauded. New acquaintances and old united to draw him out, and the bolder his remarks the better they liked them. But he was still capable of awe. In October came an invitation to dine on the 23rd at Catrine House, country home of Dugald Stewart, Professor of Moral Philosophy in Edinburgh University. The company included Basil William, Lord Daer, the flighty and consumptive but liberal-minded son and heir of the Earl of Selkirk. In an amusing set of verses Burns described how, at the prospect of meeting a peer for the first time, his knees shook as he sidled into the Professor's drawing-room, and he reverted to his old trick of watching from a corner until he had taken the measure of the company. The incident is worth mentioning because it was probably the last time Burns was ever unsure of himself in society. In later months and years he was often irritated and uncomfortable when members of the upper classes emphasized their elevation, but such feelings were the reverse of awe. Two months after the dinner at Catrine he was meeting professors and peers by the dozen instead of the brace, and was maintaining not merely self-possession but critical appraisal.

Burns's standards of social intercourse, as of so many other things, were firmly established before the surviving records become full enough for detailed study. They were as honest and straightforward as the rest of his dealings. Except for the brief embarrassment of a first meeting, rank as such meant nothing to him. What he demanded, and all he demanded, of any man was, in his own phrase, that he have something to him. That something must be native; a matter of mind and personality, not of social place. A Souter Johnie was better company than a Hugh Blair, because the cobbler's wit and wisdom were the product of native shrewdness dealing with first-hand experience; the professor's attainments were 'meerly an astonishing proof what industry and application can do'. To his cultured friends, Burns seemed to have a perverse taste for low company, whereas his real quest was genuine company. His own unbridled wit and tempestuous emotions naturally made him gravitate towards other similarly endowed people, who too often were not pillars of society, but this was not his reason for choosing them. When a pillar of society bore himself 'to all the Actors, high and low, in the drama of Life, simply as they merited in playing their parts', and excelled in telling a story—in other words, when the pillar was Dugald Stewart—Burns enjoyed his company as much as John Rankine's or Willie Nicol's. Nor was wit or waggishness necessarily demanded. Grave wisdom Burns could relish as well as gay, though not in every mood; what he could never endure was dullness, pomposity, or conceit.

As the autumn of 1786 wore on, new friends and old agreed that the success of the Kilmarnock *Poems* should make Burns abandon his flight to Jamaica. He ought to publish a second edition in Edinburgh and then settle down, either on a farm of his own, or—as Aiken suggested—in the Excise service. The poet would find plenty of friends to help him win a hearing, and publishing in the capital would give him a national instead of a local audience. Burns must have made up his mind immediately after his dinner with Dugald Stewart. Among his new friends was Alexander Dalziel, steward of the Renfrewshire estates of the Earl of Glencairn. On November 1 Dalziel wrote to congratulate Burns on abandoning the West Indian venture and to tell him that he had showed the *Poems* to the Earl himself. The Earl bought a copy, which he had richly bound, and expressed warm interest in the poems and their author.

Thus began Burns's most successful acquaintance with a peer—the only association of the sort which did not sooner or later end in apathy on one side and humiliation on the other. Though the circumstances of Burns's earliest introduction to Edinburgh society are obscure, the obscurity is lightened if we take at face value the poet's repeated statements that he owed everything to Glencairn—that the Earl, as he put it, took him by the hand and led him up to fame. Burns afterwards said that he went to the city without letters of introduction, but that can have been true only in the narrowest sense. Dalziel certainly apprised Glencairn of Burns's plans, as Dr. Mackenzie apprised Sir John Whitefoord and Andrew Erskine, and as the Rev. George Lawrie of Loudoun apprised the blind poet, Thomas Blacklock. Dugald Stewart also must have known of the decision. Within a week of his arrival, Burns was the lion of the Edinburgh season. Many new friends must have contributed to such immediate success, but the poet's emphasis on Glencairn's kindness marks the Earl as the man who secured the patronage of the fashionable Caledonian Hunt, and probably also as his sponsor in Masonic society.

All this the Earl succeeded in doing without offending the touchy poet by condescension, though Burns's pride sometimes suffered because of Glencairn's deference to people of superior rank. Once, indeed, Burns was 'within half a point' of throwing down his 'gage of contemptuous defiance' because the Earl was giving too much attention to a wealthy dunderpate, but even then he was quickly reassured as to Glencairn's sincere good wishes. Touchiness aside, Burns's position in Edinburgh recalls Benjamin Franklin's at Versailles a decade before. In each place the fashionable world thought it had discovered a child of nature; in each place the newcomer had really a shrewder mind and a quicker penetration of character and motive than most of the *élite* who patronized him. The contrast between Burns's attitude toward Glencairn and toward his fellow peer, the Earl of Buchan, shows how thoroughly the poet had learned to take men's measure regardless of rank. Buchan also had professed great interest in Burns and was lavish with advice, but Burns recognized the man as an egotistical windbag and received his advice with an elaborate irony of compliment which would have betrayed itself to anyone less conceited than the busybody who once, when Sir Walter Scott lay ill, volunteered to arrange his funeral, and who, when he himself had written some amazingly bad verses, accepted as a tribute John Taylor's publication of them in a part of *The Scots Magazine* 'distinct from the mass of vulgar poetry'.

Nevertheless, Burns's deference to Glencairn had unfortunate results. In securing William Creech, his brother's former tutor, as Burns's publisher, Glencairn thought he was doing the best possible good turn. Yet the outcome was months of vexation and delay for the poet, and the loss of all profits from later editions of his poems. Moreover, the poet had soberly decided that his best hope for a livelihood lay in securing an Excise post which would support him while he banked his profits as a reserve fund for his children. But Glencairn, like Mrs. Dunlop and other gentry whose knowledge of the lives of tenant farmers was limited to the quarterly receipt of their rents, was all for the poet's investing his capital in a farm of his own. Disapproving of the Excise scheme, Glencairn would do nothing to forward it, though a word from him in the right place—that is, in the ears of Henry Dundas—would have procured Burns the appointment he sought. As it was, all hints fell dead, while meantime Patrick Miller dangled the bait of Ellisland. When at last Burns interested a man willing to help the Excise plan, the mischief was already done; he was committed to the undertaking which swallowed all his little capital. The best intentions of his would-be patrons kept turning to evil for Burns; even Glencairn's gift of a diamond-pointed pencil made trouble by supplying the poet with the means of inscribing blazing indiscretions on window-panes.

Burns observed the rest of the Edinburgh gentry and literati as closely as he did Glencairn and Buchan. He was measuring himself and his native ability against them, and was not inclined to award himself second place. But he was not comfortable with most of them. Even if they did not offend him by overt condescension he was fully aware that they received him only because he was the fad of the moment. When the novelty staled he could not hope to continue many friendships in exalted quarters. The tide of popularity had swept him higher than he could expect to remain; its ebb might leave him stranded far lower than he deserved. It was not long, indeed, before his hosts began to find things to criticize. Burns not only said what he thought, he said it with an emphasis they found unbecoming in a man of peasant birth. The great Doctor Johnson could be as gruff as he pleased with his Scottish hosts because he was Johnson; Lord Braxfield could roar and Lord Kames rave, both bawdy, in a gentleman's home because they were Lords of Session; for Burns to express emphatic opinions argued a lack of the humility which beseemed a ploughman entertained by his betters.

The fact was that Burns lacked both the finesse which would have enabled him neatly and inoffensively to deal with snubs, and the insensitive egotism which could have ignored them. No one could snub the Ettrick Shepherd, because his magnificent self-esteem made it impossible for him to see any remark in anything but a complimentary light. One did not safely snub Charles Kirkpatrick Sharpe, because that wasp could sting. Burns's pride, unfortunately, not only made him sensitive; it made him aggressive and heavy-handed. When he flaunted the blue-and-buff of the Whigs he was going out of his way to assert his independence among people who were mostly Tories; when he told a lady, who had not waited an introduction before inviting him to her party, that he would come if she would also in-

vite the learned pig from the Grassmarket, he was
making a show of himself in one way in the very
act of resenting being made a show in another. The
consciousness that he was acting a part—whether
behaving like a country bumpkin in Smellie's print-
ing-house, or posing as the Bard of Nature in drawing-rooms—no doubt partly explains some of his
more violent outbursts. Thus when he demolished a
clergyman, whose niggling criticisms of Gray had
goaded him beyond endurance, with the Johnson-
ian thunderbolt, 'Sir, I now perceive a man may be
an excellent judge of poetry by square and rule, and
after all be a damned blockhead!' the victim was
probably drawing all the electric tension which had
been accumulating in the poet's nerves through a
long series of irritations and repressions. But such
things did him no good in Edinburgh society.

It was not that his manners were worse than gentlemen's. In some respects they were probably better. 'Swearing,' Henry Cockburn dryly records,
'was thought the right, and the mark, of a gentleman. And, tried by this test, nobody, who had not
seen them, could now be made to believe how many
gentlemen there were.' Boswell's long-suffering wife,
Margaret Montgomerie, took her husband to task
for his loud and abusive manner of asserting himself
in argument, and Boswell admitted to his journal
that she was right. Benjamin Franklin remarked
that Edinburgh was the only place he knew where
violent disputatiousness was not confined to lawyers and university men. But when a mere peasant

exhibited, in however mild a form, the traits of the gentry, he was forgetting his place, and should be put back in it.

Moreover, Burns quickly realized that these gentry scorned the national tradition which was his life-blood. If they did not all, like Dr. John Moore, urge him henceforth to write in standard English, they at least made it plain that a Scots poet could not aspire to literary equality with Dr. Beattie and Dr. Blair. Robert Fergusson was a regrettable scamp whom Edinburgh preferred to forget; Burns erected, at his own expense, a monument to Fergusson, and insisted, in speech and writing, on praising the dead poet and heaping scorn on the gentry who had let him starve. The place where Burns, after the first few weeks, really enjoyed himself in Edinburgh and where he made most of his intimate and lasting friendships, was among the Crochallan Fencibles. This was one of the numerous clubs in which lawyers and merchants carried on the old convivial traditions of their city. Edinburgh clubs were ancient institutions which arrayed bibulous functions in ceremonials ranging from the harmless High Jinks described by Scott in *Guy Mannering* to almost psychopathic debauchery in such an organization as the Wig Club. They were, in fact, along with the Freemasons, the ancestors both of the American fraternal orders and of the Rotary and Kiwanis Clubs. In the more elaborately organized groups each officer, and sometimes every member, had a special title. Thus each member in Allan Ramsay's

Easy Club took the name of an old Scottish writer; in the Cape Club, to which Robert Fergusson belonged, each member was a Knight Companion of the Cape, with titles like Sir Cape, Sir Brimstone, Sir Precenter (Fergusson himself), Sir Nun and Abbess, and Sir Pope. The Fencibles went in for military designations. William Smellie, the gruff, slovenly, and erudite printer who was handling the Edinburgh edition of the *Poems*, as Adjutant of the corps introduced the poet. Burns's publisher, Creech, proved a social disappointment as well as a financial disaster; his printer was a man after his own heart, an 'old Veteran in Genius, Wit and Bawdry'. Smellie, like Burns, concealed an inward diffidence and sensitivity beneath an aggressive manner; like Burns, too, he was self-educated. The poet was not far wrong in describing him as 'a man positively of the first abilities and greatest strength of mind, as well as one of the best hearts and keenest wits that I have met with.' He had displayed his intellectual power in his *Philosophy of Natural History*, long regarded as a standard work, and in writing large sections of the original *Encyclopædia Britannica*; his wit he reserved for conversation, where, like Burns's, it allowed no considerations of reverence or prudery to stand in its way. Despite his rough exterior, he was able to captivate an intelligent woman of the world like Maria Riddell, as well as the ebullient poet. But the records of this friendship were too much for Smellie's squeamish executors; his biographer piously relates that 'many letters of Burns to

Mr. Smellie which remained, being totally unfit for publication, and several of them containing severe reflections on many respectable people still in life, have been burnt.'

The records of another friendship which had its start among the Edinburgh bookmen fared better. Peter Hill, five years the poet's senior, was in 1787 a clerk in Creech's shop, but was soon to set up in business for himself and prove a kindly and indulgent master to an apprentice named Archibald Constable. Hill's was one of the few friendships Burns made in Edinburgh which suffered no abatement with time. From the summer of 1787, when Hill was handling some of the innumerable details of business relating to the Edinburgh *Poems*, until the beginning of 1796, when Burns sent his 'annual' gift of a kippered salmon from the Nith, their association was unclouded. Hill supplied the poet with books, sent presents to his family, and took care of miscellaneous business errands in the city. Burns secured for Hill the book-orders, first of the Monkland Friendly Society and later of the Dumfries Public Library, and interspersed his business communications with hearty blasts of execration, broad humour, and messages to all their common friends. Though the phraseology of the letters often seems stilted, behind its stiffness glows a genuine affection and esteem.

But the backbone of the Fencibles was the lawyers. Their Colonel, William Dunbar, was a jolly little bachelor some years older than the poet; their Major and Muster-Master General was Charles

Hay, friend of Boswell in the days when the latter
was striving for distinction at the Scottish bar, whose
port-inflamed countenance blinks above his judicial
robes as Lord Newton in Raeburn's superb portrait
in the Scottish National Gallery. More notable for
'law, paunch, whist, claret, and worth' than for literary interests, Hay's one poetic suggestion to Burns
had humiliating results. He was among those who
urged the poet to compose the unfortunate elegy
'On the Death of Lord President Dundas', the complete ignoring of which by Dundas's son inflicted on
Burns's pride a wound which never healed.

Among the lawyer Fencibles the most congenial
to Burns was Alexander Cunningham, a distant and
impoverished relative of Lord Glencairn. Though
Burns described him to his face as dissipated but not
debauched—a subtle distinction of which the exact
import is probably forever lost—Cunningham was
diffident and retiring. Perhaps for this reason, perhaps also because of his kinship to Glencairn, Burns
never sent him on such ticklish errands as he entrusted to Bob Ainslie, but their literary and intellectual fellowship was sincere. Unlike Hay and
Ainslie, Cunningham had real fondness for the higher
types of poetry, though to offset this he had the anglicized Scotsman's inability to see anything but the
ludicrous and the low in folk literature. Burns felt
that in offering 'My Love is like a red red rose' to
Cunningham he had to apologize for its simplicity;
Popean imitations would have been more in his line.
The young lawyer, in short, belonged to the genera-

tion which was trying to live down the national characteristics that meant most to Burns. In Edinburgh the legal profession was the last stronghold of the rich old gusto of Scottish life, the last group of men unashamed of being 'characters'. But even there such traits belonged mainly to the generation passing or past which included men like Braxfield, Monboddo, and Kames, or to the already mature generation of Charles Hay and Henry Erskine. Cunningham belonged more nearly to the generation of Henry Cockburn, without Cockburn's relish for the memories of traits which he did not share.

Within the limits imposed by his diffidence and his tastes, Cunningham had no reason to complain of lack of sympathy or confidence from Burns. When his first sweetheart jilted him with humiliating publicity, Cunningham told his sorrow to Burns, who had previously supplied him with a poor song in furtherance of his suit, and who now condoled in terms which bore hard on the young lady. The poet's letters ranged from gay impromptu verses to the confession that as a result of the fiasco of the elegy, 'I never see the name, Dundas, in the column of a newspaper, but my heart seems straitened for room in my bosom; & if I am obliged to read aloud a paragraph relating to one of them, I feel my forehead flush, & my nether lip quivers.' On his part, Cunningham obtained for Burns the last national honour which Edinburgh conferred in his lifetime—election to membership in the socially exclusive Royal Company of Archers. And at the end

Cunningham received one of the poet's desperate appeals for help—not for money, but for intercession with the Commissioners of Excise not to put him on half-pay during his illness. Cunningham, moreover, shared with John Syme the credit for setting on foot the subscription for Jean and the children after Burns's death, though his diffidence made him a poor collector of funds. Through diffidence, also, he permitted George Thomson to prepare for the newspapers the obituary he should have written himself, and by this neglect did injury to his friend's memory.

But the names of three other friends are associated with much more damage to Burns's reputation during his life and after his death. Only one of the three was a Fencible—Robert Cleghorn, a jolly gentleman farmer from Corstorphine. Cleghorn had what Cunningham lacked, a strong relish for vernacular literature, publishable or unpublishable. Thus he became the recipient of many choice bits of verse, sometimes traditional and sometimes original, for his own and his friends' edification. The correspondence harmed Burns's reputation not through its publication but through its long suppression. That remarkable moralist, Lord Byron, read the Cleghorn letters in manuscript and set down in his journal a highly-coloured summary of them as 'full of oaths and obscene songs' which stimulated the imaginations of several generations of readers. Now that the surviving letters can be read in full, they produce no such revulsion as do some of the things Burns wrote about Jean Armour and Maria Riddell. For readers who do not relish broad humour they may be distasteful, but beneath their coarseness is the record of a genuine friendship with an honest, hearty, and generous man. One suspects that had Cunningham, for instance, visited Burns at Ellisland or Dumfries, he would have felt the same disillusionment at sight of the poet's narrow and primitive domestic life which the pettier Robert Ainslie recorded. Cleghorn made such a visit in 1795, when Burns's health and spirits were already declining, and left behind him a warm glow of renewed and strengthened friendship.

It is regrettable that Cleghorn's name should be, for most readers of Burns, associated with the poet's collection of 'cloaciniad' verse. In fact, Cleghorn received no more of such work than did a dozen other friends, but John Allen, his stepson and heir, had ideas about the treatment of a great poet's manuscripts which differed from those of William Smellie's executors. Allen did not feel free, by mutilating some of his most characteristic letters, to 'protect the memory' of a poet who had never tried to disguise any side of his own nature. And Cleghorn's tastes were as catholic as David Herd's, or as Burns's own. He measured the merit of a song by its singing quality, and not by its suitability for use in a young ladies' seminary. Burns sent him the charming 'O wat ye wha that lo'es me' with the certainty that it would please him as much as the broadest ribaldry. The male who in male company does not occasionally relish crude humour is a scarce creature in any age or nation; was perhaps unusually scarce in eighteenth-century Scotland. The songs which went to Cleghorn went also to Graham of Fintry and Provost Maxwell, to Collector Mitchell and John M'Murdo and John Syme—in other words, to some of the best and most loyal characters in Burns's circle. Boswell's journals are crammed with proof that similar tastes prevailed in still higher ranks of society.

To avoid misunderstanding both Burns and his friends, a brief digression is necessary regarding the book entitled *The Merry Muses of Caledonia*. Burns was well aware that his own work, like the folksongs he collected, was divided into the publishable and the unpublishable. But he did not draw the line where his later editors did. To him, 'The Jolly Beggars', 'A Poet's Welcome', and 'Holy Willie' were no fitter for general circulation than were 'When Princes and Prelates' and 'The Court of Equity'. They were *jeux d'esprit* intended for private circulation among a few intimates. His riotous imagination respected no boundaries when it began to play; what distinguishes most of his bawdry from the common sort is its wit. And this wit as frequently saw how an improper folk-song could be made more brilliantly improper as it saw how a halting one could be made lyric. Much of his folk collection, together with 'a very few' of his own composition, was written into a manuscript volume which he sometimes lent about, with strict injunctions as to secrecy. According to tradition, that volume fell after his death into unscrupulous hands and formed the basis of the earliest of the various collections called *The Merry Muses*. The tradition is almost certainly wrong. The ultimate source may have been Burns, but not the immediate one. In all the editions the authentic Burns verses are too garbled to have been printed from his own copies. They bear every sign of oral transmission or hasty transcription at several removes from the original. The real manuscript was probably destroyed after Burns's death; certainly it was never printed. It would have been better for his reputation if it had, for he now stands father or godfather to a garbled mass of Scottish, English, and Irish filth, little of which he wrote, and some of which he never even saw.

Neither Robert Ainslie nor William Nicol needed the chance association of their names with fescennine verse to bring discredit on Burns. Their own conduct sufficed. Ainslie, like Cunningham, was a young lawyer, but the two moved in different orbits, and were never brought together even by their friendship for Burns. They appealed to different facets of the poet's nature, Ainslie's relation to him being that of Smith and Richmond in the days of the Fornicators' Court. The son of a good family in the Border village of Dunse, Ainslie was celebrating his recent emancipation from parental government by sowing a plentiful crop of wild oats. Full of the high spirits of twenty-one, he furnished the same ready chorus of laughter the Mauchline cronies had

provided, and was rapidly qualifying himself to dis-
cuss with Burns the pleasing topic of comparative
bastardy. The most enjoyable part of the poet's
Border tour in May, 1787, was his visit to Dunse;
after Ainslie left him he complained that he never
had a mouthful of really hearty laughter on the trip.

Even the mutilated letters which survive show
that Burns freely confided his past and present peccadillos to Ainslie; the sequel proves the confidence
to have been ill bestowed. At the end of the Border
tour, for instance, Burns found awaiting him in
Dumfries post-office a letter from Meg Cameron, an
Edinburgh servant girl who was to bear a child
which she claimed was his. Ainslie was commis-
sioned to 'send for the wench and give her ten or
twelve shillings' against the poet's return to the city.
In reply, Ainslie broke the news that he had himself
just become the father of an illegitimate son, and received from his friend a roaring welcome to 'the venerable Society of Fathers'. Again in the following
year Burns favored Ainslie with a highly-coloured
account of his final reconciliation with Jean Armour,
and early in 1789 instructed his young friend to lo-
cate Jenny Clow so that Burns, on his arrival in
Edinburgh, could settle the suit Jenny had brought
against him. More creditable matters also occupied
the correspondence. Some of Burns's earliest doubts
about Ellisland, some of his deepest gloom about his
own and his family's future, were told to Ainslie.
But the friendship died before Burns did, and
through Ainslie's fault.

On Friday, October 15, 1790, Ainslie came to Ellisland for the week-end. On Monday he reported the visit to Agnes M'Lehose, with whom he was by this time on confidential, and even flirtatious, terms. The warmth of Burns's welcome was gratifying, but the house, he noted, was 'ill contrived—and pretty Dirty, and *Hugry Mugry*', and its other inmates pleased him little. Jean was 'Vulgar & Common-place in a considerable degree—and pretty round & fat', but 'a kind Body in her Own way, and the husband Tolerably Attentive to her'. Also present were Burns's sister and sister-in-law—'common looking girls'—and '3 Male and female cousins' who had been helping with the harvest.

Burns rejoiced that his friend had arrived 'upon his *Kirn* night, when he Expected some of his friends to help make merry', but sight of the guests deepened Ainslie's depression, for they were 'a Vulgar looking Tavern keeper from Dumfries; and his Wife more Vulgar—Mr. Miller of Dalswinton's Gardener and his Wife—and said Wife's sister—and a little fellow from Dumfries, who had been a Clerk'. Burns and the rest had a good time, 'Dancing, and Kissing the Lasses at the End of every dance', while Ainslie shuddered to the depths of his paltry little soul. Burns the peasant was enjoying himself in the world of his birth, and the young snob from Edinburgh couldn't understand him at all:

'. . . Our Friend himself is as ingenious as ever, and Seems very happy with the Situation I have described—

His Mind however now appears to me to be a great Mixture of the poet and the Excise Man—One day he sits down and Writes a Beautiful poem—and the Next he Seizes a cargo of Tobacco from some unfortunate Smuggler—or Roups out some poor Wretch for Selling liquors without a License. From his conversation he Seems to be frequently among the Great—but No Attention is paid by people of any rank to his wife. . . .'

After such a letter—withheld from complete publication until 1938—it is plain enough why the friendship went into a swift decline. For another year or two Burns continued to write, gaily or confidentially, but got small response. Ainslie's last letter, early in 1794, 'was so dry, so distant, so like a card to one of his clients', that the poet 'could scarce bear to read it', and never answered it. The lawyer was already on his way, via the fashionable *Werther* melancholy, back to the orthodox piety which led him, early in the nineteenth century, to compose a couple of devotional pamphlets. But neither piety nor loyalty sufficed to make him protect the memory of the friend whose name has kept his alive. Preserving the reckless letters Burns had written him, he allowed them to pass into circulation, once at least accompanied by a formal docket certifying that Burns was the author of a letter signed with a humorous pen-name. The mutilations which so many of the manuscripts have suffered were the work of later owners.

Ainslie's chief injury to Burns's fame was inflicted after the poet's death; William Nicol, Latin master in Edinburgh High School, harmed him in life. A coarse, egotistical, drunken man of violent temper, Nicol was also one of the foremost Latin scholars of his day. In his bawdy violence of language Burns saw wit; his emphatic dislike of his superiors Burns interpreted as proof of an independent spirit. No great harm might have come of the friendship had it been confined to drinking bouts in Edinburgh and to correspondence thereafter. Unfortunately Burns took Nicol as his travelling companion on the tour of the Highlands in September, 1787. This tour was Burns's chance to meet influential folk in their homes and to show himself at his best. Thanks to Nicol he came near to showing himself at his worst. Among the people from whom he had invitations were the Duke and Duchess of Athole. Their reception of him at Blair Athole was all the touchy poet could desire. The Duke and Duchess were cordiality itself; among the guests was Robert Graham of Fintry, Commissioner of Excise, whose friendship and influence could be of the utmost importance to Burns; a still more influential person, Henry Dundas, dispenser of patronage for all Scotland, was expected next day on one of his periodical inspections of his political fences. Everything seemed to be going well for Burns when Nicol, the 'most unprincipled savage', intervened. The boorish schoolmaster, finding himself neglected in favour of his companion, decided to move on at once, and insisted on Burns's going with him. The poet's pride made him guilty of outrageous bad manners. In reply to Nicol's insistence, Burns should have bidden him go to the devil his own gait. But that might have been interpreted as subservience to the Great. Through what can only be described as inverted snobbery, Burns allowed Nicol to drag him away. The scene was repeated at Castle Gordon, where the merry Duchess, who had declared in Edinburgh that Burns swept her off her feet, pleaded in vain against Nicol's urgings. Though he afterwards wrote complimentary and apologetic letters, and cursed the 'obstinate son of Latin Prose', Burns could not efface the impression he had made. He never saw the Atholes or the Gordons again.

Throughout the trip Nicol's conduct was the same; he even snatched Burns away before breakfast from the home of his cousin, James Burness of Montrose. The Highland tour, though he did not then realize it, was Burns's last opportunity to enlist the active friendship of people whose influence might have changed his life. His failure was largely Nicol's fault. Reports of his abrupt and ungracious conduct undoubtedly came back to Edinburgh and contributed to the comparative neglect he suffered during his second winter in the city. Edinburgh was too small a place for misconduct to hide in; every lawyer in the old Parliament House would have heard that a servant girl had brought suit against the Ayrshire Bard; the stories from the Highlands, losing nothing in the telling, would add to the swelling tide of hostile gossip. The talk, indeed, reached so far, and was believed so implicitly, that not even

death could alter Edinburgh opinion. Cunningham's efforts to interest prominent citizens in the
subscription for Burns's widow and children met repeated snubs and refusals; to this day, despite the
monument on the Calton Hill, the city pays only a
half-hearted tribute to his memory.

Of course all blame for the hostile talk cannot be
shifted to Nicol, or even to Meg Cameron and Jenny
Clow. Burns was indiscreet enough to start plenty of
tales without help. But his too long stay unfortunately predisposed many people to believe the worst
not only of his conduct in the city but afterwards.
Henry Mackenzie and Dugald Stewart, for instance,
both accepted at face value the second-hand reports
of Burns's alleged misdoings in Dumfries, and wrote
him off their books. For years anecdotes showing
Burns in an absurd or discreditable light circulated
in Edinburgh. Some may have been true; others
were malicious distortions which point the direction
taken by city opinion. Thus Lockhart told how
Hugh Blair had suggested, when a party of gentlemen were discussing possible changes in the Kilmarnock *Poems*, that 'tidings of salvation' might advan-
tageously be emended to 'tidings of damnation'.
Thereupon the poet, according to Lockhart, embar-
rassed the professor by asking permission to acknowledge his improvement in a footnote. The basis
of the story is truth; its details are not. Blair did
suggest the change; Burns did, in conversation with
other people, acknowledge his help. But Blair's suggestion came in writing, as a carefully veiled hint

amid other criticisms of the poems. The episode as
Lockhart told it is city gossip intended to display
Blair as the urbane professor and patron and Burns
as a clumsy rustic. Of no importance in itself, the
story is symptomatic of the attitude of cultured
Edinburgh after the first enthusiasm over Burns had
waned.

But no realization of the trouble Nicol was helping to make, no recognition of the schoolmaster's
real character, affected Burns. He continued, after
he left the city, to correspond with Nicol; when the
obstinate son of Latin Prose got into the row which
finally led to his resignation from the High School,
Burns championed him against his amiable principal, Dr. Alexander Adam. By christening one of his
sons William Nicol, Burns proclaimed his friendship
to the world at large, and during the years at Ellisland performed such services as getting appraisals
of a farm Nicol was buying, and maintaining a
broken-down mare which a horse-coper had passed
off on the schoolmaster. The friendship lasted until
February, 1793, when Burns was suffering from the
rage and humiliation which followed the official inquiry into his revolutionary sympathies. Some report of the matter having reached Nicol, he undertook to rebuke Burns in a would-be facetious vein.
The poet was in no mood for rebuke or good advice,
facetious or not, and with his heavily satirical reply
to Nicol their correspondence ended—too late.

In any case Edinburgh friendships, good or bad,
however much he might try to maintain them by

correspondence, could not supply companionship when Burns moved to Ellisland. Though on his first visit to Dumfries he had professed himself enchanted with the company he met, he was lonely enough when he actually settled there. He made acquaintances, no doubt 'men of talent and humour', among the tradesfolk and professional men of the town, but people like Dr. James Mundell, Walter Auld the saddler, Henry Clint of the King's Arms, William Hyslop of the Globe Inn, and Thomas Boyd, the contractor who built Ellisland, are names and little more. Apart from his landlord, Patrick Miller, with whom his relations were soon strained, the most congenial friend he had during the three years on the farm was Robert Riddell of Glenriddell, whose estate of Friars Carse marched with Ellisland.

Riddell was a country gentleman turned amateur antiquarian. He had embellished his grounds with a 'Druid Circle' and a 'Hermitage'; he dabbled in numismatics and church architecture. These would scarcely have interested Burns—though he remained in the hermitage long enough to inscribe some verses on the window with Glencairn's diamond-pointed pencil—but Riddell was also a musician in a small way. Besides composing a few commonplace airs of his own he professed great interest in the traditional music of his country. Here Burns shared his enthusiasm and far excelled his knowledge. The laird, perhaps at Burns's suggestion, subscribed for Johnson's *Museum* and had his set bound with blank interleaves for notes on the songs, their authors, and their

history. The number of his annotations gives the
measure of his knowledge. Out of four hundred
songs, one hundred and seventy have notes. Of
these, one hundred and fifty-two were written by
Burns, who must have spent many evenings at the
task in his friend's library; eighteen were by Riddell
himself or an amanuensis. Sir Walter Scott summed
up the laird's prose writings as 'truly the most
extravagant compositions that ever a poor Man
abandoned by providence to the imaginations of his
own heart had the misfortune to devise.'

The company which sometimes came to Carse,
including as it did men like Joseph Farington the
painter—who noted that 'Mr. Burns the Scottish
Poet' was 'a middle-sized man, . . . black com-
plexioned, and his general appearance that of a
tradesman or mechanick', had 'a strong expressive
manner of delivering himself in conversation', and
knew no Latin—and Francis Grose, the antiquary
whose inspiring enthusiasm was the real source of
'Tam o' Shanter', was more important than Riddell
himself. The laird's real tastes and aptitudes were
convivial. A man of powerful physique and a rather
overwhelming robustiousness of manner—William
Smellie spoke of 'his immense fist and stentorian
voice'—he succeeded, like so many gentlemen of his
day, in wrecking his health at an early age. The
notorious 'Whistle' contest, in which Riddell and
his kinsmen Sir Robert Laurie and Alexander Fergusson of Craigdarroch undertook to drink each
other under the table for the possession of a family

heirloom, was probably more typical of the laird's true aptitudes than the annotations were. Even at that, though, he was outdone by Craigdarroch, who won the whistle by drinking 'upds. of 5 Bottles of Claret'. Burns, like most of the friends of the contestants, found the incident vastly amusing; Burns's biographers have argued the question of his real presence at Friars Cárse with an almost theological fervour; nevertheless its only interest or value for posterity lies in the light it sheds on Robert Riddell's character. According to biographical tradition, Robert Riddell was the staid member of the family and his brother Walter the wild one; actually such distinction between them seems as baseless as the kindred legend that Gilbert Burns was a better farmer than his brother. But whether Glenriddell led or followed in the events which for a time estranged the poet from the whole Riddell family, the circumstances of the breach resemble with painful clarity many other episodes in Burns's contacts with the gentry.

The full story of the 'Rape of the Sabines' is Maria Riddell's more than her brother-in-law's, but Robert Riddell had a share in the trouble. During 1792 and 1793, when Walter Riddell and his wife Maria were occupying the estate of Goldielea or Woodley Park, family relations were not always harmonious. At a guess, Walter wanted to borrow from his elder brother the funds to complete payment for Woodley Park; at a guess, the wives failed to charm each other. Whatever the causes, by the autumn of 1792

Burns had to assure Maria that he would listen to no stories about her from Glenriddell—and presumably also from Glenriddell's wife. Yet for another year or more the poet managed to stay on good terms with both families. The year 1793 was, poetically and flirtatiously, the highest point of Burns's friendship with Maria; the same year produced asseverations of friendship as 'ardent & grateful' on Burns's part as Robert Riddell's was 'kind and generous'. In leisure moments the poet was transcribing a collection of his letters as a companion volume to the collection of unpublished verse he had given the laird in 1791. On Christmas day he was still transcribing. On January 12, 1794, his quarrel with Maria had reached its climax. Somewhere between those two dates had occurred the mysterious brawl in which Robert Riddell's part is still a matter of controversy.

If Robert Riddell was the host, who, by compelling Burns to drink more than he wished to, reduced the poet to a state in which he insulted his hostess, the laird's conduct admits of small excuse; if, as report has it, the scene occurred at Woodley Park and Robert Riddell subsequently took up the quarrel, he is even less excusable. Whichever version one accepts, Riddell was displaying innate snobbishness towards a man he considered, after all, a social inferior. If he was the host, realization of his own share in the matter should have made him charitable; if his brother was the host, Glenriddell was indulging in violent and uncalled-for partisanship. He held, it would seem, the same theory of a gentleman's privileges as was enunciated a few years later by Sir John Graham Dalyell: 'I am a gentleman, and I will be treated as such; and if any person presumes to pervert my meaning in any way whatever, if his rank is not equal to mine I will kick him; and if it is equal I will shoot him.' Burns, as a plebeian, was kicked. There is a little satisfaction in knowing that the poet held to his resolution not to apologize to his host. The 'Remorseful Apology' supposed to have been addressed to a Riddell was really sent, early in 1796, to a Mr. S. Mackenzie. Four months after the quarrel Glenriddell was dead, still unreconciled to the poet who had done more for him than he could ever have done for the poet. A loud blustering squire, a hollow and unsubstantial mind; that was Robert Riddell.

For the last five years of his life Burns's social world centred in Dumfries. About it cluster dark stories and darker hints, in the effort to refute which the poet's defenders have sometimes been led to dangerous extremities of special pleading. The truth is that Burns in Dumfries was neither better nor worse than Burns in Tarbolton and Mauchline. Such a report as James Gray's of finding Burns reading poetry with his children and hearing the older boys recite their lessons does not refute the tales of boisterous revelry in taverns; both are true. The sole difference is that Burns in Tarbolton was an unimportant young man amid a group of other youths; in Edinburgh he was partly lost in the crowds; in Dumfries he was a prominent figure whose every action was noted. He did not degenerate in Dumfries, but neither did he become a chocolate seraph.

Fortunately it is no longer necessary to rely on conjecture and second-hand reports in studying Burns's last years. The letters which passed between two of his most intimate friends, John Syme of Dumfries and Alexander Cunningham of Edinburgh, are now available to replace guess-work with facts. Of all the friends of Burns's last years, Syme is now the one who emerges most clearly, and with most credit to himself. A man of good education, a college friend of Dr. James Currie, the poet's first biographer, Syme regarded Dumfries as a place of exile in which Burns's society was almost the only redeeming feature. Having lost his small paternal estate of Barncailzie near Kirkcudbright, he had managed to recoup his fortunes by getting appointed to the sinecure post of Collector of Stamps at Dumfries. He first met Burns in 1788, but not until two years later did they become intimate. Syme was a man of sentiment in the best tradition of Henry Mackenzie and *The Sorrows of Werther*. He went into raptures over thunderstorms and desolate scenery; he read Zimmermann's *Treatise on Solitude*; he thought Clarinda's the finest love-letters ever written. Rhapsodic and absent-minded, he was the sort who could set off on a long-planned hunting-trip and find on arriving at his destination that he had forgotten his dogs. Maria Riddell paid warm tribute to his good head and excellent heart, but added that in matters of business he wanted method: 'He is always in a labyrinth of papers and accounts, and, somewhat like the cuttle-fish, he obscures himself altogether in a mist of his own creating.'

Burns admired Syme's education and literary taste; Syme thought the poet 'a noble fellow', admired his wit and brilliant conversation, but could not admire his wife. 'Methinks he has exhibited his poetical genius when he celebrated her', he said to Cunningham after his first sight of Jean. Before long Burns was submitting his new poems to Syme and expressing implicit confidence in his judgement, though Syme avowed that he scarcely dared to touch a line of them. Sometimes the two would meet in a boisterous crowd at a tavern; again they would spend a quiet evening over a single bottle of wine in the little croft of Ryedale which Syme regarded as his refuge 'from the frivolous and dissipated society' of Dumfries. Without Burns, said Syme, his life in the town would be 'a dreary blank'. Syme had set himself up as a clearing-house for humorous and satirical verses written or collected by his friends, and Burns quickly became the chief contributor to the hoard. Some of the verses compelled caution in sharing them. Of the epigram on the Loyal Natives Club, for instance, Syme told Cunningham that, though he and Burns were 'far from differing from them on sentiments of loyalty, we differ on *sentiment*, abstractly considered. They scarcely know the meaning of the word Sentiment, & their Society consists in roaring & drinking.' 'Don't,' he added after quoting the epigram, 'let any Dumfries person see this, for one of the Savages, if he heard it, might cut Robin's pipe.'

Syme's letters abundantly illustrate what he meant by 'frivolous and dissipated society'. When the Caledonian Hunt met at Dumfries in November, 1794, 'Baker, one of the knowing english Squires on the Turf, made an elegant appearance by insulting in the grossest manner Squire Walter Riddel of this place, who pursued him to Durham and made him ask pardon, which is published in our papers of last week.' On the same occasion the Honourable Ramsay Maule of Panmure showed that for once at least Burns was justified in the tone of a satirical epigram, for Panmure and some drunken companions smeared a helpless underling's hair with mustard and stuck it full of toothpick quills, 'by way of hedgehogging him'. That Burns gnashed his teeth and passed by on the other side when he encountered such members of the organization to which he had dedicated his Edinburgh *Poems*, is no ground for wonder. He had larded the Caledonian Hunt with flattery, and they were behaving like cads and bullies.

But though Burns shrank from the Caledonian Hunt he did not always avoid similar company. There were meetings at which he and Syme drank bumpers out with wild Irishmen—such meetings as led Thomas Telford the engineer jovially to warn Burns that if he went on 'in his old way, not even a *she Devil* will be able to meet with a Milt in him.' There was a drunken brawl with one Captain Dods, who took hot exception to the poet's toast, 'May our success in the present war be equal to the justice of our cause.' That Burns escaped a duel only because he was not the Captain's social equal did not lessen his humiliation. Most biographers have held that such a toast in the presence of gentlemen holding the King's commission was a huge breach of the proprieties, and so it was—if Burns was not goaded into giving it. Nothing in the record as it stands forbids belief that Dods, or some other officer who knew that Burns was suspected of sympathy with the French, may have called for a round of loyal toasts with the deliberate intention of embarrassing the poet. In that case, nothing could have been neater than Burns's evasion, and since nothing came of the episode it is to be presumed that Samuel Clarke succeeded in making the sobered Dods realize what his objection to the sentiment implied.

But there were other similar episodes which cannot be so favourably explained, and which multiply proof that Burns had never acquired finesse, whether in toasting, flattering, or sinning. Whatever he did was done so forthrightly that it attracted attention. And the moment he attracted attention his companions recollected that after all he was a peasant received on sufferance into gentle company. The outcome might be expulsion from the house for conduct which a gentleman born need not even have apologized for, it might be a verbal attack like Captain Dods's, or it might be merely a tacit resolve to drop him forthwith. The Edinburgh experience repeated itself in Dumfries. Burns's ill-repute in certain quarters during his life and after his death was not owing to his being a sinner above the other Caledonians, but simply to his lack of the social standing which enabled Kames and Braxfield and Boswell to misbehave without penalty, and which would have tempered the sting of his satirical outbursts.

Occasional public drunken squabbles are not the only evidence that during these last years Burns's nerves were often exacerbated. The loyal Syme once undertook to rebuke him for some of his wild doings and sayings. His language was too strong— telling the story afterwards he admitted, 'I may have spoken daggers, but I meant none.' The poet, his face black with anger, fumbled with his sword-cane. Syme, half laughing, half serious, exclaimed, 'What! and in my own house, too!' The conscience-stricken Burns flung away the cane, burst into tears, and positively grovelled in contrition on the flag-stone floor. It is not a pleasant scene, and though the vividness with which it stayed in Syme's memory is indication enough that it was exceptional, it cannot be ignored. No man, drunk or sober, whose nerves were normal could have behaved so.

Fortunately the vividness of Syme's memory is not the only proof that such conduct was exceptional. Others besides Syme who were nearest to Burns in his last years concur in their loyalty and affection. At the end of 1790 Alexander Findlater reported to his official superior, Supervisor Corbet, that Burns was 'an active, faithful & zealous officer', gave 'the most unremitting attention to the duties of his office (which, by the bye is more than I at first looked for from so eccentric a Genius)', and might 'be considered a credit to the profession'. And the judgment which Findlater thus expressed at the beginning of the poet's Excise career he reaffirmed after his death. Others testified to their regard in deeds as well as words. Though Burns continued to display his lifelong preference for the company of extravagant and *outré* sorts of people the best men in the Excise were the ones who esteemed him most. John Lewars, for example, brother of the Jessie of the songs, was a man of some education, and above the level of the common riding-officer. His father had been Collector at Dumfries, and thus a man of standing in the community. Burns called Lewars 'a young fellow of uncommon merit—indeed, by far the cleverest fellow I have met with in this part of the world', and Lewars reciprocated the poet's affection by service to him and his family during his illness and after his death. And that Burns's long absence from duty did not bear more heavily on him was due to the kindness of Adam Stobbie, a young expectant who throughout the spring of 1796 performed Burns's rounds without pay, that the poet might continue to draw his full salary.

Fortunately, too, Syme records bright passages as well as dark in the last years. There were evenings at Ryedale when they consumed more cups of tea than bottles of wine, and when 'Robin's confound-

ing wit' played as sharply as it ever did over a
punchbowl. In 1793 and 1794 there were brief ex-
cursions with Burns into Kirkcudbright on which
the mercurial poet displayed every facet of his nature, bursting into furious rage over a spoiled pair
of boots, fulminating brilliantly satirical epigrams
against the Earl of Galloway, announcing that he
would dine nowhere where he could not 'eat like a
Turk, drink like a fish and swear like the Devil', and
anon proving a decorous and fascinating house-
guest at St. Mary's Isle, seat of the Earl of Selkirk,
whose son Lord Daer had given Burns his first
glimpse of the peerage. Burns still shrank from the
ordeal of encountering such exalted folk—'I am
indeed ill at ease whenever I approach your Honorables & Right Honorables'—though now for a different reason. In 1786 the consciousness of his own
rusticity had been uppermost; in 1794 he did not
wish to be laid open either to a fresh snub or renewed
condescension. But his last recorded intercourse with
the peerage was as pleasant—and as dangerous—as
his first. The Earl of Selkirk was one of the few Scottish peers who were Whigs at a time when all power
belonged to the Tories; thus meeting Burns on congenial grounds he helped to draw him into the last
of his ill-advised meddlings with politics by interesting him in the parliamentary campaign of Patrick
Heron of Heron. So to the last the peerage influenced Burns against his own best interests. Nevertheless this visit to St. Mary's Isle is refutation
enough of the charge that in his last years Burns

had sunk so low that gentlefolk shunned him. The man who so charmed the Earl's young daughter, Lady Mary Douglas, that she lent him a volume of music and entered into correspondence about his task of fitting Scottish airs with words, can scarcely have been the social outcast some biographers have portrayed. In fact, he strikingly resembles the man who in 1787 swept the Duchess of Gordon off her feet, and won the esteem of Lady Harriet Don and the Dowager Countess of Glencairn.

Despite their intimacy, it would be false to claim that Syme shared all Burns's interests. No one man could do that. The very topic on which Burns and Lady Mary found common ground was outside Syme's range. He never could understand what Burns saw in the crude and half-literate James Johnson, because he never understood the bond of fellowship established by mutual devotion to Scottish folksong. Nevertheless, Syme was probably the closest to Burns of all his Dumfries friends, and knew—as certain impassioned defenders like Anna Dorothea Benson could not—the worst as well as the best in his later conduct. The man who noted that 'Robin's temper is not cold and frugal', and who did not hesitate to record the sword-cane story and certain other episodes, cannot be charged with allowing affection to obscure the full truth about his friend. Hence Syme's deeds and words at the time of Burns's death give as reliable a verdict on the poet's last years as can now be reached.

As Burns's health failed in 1796 Syme watched

him with increasing anxiety. As long as he could he hoped for recovery, but when the poet returned from the Brow Well his 'cadaverous aspect and shaken frame' told the truth which the doctors confirmed. On July 17 Syme wrote to warn Cunningham and to urge him to press their friend's petition to the Commissioners of Excise that they continue his full salary. Two days later, when Syme called at the little house in Mill Street, he saw the hand of Death visibly fixed on Burns:

'I cannot dwell on the scene. It overpowers me—yet gracious God were it thy will to recover him! He had life enough to acknowledge me, and Mrs. Burns said he had been calling on you and me continually. He made a wonderful exertion when I took him by the hand. With a strong voice he said, "I am much better today—I shall soon be well again, for I command my spirits & my mind. But yesterday I resigned myself to death." Alas it will not do.'

Syme was already consulting with Patrick Miller, John M'Murdo, Dr. Maxwell, and other Dumfries friends to set measures afoot for the welfare of Jean and the children; when he wrote again on the 21st, shaken by the 'variety of distressful emotions' stirred by Burns's death, he gave further details of their plans, and urged Cunningham to launch a similar plan in Edinburgh and to see that a proper obituary was prepared. Here Cunningham blundered. He entrusted the obituary to George Thomson, and the latter's remark that Burns's 'extraordinary endowments were accompanied with frailties which rendered them useless to himself and his family' roused the Dumfries friends to indignation. 'We were much hurt at this,' said Syme, '& reckoned it indelicate, if not unfeelingly superfluous on that occasion.'

These feelings were intensified by the appearance in the London *Chronicle* of a longer article, also by Thomson, which included assertions that Burns's 'talents were often obscured and finally impaired by excess,' that 'his conduct and his fate afford[ed] but too melancholy proofs' of his possessing the failings as well as the powers of genius, and that, 'like his predecessor Fergus[s]on, though he died at an early age, his mind was previously exhausted.' Thomson had never been in Dumfries, and had never met Burns. The friends in Dumfries who read his article did not concur. Syme's comment was brief and pointed. These statements were 'd—d illiberal lies'. On that comment, by the man who knew him best in his last years, the case for the defence of Burns against the stories of his deterioration in Dumfries may be allowed to rest.

IV

WOMEN

BURNS was twenty-six before he ever entered the home of a woman sufficiently well-to-do to have carpets on her floors. Though the last ten years of his life included many friendships with ladies, his basic ideas of the other sex were the fruit of the peasant environment he was reared in. His sentiment and chivalry were literary by-products; underneath them was always the crude realism of the Ayrshire countryfolk. In moments of stress it was only too apt to come to the surface.

The only subtlety the peasant women of Burns's youth could claim was that native to every daughter of Eve. Schooling was too expensive to waste on girls. The majority, like Agnes Broun, could not write their own names; many could not even spell out the Scriptures or the Psalms of David in metre. Their fathers, their husbands, or the minister could read the Bible to them, and thus they could obtain the light of salvation at second hand. But this is not to say that they knew no literature. In fact it was only among an illiterate population that the songs and ballads of popular tradition were living realities. James Hogg's mother spoke for her whole class when she told Sir Walter Scott that he had killed her ballads by writing them down. Learning to read destroyed both the sense of reality in the traditional literature and the retentiveness of memory which made its transmission possible. Had Betty Davidson, Agnes Broun, and Jean Armour been literate women they would not have furnished Burns with the mass of traditional literature he owed to them.

A girl's real education in rural Scotland was obtained in the kitchen, the dairy, and the fields. Almost as soon as they could walk boys and girls alike helped with the sheep and cattle and in all the work of seedtime and harvest. As they grew older the girls were trained more and more for the indoor duties of which cooking was the smallest part. Most of the clothing was made at home, from the carding and spinning of the wool and flax to the sewing of the finished webs into garments. Itinerant tailors made the Sunday clothes of the men; all the rest was the work of the women of the household. Add to these activities the manifold duties of kitchen and dairy and poultry yard and no peasant woman could have reason to complain of lack of occupation. At harvest time men and women alike turned out into the fields, the men to mow with scythe and sickle, the women and boys to bind and stack the sheaves and to glean after the reapers.

It was from these barefooted illiterate lasses that Burns got his first experiences in love and his whole simple theory of the relations of the sexes. Woman as the peasant knows her, sharing his daily toil, is not a superior being set apart for adoration. There is no mystery about her except the endless mystery of sex. There may be companionship and a more intimate sharing of the man's interests than women of higher rank attain. But the peasant woman cannot expect and does not get the graces of deference. Burns's attitude towards the girls of his class differed in one respect only from that of any other possessive young male. He was a poet, and from the very beginning poetry and sex were inextricably mingled. When as a fifteen-year-old boy he helped Nellie Kilpatrick to bind sheaves in the harvest field, and experienced the primitive coquetry which sought his help in extracting nettle and thistle stings from her fingers, his first impulses were those of any adolescent just becoming conscious of desire. But the second impulse was different. Unable to possess Nellie, he made a song about her.

As we have seen, courtship among the peasantry was no private matter. Not only did everyone know who was courting whom, but the aid of interested friends was habitually enlisted in arranging trysts. While still in his teens Burns displayed a command of the written word—insufferably turgid though the few surviving specimens of his early love-letters seem to us—which made him the chosen secretary for his less fluent cronies. He himself fell into love and out again with ease and frequency. But his early sweethearts are, like Nellie Kilpatrick, names and nothing more. Burns's statement that his relations with women were entirely innocent until after he met Richard Brown in 1781 is countered by Brown's charge that he was already fully initiated. As Henley says, it is one man's word against another's; since Burns was not in the habit of lying about his own conduct we may believe him. Where, when, or with whom his initiation took place is both uncertain and unimportant. His own assertion that he 'commenced a fornicator' with Betty Paton is subject to the discount always to be charged against poetical versions of prose facts. The certainty is that the years following his return from Irvine were loaded with emotional tension by three women—Elizabeth Paton, Mary Campbell, and Jean Armour. Of the three the one who has received the most attention probably deserves the least.

No glamour of romance shields Betty Paton. A servant of his mother's at Lochlie and Mossgiel, she succumbed willingly enough to the advances of the young farmer whom his father's death had just released from tutelage, and in due course bore him a daughter in the spring of 1785. According to Gilbert Burns, Robert wanted to marry her, but was dissuaded by his family, who feared that her coarseness would soon disgust him. Perhaps so, but the only contemporary letter does not include matrimonial desire among the feelings it hints at. After the first embarrassment wore off and he and Betty had duly stood thrice before the congregation of Mauchline Kirk to be admonished for their sin, Burns brazened it out to the scandal of his stricter neighbours, and Betty accepted it resignedly, knowing that such accidents would happen and that they need not neces-

sarily impair her future career. Part of her resignation, however, may have been conviction that
Robert Burns had insufficient prospects to make
marriage worth fighting for. In the fall of 1786,
when the Kilmarnock *Poems* had supplied her erst-
while lover with a little ready cash, Betty promptly
demanded maintenance for herself and her child.
In settling the claim Burns apparently had to pay
over rather more than half his profits, besides legally
binding himself for the complete support and education of his daughter. When on December 1, 1786,
she signed with her mark the legal discharge of her
claim, Betty Paton disappeared from Burns's life.
She was a merry lass; her lover had paid for his fun;
the account was closed—except for the black-eyed
little girl being reared by a long-suffering grandmother at Mossgiel.

Jean Armour's case was different, though it commenced, like Betty's, in purely physical attraction.
To begin with, the status of the girls was different,
even though both were red-knuckled, barefooted
country lasses. Betty was merely a farm servant
whose family ties, whatever they were, were already
broken. Jean was the eighteen-year-old daughter of
James Armour, a well-to-do master-mason and contractor in Mauchline. She was educated to the extent of being able to read the Bible and write her
own name. The story of her first meeting with Burns
is probably legend, yet in spirit the anecdote is at
least partly true. Burns at a village dance, embar-
rassed by a too-faithful collie which followed him

about the floor, remarked as he expelled the animal that he wished he could find a lass to love him as well as his dog did. Whether or not Jean actually asked him a few days later, when he found her bleaching linen on the green, if he had yet found such a lass, the fact was that he had. From that moment until his death Jean lavished upon him a docile and much-enduring devotion which leaves nothing derogatory in the comparison. She was playing with fire and must have known it. The scandal of Betty Paton was still fresh; Burns was a notorious man, glorying in the reputation of village Lothario and writing verses to warn the Mauchline belles how devastating he was. Experience had convinced him that all women are sisters under the skin—a dangerous half-truth which made trouble for him when he met women of another social level. They may all be sisters under the skin, but not on it or outside it. The fascination exerted so successfully over girls of his own class was in fact disastrous training for subsequent encounters with ladies. A lady may yield to a lover like any peasant lass, but she expects some finesse in his approach. But in the summer and autumn of 1785 Burns seemed as likely to enter Edinburgh drawing-rooms as to enter Parliament. He was merely an unsuccessful tenant-farmer with a dangerous talent for writing satirical verse and a dangerous light in his eye when an attractive young woman was in sight.

Between the tradition of his first meeting with Jean in 1785 and the beginning of surviving refer-

ences to the affair in February, 1786, its history is a
blank. On the surface Jean's experience merely repeated Betty Paton's. She surrendered to Burns and
in due course endured the consequences. Yet on
Burns's side the cases were not alike. However
brazenly he may have begun his courtship he soon
found that Jean roused deeper emotions than Betty
ever had. His first extant reference to the affair,
apart from verses in praise of Jean's charms, was on
February 17th, 1786, when he told John Richmond
—who after a similar scrape had fled to Edinburgh—that he had important news 'not of the
most agreable' with respect to himself. In other
words, Jean had told him she was pregnant. Entirely on his own initiative Burns undertook to do
the right thing he had successfully avoided, or been
dissuaded from, doing for Betty Paton. Sometime
in March he gave Jean, if not marriage lines, at
least some written acknowledgement that she was
or would be his wife. That he acted in a certain glow
of self-righteousness is a fair deduction from the
violence of his subsequent reaction. Rab Mossgiel,
the village Lothario, had behaved like a man of
honour and expected due recognition of his conduct.

The recognition he got was humiliating in the
extreme. The details can be reconstructed only by
inference from the result. Apparently Jean's parents,
suspecting her condition, began to question her.
She produced Burns's written pledge. A domestic
storm burst, not so much because Jean was to bear
Burns's child as because he expected Jean to bear

his name. To James Armour an illegitimate grand-
child was preferable to such a son-in-law as Robert
Burns. Jean meekly surrendered her lines to her
father—throughout her life she was usually passive
in the hands of male authority—and Armour carried
the document to Burns's patron and friend, Robert
Aiken, whom he persuaded to cut out the names.
Not the least extraordinary element in the affair is
the apparent belief of a successful lawyer that a contract could be voided merely by mutilating the
written evidence. Armour's desire publicly to humiliate Burns was greater than his desire to protect his
daughter. He succeeded admirably. In the same
letter in which the poet told Gavin Hamilton that
the document was mutilated he declared he 'had
not a hope or even a wish to make her mine after
her damnable conduct', yet amid his execrations he
paused to invoke a blessing on his 'poor once-dear
misguided girl'. The letter was the first of a series of
denunciations and repudiations of Jean much too
loud and too shrill to be convincing. They suggest
that Burns had to talk at the top of his voice to
maintain the degree of indifference which he felt
self-respect called for.

Perhaps nothing in Burns's whole life more completely demonstrates the impossibility of judging
him and the society in which he was reared by the
standards of nineteenth-century middle-class respectability. When James Armour learned that the
subscription for the Kilmarnock *Poems* was a success
he showed that, though unwilling that his daughter

should bear Burns's name, he was quite willing she
should share Burns's money. Accordingly he sued
out a writ *in meditatione fugae* to require Burns to
guarantee the support of Jean's expected child. The
news reached Burns, probably from Jean herself,
and he acted promptly. By formal deed of assignment he conveyed to Gilbert not only his share in
Mossgiel, but also the entire proceeds of his forth-
coming poems in consideration of Gilbert's undertaking to provide for Betty Paton's child. Burns had
checkmated James Armour, and so doing had almost evened the honours for ungenerous conduct. By
nineteenth-century standards his conduct was caddish, but by the same standards Armour could have
done only one of two things—either expel his daughter from his home, or protect her technical good
name by insisting upon marriage however distasteful
the prospective son-in-law was. But even by his own
standards Burns was acting ignobly. The man who
had written

> 'But devil take the lousy loon
> Denies the bairn he got
> Or leaves the merry lass he lov'd
> To wear a ragged coat,'

and who less than six weeks after the deed of assignment eloquently reproached John Richmond for
neglecting his late mistress and future wife and her
baby daughter, was allowing spite to degrade him
below the standards of the class to which he belonged
by birth, and much further below the standards he

had consciously set for himself. This was not acting according to the example of Harley the Man of Feeling. If the episode stood by itself it might be easier to condone. Unfortunately it is merely the first conspicuous incident in a series which includes his remarks about Jean to Clarinda and Bob Ainslie, his neglect of Jenny Clow, his attack upon dead Mrs. Oswald of Auchencruive, and his lampoons of Maria Riddell, and which justifies Henley's phrase that such things 'roused the cad' in Burns. Where women were concerned, it was always too easy for him to drop the thin cloak of acquired culture and revert to his peasanthood.

Alongside the Armour quarrel runs the mystery of Mary Campbell. Burns himself began the mystery by his curiously veiled allusions to the affair, but the real work of obfuscation was done by biographers who erected upon exiguous foundations of fact an ornate superstructure of legend.

The exact date at which Burns composed the 'Jolly Beggars' is uncertain—if it was really written after a slumming frolic with John Richmond it must have been in 1785—but the closing episode is either autobiography or prophecy. The Bard, whose sentiments in the closing chorus are definitely Burns's own, is depicted with a doxy upon either arm. After the stormy spring and summer of 1786 Burns confessed to Robert Aiken that he had plunged into all sorts of riot, Mason meetings, and dissipation, to distract his mind from the humiliation of the Armour affair. What form his dissipation took may reasonably be guessed not only from Burns's own temperament but from human nature in general. Yet nothing about his relation with Mary Campbell is free of doubt. All that can definitely be proved is that there was a servant-lass of that name to whom Burns apparently addressed certain lyrics and to whom he certainly gave a pair of Bibles bearing peculiar inscriptions. It is useless to rehearse the endless controversy between the romantics to whom Mary Campbell was a Lily Maid of Astolat and the realists to whom she was just another girl who couldn't say no. But a few facts must be underscored. The critical analysis of the legend made with caustic humour by Henley in 1896 and subsequently elaborated by Professor Snyder has never been rebutted nor even answered. The scripture texts Burns wrote on the fly-leaves of that Bible are such as would have been chosen by a man to whom a frightened girl was appealing for protection and who was impulsively promising it on his word of honour as a man and a Mason. That he also sang Mary's praises as 'Highland Lassie' and in another lyric asked—for poetic effect at least—if she would go to the Indies with him means little, if anything. The enthusiasts prefer to forget that during the same summer Burns said farewell to Eliza Miller in a lyric quite as fervid as any of those addressed to Mary.

Out of the mass of legend and conjecture the only solid facts which emerge are that during this spring of 1786 Burns was having some sort of a love affair with Mary; that she left Ayrshire in May, and that she died in the early autumn. Burns may have turned to her for consolation after the breach with Jean; the affairs may have been simultaneous. Most biographers incline to the sequel theory on the naïve assumption that love affairs, unlike electric batteries, are always mounted in series and never in parallel. In view of the social attitude of the Ayrshire peasantry the question of whether or not Mary was technically chaste is both metaphysical and irrelevant. Burns's attitude toward the other sex was direct; perhaps the strongest argument for Mary's chastity would be the complete lack of reference to her in his contemporary letters, were it not for his subsequent description of her as 'as charming a girl as ever blessed a man with generous love'. Burns ordinarily meant such expressions in the most literal sense. Despite the evidence in the Bibles that he had tried again to do the right thing it is hard to believe that in retrospect Mary would have touched him any more deeply than Jenny Clow or Anne Park later did had it not been for her untimely death. She certainly meant little in May and June of 1786. In the same month in which he gave her the Bible he composed the long and bawdy 'Court of Equity'; throughout the summer his letters to his intimates mingle execration, devotion, and regret for Jean Armour in precisely the same tones he had used in April. A man who had really found an adequate new love might be supposed to speak of the old one as Burns had spoken of Peggy Thomson in 1784. Resentment of the Armours' conduct might explain the execration, but hardly the regret and certainly not the devotion. If Burns really intended to make a new start in Jamaica with Mary Campbell, it is strange indeed that he never hinted of it to his friends—unless we accept the tradition, reported at second hand from John Richmond, that Mary was a light-skirts whose character Richmond and some other friends exposed to the poet. In that case, he would have had good reason for silence.

When in October he summed up his situation in a long letter to Robert Aiken it was still Jean who was the cause of his secret wretchedness and who was the source of 'the pang of disappointment, the sting of pride, with some wandering stabs of remorse'. The sole passage in the letter which Snyder thought might apply to Mary—'I have seen something of the storm of mischief thickening over my folly-devoted head'—may now be interpreted as referring instead to the disconcerting reappearance of Betty Paton as a claimant for support. The sole evidence surviving from 1786, apart from Burns's lyrics, is his sister's story, told many years after his death, that one day in October he received a letter which he read with a look of agony and then crushed into his pocket as he silently left the house. Connecting this story with Burns's later statement that 'a malignant fever hurried my dear girl to her grave before I could even hear of her illness', biographers have assumed that the painful letter bore the news of Mary's death. But this, even granting perfect reliability to Isabella Begg's memory, is pure assump-

tion. Burns's sole references to her were written from
three to five years after the supposed event. With
one exception they were intended for the mystifica-
tion rather than the enlightenment of Robert Riddell and George Thomson. That exception is the
composition of 'Thou Lingering Star' and the letter
to Mrs. Dunlop which accompanied it—both of
them written in a neurotic state close to complete
nervous breakdown. The Highland Mary we know
is the creation of biographers, and should be suffered to abide in the Never-Never Land of romance.
The truth about the Burns of flesh and blood had
better be sought in his relations with flesh and
blood women.

In these relations there were three main degrees.
The foremost group consists of women who pro-
foundly stirred him, and on whom for a time at
least he concentrated his intellect and his affections
as well as his desires. In this group belong Jean
Armour, Margaret Chalmers, Clarinda, and probably Maria Riddell. Next come the women who
engaged his passing fancy, and for whom he felt
some tenderness, but who did not influence him
deeply or long. Among these are Betty Paton, Anne
Park, Jean Lorimer, and Jessie Lewars. A woman
who appealed to Burns on either of these bases need
not have been his mistress; in fact, only three of those
named ever yielded to him. But below these was a
third group, represented by Meg Cameron and
Jenny Clow, who were mistresses and nothing
more—the mere conveniences of the moment. These

last never roused even a momentary spark of poetry
in their lover. Judged purely on the basis of literary
by-product, Mary Campbell belongs in the second
group, but not in the first. Even her most ardent
champion might hesitate to assert that any lyric
addressed to her is the equal of 'Ae fond kiss' or 'Of
a' the airts'. Jessie Lewars and Jean Lorimer both
inspired better songs than Mary ever did.

But Burns's tenderness, even for the women who
meant most to him, was often of a peculiar sort.
Though he told Deborah Davies that 'Woman is the
blood-royal of life; let there be slight degrees of
precedency among them, but let them all be sacred', his practice was more accurately summarized
in what he said about love in confiding to George
Thomson his admiration for Jean Lorimer:

'. . . I am a very Poet in my enthusiasm of the Passion.—The welfare & happiness of the beloved Object, is
the *first & inviolate* sentiment that pervades my soul; &
whatever pleasures I might wish for, or whatever might
be the raptures they would give me, yet, if they interfere
& clash with that *first* principle, it is having these pleasures at a dishonest price; & Justice forbids, & Generosity
disdains the purchase!—As to the herd of the Sex, who
are good for little or nothing else, I have made no such
agreement with myself; but where the Parties are capable
of, & the Passion is, the true Divinity of love—the man
who can act otherwise than as I have laid down, is a
Villain!—'

One fears that Burns remained on these chivalrous
heights only when the woman was unattainable;

should she yield to him, she would too readily take her place among 'the herd of the Sex'. Certainly he freely discussed his loves not only among his male friends but with a patroness like Mrs. Dunlop. When, for instance, after his conquering hero's return to Mauchline in June, 1787, the Armours bade him welcome and Jean succumbed once more, he lost no time in reporting the victory to Smith and Ainslie. To put it briefly, beneath the veneer of sentiment, beneath even the poetic response, Burns's attitude towards women of his own age was the elemental possessiveness which regards sex primarily as a ribald jest. His sincerest tenderness belonged to no woman as deeply as it did to his children, however or wherever begotten.

Burns never revealed more truly his own feelings than in the 'Poet's Welcome to his Bastart Wean' which hailed the birth of his eldest child, Betty Paton's daughter. Its mixture of bawdry with affection, of rollicking defiance of the unco guid with exultant pride in paternity, may distress the tender-minded who prefer not to admit the existence in parental relations of even a sublimated carnality, but it is the very essence of Burns himself. His plainest expressions of his love for his children occur not in letters to women but in letters to his most intimate male friends, and often amid flagrant ribaldry. It was not to Mrs. Dunlop that he wrote that Jean's first twins 'awakened a thousand feelings that thrill, some with tender pleasure and some with foreboding anguish, thro' my soul'; it was to Robert Muir, com-

panion of his revels and recipient of broad jests.
Robert Aiken was told that the feelings of a father
outweighed in Burns all the sound reasoning and all
the bitter memories that joined in urging him to
carry through the Jamaica project. 'God bless them,
poor little dears!' he exclaimed to John Richmond
on reporting the birth of the twins. Such remarks to
men before whom he had no motive for acting a
part, are more convincing proof of real feelings than
are the dissertations, garnished with quotations from
James Thomson's dramas, on parental anxieties in
his letters to Mrs. Dunlop.

Especially notable is the letter he wrote to Bob
Ainslie on August 1, 1787, in response to the latter's
announcement of the birth of an illegitimate son.
Beginning, 'Give you joy, give you joy, my dear
brother!' he goes on to say that he has 'double
health and spirits at the news', and to welcome
Ainslie to 'the society, the venerable Society of
Fathers'. There follow eight lines of the metrical
version of Psalm 127, obviously quoted with as much
sincerity as when he later used it, in quite different
context, in writing to John M'Auley. He continues,
'My ailing child is got better, and the Mother is
certainly in for it again, and Peggy [Meg Cameron]
will bring me a half Highlandman', and announces
his intention of getting a farm, bringing them all
up in fear of the Lord and of a good oak stick, and
of being the happiest man alive. Then the letter
shifts to snatches of bawdy song, some quoted, others
apparently impromptu. This primitive joy in pa-

ternity, this exultation over the mere fact of birth,
whether the child was his own or another's, was
part of his heritage from the Scottish soil. The same
spirit shows three years later in his reply to
Mrs. Dunlop's news that her widowed daughter
Mrs. Henri had borne a posthumous son:

'. . . I literally, *jumped for joy*—how could such a
mercurial creature as a Poet, lumpishly keep his seat on
the receipt of the best news from his best Friend—I seized
my gilt-headed Wangee rod, an instrument indispensably
necessary in my left hand in the moment of Inspiration &
Rapture—and stride—stride—quick & quicker—out
skipt I among the broomy banks of Nith to muse over my
joy by retail.'

Nor did his paternal emotions dissipate themselves
in rejoicings over birth. Testimony abounds of his
devotion to his children, his concern over their
proper education, his anxiety for their futures.
James Gray on evening visits in Dumfries found him
explaining poetry to the eldest boy and hearing him
recite his lessons; Maria Riddell was impressed by
his constant devotion to the children's welfare. But
towards their mothers, once the fancy had passed,
he was indifferent. 'I am very sorry for it, but what
is done is done', he said of Meg Cameron, and
though Clarinda's rebuke stung him into something
like remorse for his treatment of Jenny Clow, even
there his last thought was for his son: 'I would have
taken my boy from her long ago, but she would
never consent.' The one possible exception to his

generalization was Jean Armour, but Jean's later history belongs elsewhere, beside Clarinda's.

In brief, Burns's experience among women up to his departure for Edinburgh had made him the 'magerfu'' man Sentimental Tommy had longed to be. His love-making might involve him in tangles which he was neither astute nor callous enough to avoid, but he had found his attraction enhanced by his reputation as a dangerous man. He had learned the value of aggressiveness; he had not learned finesse. When he met ladies his lack sooner or later became painfully evident.

Among women of the upper classes he was at his best in association with those whose interest was motherly rather than actually or potentially amorous. Before going to Edinburgh he had charmed middle-aged Mrs. Stewart of Stair as well as mature Mrs. Lawrie, wife of the minister of Loudoun, and had begun with Mrs. Dunlop a correspondence which ended only on his deathbed. In its progress this friendship reveals much of what was best in his relations with women; in the estrangement which interrupted it it reveals also his shortcomings. Since, moreover, it is the only one of his friendships in which both sides of the correspondence have been preserved, no guess-work is required in tracing its rise and decline.

Frances Anna Wallace Dunlop belonged by both birth and marriage to the old landed gentry of Scotland, and claimed collateral descent from Sir William Wallace. In the autumn of 1786 her mind was 'in a state which, had it long continued my only refuge would inevitably have been a mad-house or a grave; nothing interested or amused me; all around me served to probe a wound whose recent stab was mortal to my peace, and had already ruined my health and benumbed my senses.' Grief at her husband's recent death had something to do with it, but the chief wound was her eldest son's extravagance and marital scandals. About the beginning of November a copy of the Kilmarnock *Poems* reached her and her reading of them—significantly enough it was 'The Cotter's Saturday Night' and other poems based on the genteel tradition of eighteenth-century poetry that won her admiration—roused her to fresh interest in life. 'The poignancy of your expression', as she put it, 'soothed my soul.' To one reading her letters without reference to her age she often sounds like a decrepit and almost dying woman. Actually when she began writing to Burns she was only fifty-six, and she outlived him by nineteen years. She opened the correspondence with an order for six copies of the poems; the flattered poet could scrape together only five, which he dispatched with a complimentary letter that included the news that he was planning a second edition in Edinburgh. Mrs. Dunlop immediately elected herself one of his chief advisers, and among other things suggested that in revising his poems he should avoid describing her great ancestor as 'unhappy Wallace' and should make the Twa Dogs sit down more decorously. Later she offered the two

most inept of all the recorded plans for the poet's
future. In February, 1787, she proposed that he
should use the proceeds of his Edinburgh subscription to buy a commission in the army. The man
who wrote 'I murder hate by field or flood' and
whose dislike for 'the lobster-coated puppies' of the
army more than once got him into hot water would
have cut a strange figure in any officers' mess. On
April 1, 1789, she suggested his applying for the
newly established Professorship of Agriculture at
Edinburgh University. The self-taught peasant
would have cut a still stranger figure as the colleague
of Robertson, Cullen, and Blair.

The history of the first few months of his friendship with Mrs. Dunlop reveals how far Burns was
from understanding the finer points of etiquette. To
begin with he ignored her suggestions for altering his
poems. True, he could do nothing else. Her advice
was merely typical of what genteel Scotland thought
about his work. To accept all emendations would
have reduced his poems to namby-pamby; to accept some and reject others would have doubly
offended those whose criticism he ignored. But he
should have explained this to Mrs. Dunlop, and did
not. Her vexation at the discovery was intensified by
an innocent blunder he made in arranging for the delivery of copies she had ordered for her stepmother, the
dowager Lady Wallace of Craigie. The copies went
instead to the estranged wife of her eldest son, also a
Lady Wallace but regarded by her mother-in-law as
the worst blemish the family tree had ever suffered.

Their relations were first put on a really cordial basis when Burns visited her at Dunlop House in July, 1787. Annoyance at his social blunders evaporated before the charm of his personality, and thereafter the correspondence on both sides took a new tone of affection and esteem. Her interest in Burns was generous and motherly. She plied him with good advice, which he generally ignored, and frequently added substantial help with both money and influence. Towards her Burns seems to have felt as many a man does towards his mother—she bored him but he loved her. She often accused him, no doubt justly, of not reading her letters. They were long, tedious, and wholly unpunctuated; he probably glanced over them when they arrived and then laid them aside for more careful reading at a leisure hour which never came. But though he seldom answered her questions he took her unreservedly into his confidence—or almost unreservedly. He never did more than hint about Clarinda, but he told her everything about Jean. In fact he must have told almost too much; it is hard otherwise to explain his embarrassment over breaking the news that he had finally married the girl who had borne him 'twice twins in seventeen months'.

By the beginning of 1788 the friendship was so firmly established as to survive a most humiliating incident. When he visited Dunlop House on his way back from Edinburgh in February his reception was warm and flattering. Mrs. Dunlop's unmarried daughters were agog with admiration. Miss Rachel was hard at work on a painting of his muse, Coila, as to whose appearance she sought the poet's expert advice. Miss Keith discussed poetry with him and revealed the somewhat surprising fact that she had never read Gray. Before he left he had promised to lend the ladies his copy of Spenser, a recent gift from William Dunbar of Edinburgh. When a few days later he fulfilled his promise he added to the parcel a copy of Gray as a present for Miss Keith, only to learn that a plebeian poet must not presume too far. Mrs. Dunlop replied that she did not allow her daughter to receive presents from men who were not members of her own family, and proposed either to return the whole book or at most to permit Miss Keith to tear out the pages containing the poems she liked best. That Burns continued in friendship with Mrs. Dunlop after this rebuff is eloquent proof of the esteem in which he held her; he had lampooned others of the gentry for less.

Not that this was the only time when Mrs. Dunlop made him conscious of the difference in their ranks. Her occasional gift of a five-pound note, though usually tactfully designated as for some special purpose or occasion, always hurt his pride— the more so because he could not deny that he needed the money. He silently drew the line, however, when she proposed, in one of those fits of economy which sometimes afflict the well-to-do, that he help to sell some decorative fringe which she had been manufacturing. Over this as over others of his sins of omission she displayed an irritability more like a schoolgirl's than a grandmother's; most schoolgirlish in its evanescence. A thorough scolding which sounded like a total breach of relations would be countered by some new poems or new compliments from Burns, and her next letter would contain a five-pound note for the latest baby.

Though as Burns became more heavily burdened with labour and responsibility his letters grew shorter and fewer than at the peak of the correspondence during the summer of 1788, no serious rift appeared until December, 1792. When it came it was the result of Burns's pride working in combination with his want of tact. Among the servants on Mrs. Dunlop's estate was a milkmaid named Jenny Little, whom Burns's success had inspired to burst into rime. Burns had already endured a good deal of her output, both from manuscripts sent to him by Mrs. Dunlop and from a pilgrimage of adoration which Jenny had made to Ellisland in 1790—an unsuccessful pilgrimage, for she had found the poet laid up with a broken arm and in no mood for entertaining an aspiring poetess. When Burns reached Dunlop in 1792 he found his patroness's interest in her protégée still unshaken. With her assistance Jenny had recently printed her poems, and Mrs. Dunlop produced the volume with the request that Burns give his opinion of certain of the verses which she pointed out. He said, 'Do I have to read all those?' in a tone which she afterwards described as the equivalent of a slap in the face.

It was supreme tactlessness. Burns was bored and

showed it. A more politic man would have waded through the verses however much his jaw might ache with suppressed yawns. But boredom was not the worst aspect of the incident from Burns's point of view: his pride was wounded. Of all his patrons in the upper ranks of society Mrs. Dunlop alone had kept up her interest in him and had appeared to treat him as an equal. Now she unconsciously revealed that she saw no *essential* difference between his writing and Jenny Little's. To her he was after all merely a peasant poet with the accent on the adjective; the difference between him and Jenny Little was a difference in degree and not in kind. Both wrote in dialect; she failed to see that one wrote Scots poetry and the other Scots twaddle.

The incident illustrates once more what Maria Riddell meant when she described Burns as devoid in great measure of refinement and social graces. The abrupt and masterful manner, successful with the girls of his own original class, sooner or later annoyed other ladies besides the Duchess of Gordon. Mrs. Dunlop, however, did not allow her vexation to cause an immediate coolness; she contented herself with a lengthy silence followed by an explanation of her reasons for being offended. Yet when the real break came two years later Burns's unbridled tongue and pen were again at fault. Mrs. Dunlop heartily disapproved of his sympathy with the French Revolution, and had warned him more than once to drop the subject in his letters. Inasmuch as four of her sons and one grandson were or had been in the army and two of her daughters were married to French royalist refugees, Burns should have known that her sympathies would be Tory. Yet in face of her warnings he wrote in January, 1794, the most outspoken of all his political remarks, describing Louis XVI and Marie Antoinette as a perjured blockhead and an unprincipled prostitute who had met their deserved fate at the hangman's hands, and adding a guarded hope that revolutionary principles might have more scope in England. This time Mrs. Dunlop broke off the correspondence. Though Burns made two attempts during the next year to reopen it, she maintained dogged silence until his pathetic letter of farewell, written on his deathbed, at last broke down her reserve. Her letter of reconciliation was almost the last message which reached him before his death. For a century charitable biographers conjectured that the estrangement must have been due to the lady's hearing reports that Burns was living an evil life in Dumfries. The recovery of the complete text of his letter of January, 1794, revealed the simple truth that the breach resulted from nothing more serious than a failure in tact. There, as always, his trouble came because he had not taken heed to his ways, that he offend not with his tongue.

The same trouble underlay his relations with other women of a rank above his own—Margaret Chalmers, Agnes M'Lehose, and Maria Riddell, though in different ways and different degrees. With Margaret Chalmers, indeed, he maintained for a

couple of years the nearest approach he ever made
to a non-flirtatious friendship with a woman of his
own age, but of the three just named this clever
daughter of a gentleman farmer in Ayrshire was the
least removed in station from himself. Unfortunately, only Burns's side of the correspondence sur-
vives, and that in fragments. Apparently it began,
as usual, with love-making, but when Margaret
gently put a stop to that—probably by telling Burns
that she was already engaged to Lewis Hay, whom
she married in 1788—their relation ripened into a
genuine friendship which produced what Cromek
rightly called some of the best letters Burns ever
wrote. The poet took her unreservedly into his confidence about his troubles with Creech and his
anxiety over his future, so that his three or four letters to her during the height of his correspondence
with Clarinda come like a breath of bleak but pure
air in that hothouse atmosphere. But the friendship
ended, apparently through Burns's neglect. Two
years after her marriage he sent regards to her
through another friend, and called himself a wretch
for not writing her, but seemingly he could not
write when he felt that his confidences might be
shared with her husband. An estranged husband
would not have mattered, as his flirtation with Agnes
M'Lehose proved.

The Clarinda episode has more prominence in
most accounts of Burns than it deserves. In its beginning and growth it was in fact quite untypical
of the man—his one intensive effort to act a part

not natural to him. Its development in this way was mainly the result of the accident which threw him back on letter-writing instead of speech in conducting his suit. Agnes M'Lehose when Burns met her was a plump young matron about his own age. Born Agnes Craig of Glasgow and a relative of one of the Lords of Session, she had married in romantic haste at the age of seventeen a young lawyer named James M'Lehose, and when Burns met her had already had eleven years of leisure to repent. Her husband, after abusing and neglecting her and getting into debt and disgrace, had at last been exiled by indignant relatives to Jamaica—that tropical refuge for Britons who had made their native climate too hot for them. His wife, trying to rear three sickly children on a microscopic annuity, had turned for consolation to literature and religion. In the latter she had espoused under the dynamic preaching of the Rev. John Kemp the strictest tenets of Calvinism; in the former she had familiarized herself with the most elegant authors of the day and had taken to versifying occasionally with the fluency and inaccuracy prevalent among women poets prior to Christina Rossetti and Emily Brontë. Like most of Edinburgh in 1787 she had been eager to meet Burns. When at last she did so at a tea-party given by her friend, Miss Erskine Nimmo, she and Burns became so visibly absorbed in each other as to rouse the amusement of the other guests. The poet's experiences hitherto with young women of the upper classes had been disappointing. They were polite and attentive, but reserved. Here at last was an indubitable lady, and a young and attractive one at that, who displayed something like the enthusiastic attention he had been accustomed to receive from the belles of Mauchline. Before the tea was over Burns had accepted Mrs. M'Lehose's invitation to a party of her own. If ever a woman threw herself at a man's head Agnes M'Lehose did, and Burns was not the man to refuse such a challenge. A letter to Richard Brown in the early days of his infatuation leaves no doubt that he thought he had made a conquest; but he had reckoned without Clarinda's Calvinism and her social traditions.

The affair might have spent itself in a passing flirtation had not chance, in the form of a drunken driver who overturned a coach and dislocated the poet's knee, confined him to his room for several weeks. His note explaining and deploring his inability to attend the tea-party was answered by one offering sympathy and regret. Burns and Mrs. M'Lehose both wielded free-flowing pens; their correspondence rapidly gained momentum and fervour. By the third exchange of letters she felt it her duty to remind him that she was a married woman. The result may or may not have been what she intended. Assuring her that his intentions were strictly honourable Burns seized the opportunity to express far more ardent chivalry and devotion than he would probably have ventured on had she been free. In reply she suggested their writing under Arcadian pseudonyms—no doubt as evidence of the strictly Platonic nature of their sentiments; displayed her acquaintance with *The Spectator* by calling herself Clarinda; and suggested Sylvander for Burns. Having thus safely wrapped their correspondence in asbestos they relaxed in a vapour-bath of emotion.

Less than three weeks after Burns's accident he was assuring Clarinda that she was a gloriously amiable fine woman and was promising lifelong devotion. But he was not admitting her as yet into his inner doubts and perplexities. Margaret Chalmers was the only woman who shared those. In fact both Sylvander and Clarinda seemed to have reserved their more intimate communications for personal speech. Apparently not until their long-deferred second meeting in January did Burns tell her about Jean and his children and Clarinda give him the whole tale of her unhappy marriage. She also sought in both speech and writing to convert him to Mr. Kemp's particular brand of Calvinism. But here even at the height of his infatuation she failed. The most she got was a partial recantation of his liking for the heroic qualities of Milton's Satan.

So long as communication was limited to pen and ink the affair for Burns was little more than a literary exercise. After they began to meet it became different and, in its effects on him, worse. Physical nearness could not fail to stir a man of his temperament. Soon their conversation was supplemented by caresses which Clarinda, however, managed to keep within bounds. As a result, Burns left these interviews with his blood at fever heat. A servant-girl

named Jenny Clow, successor to the Meg Cameron
of the previous winter, provided the consummation
which Clarinda denied, and in due course added
yet another to his growing list of paternal, legal,
and emotional perplexities.

Clarinda was of course unaware of Jenny's existence, but she soon had other reasons for being uncomfortable. Edinburgh was not a city in which a
gentlewoman could be indiscreet and get away with
it. More than a dozen years later Euphemia Boswell
told Joseph Farington that Edinburgh's chief draw-
back was that everybody knew all his neighbours'
affairs. The poet's visits to the Potterrow were freely
discussed. Lord Craig heard of them and was annoyed by his kinswoman's indiscretion; the Rev.
Mr. Kemp heard of them and felt it his duty to admonish his parishioner. When Clarinda confided
these troubles to Burns they of course roused him to
new fervours of knight-errantry. Moreover, other
agitations were intensifying the emotional stress of
the love affair. A great lady named Mrs. Stewart
who was expected to help his Excise project chose
to lecture him on the error of his ways; rumours
were afloat that William Creech was insolvent;
above all there was bad news from Mauchline.
Jean's parents had this time chosen the heavy
melodramatic role and had bidden their erring
daughter not to darken their doors again. She was
being sheltered by friendly Mrs. Muir of Tarbolton
Mill, but her future was black. In these circumstances it is unjust in the extreme to judge Burns's

conduct by the cool standards of sobriety and sanity. The man was in such a state of frenzy that he cannot be held accountable for his words nor even for all his actions.

What had begun as a flirtation and had continued, in part at least, as a piece of play-acting had by the middle of February become an imbroglio. Burns and Clarinda, both of them sentimentalists whose roused emotions were stronger than their reason, had gone so far that they could no longer regard their relations as simple friendship. By the time Burns set out on the 18th for Mauchline by way of Glasgow he had indulged in a perfect delirium of sentiment and rash vows. If he had not actually pledged himself to wait until James M'Lehose should be considerate enough to die and leave Clarinda free to marry Sylvander it at least appears that she expected him to wait. Meanwhile they were to write to each other every day.

The artificial and hot-house nature of the affair is fully demonstrated by the change which came over Burns's letters as soon as removal from Edinburgh plunged him into the chilly air of everyday. The promise of a daily letter was the first to fail. Burns reached Glasgow on the evening of the 18th to find Richard Brown awaiting him at the Black Bull Inn in the company of young William Burns, who had ridden up from Mauchline with his brother's horse. Before settling to a convivial evening Burns managed to dispatch a hurried note to Clarinda, but it was four days before he found time to write again.

His next letter shows how effectively those four days had brought him back from a sentimental dream-world to crude reality. Doubtless William had brought the latest bulletins about Jean, but no hint of them was passed on to Clarinda. A feverish day of entertainment among the prosperous weavers of Paisley was followed by two days of more decorous pleasure at Dunlop House and then by another wild bout at Kilmarnock. The letter from Kilmarnock is devoted mainly to a broadly humorous account of his Paisley host's troubles with a daughter who had been to boarding school, a son who wanted a latch-key, and himself who thought it better to re-marry than to burn. Not a word about Jean, scarcely a word about worthy Mrs. Dunlop and none about artistic Miss Rachel and poetic Miss Keith—in short, just such a letter as Burns might have written to Bob Ainslie or Alexander Cunningham, and in comparison with all the previous Clarinda correspondence as inappropriate as Falstaff in love.

But this letter jars on the reader only because it is wrong in its context. Two which he wrote after his arrival at Mauchline on the 23rd jar for a different reason. Only one of these, however, was to Clarinda. She had given him a couple of little shirts for Baby Robert, who was being cared for at Mossgiel. As soon as he had delivered these and seen his family, Burns set off to interview 'a certain woman' at Tarbolton Mill. 'I am disgusted with her; I cannot endure her! I, while my heart smote me for the prophanity, tried to compare her with my Clarinda:

'twas setting the expiring glimmer of a farthing taper beside the cloudless glory of the meridian sun. Here was tasteless insipidity, vulgarity of soul, and mercenary fawning; there, polished good sense, heaven-born genius, and the most generous, the most delicate, the most tender Passion. I have done with her and she with me.'

Of the many things in Burns's life which might better have been left unsaid or undone this letter might claim first place were it not for the one he wrote to Bob Ainslie ten days later. Here he describes his reconciliation with Jean. What makes this letter revolting is not so much its biological detail as the realization that the alleged events which Burns describes occurred less than a fortnight before Jean's confinement. On March 3 she again bore her lover twins, who did not live even long enough to be baptized. Still worse, if it is true, is his assertion that he had sworn Jean 'privately and solemnly never to attempt any claim on me as a husband, even though anybody should persuade her she had such a claim, which she has not, neither during my life nor after my death. She did all this like a good girl'. . . . Here, however, it is more than possible that he was talking brazenly for Ainslie's edification; Henley's doubt that Mrs. Armour could have been reconciled to her daughter without a promise of marriage seems well founded. Moreover the statement proves that by this time, whatever he may have thought in 1786, Burns realized that the destruction of the original marriage lines had not necessarily voided the contract.

Whatever he said or did at his first interview with Jean he must, before he returned to Edinburgh in March, have made up his mind that sooner or later he would acknowledge Jean as his wife. The letters to Clarinda during the remaining two weeks of his absence were noticeably lacking in fervour. They contained, however, more news about his personal affairs, especially the doubts and uncertainties that still kept him hesitating between farming and the Excise, than any of the earlier ones did. An unsolved mystery in his life is the nature of his relations with Clarinda during the fortnight he spent in Edinburgh in March. To the modern reader with full knowledge of the facts the fervour of his latest letters seems still more forced and artificial than before, but it may be questioned if this truth was equally obvious to Clarinda. Indeed their final meeting, at which Burns presented her with a pair of drinking-glasses, a poem, and an inscribed copy of Young's 'Night Thoughts', clearly had enough romantic intensity to satisfy even Clarinda. Herein lies the mystery. The later developments prove that Burns had told her nothing of his reconciliation with Jean, yet Burns was not a man who could ordinarily act a part convincingly. This time he must have tried. The results, combined with anxiety over livelihood, are displayed in a letter of March 20, in which he told Richard Brown that worry over his lease, 'racking shop accounts' with Creech, 'together with watching, fatigue, and a load of care almost too heavy for my shoulders, have in some degree actually fever'd me. . . . These eight days, I have been positively crazed.'

He returned to Mauchline on the 22d to receive his six weeks of Excise instructions, publicly to acknowledge Jean as his wife, and incidentally to compose a formula whereby to explain his action to his friends and patrons:

'I had a long and much-loved fellow creature's happiness or misery in my determination, and I durst not trifle with so important a deposite.'

This statement with only slight variations he used to half-a-dozen different correspondents. Whether he used it to Clarinda or not is uncertain; he may have entrusted Ainslie with the delicate task of breaking the news. However the news reached her, it quite naturally angered her. If Burns wrote it to her she destroyed the letter, and we know that he destroyed her reply calling him a Villain and accusing him of perfidious treachery. When he visited Edinburgh again in February, 1789, she refused to see him and told Ainslie that she intended to keep away from her windows while he was in town lest she catch a glimpse of him in the street.

In the fall of 1791, however, she had a chance to reopen the correspondence. Jenny Clow in June, 1788, had undertaken some sort of legal action against Burns and one purpose of his return to Edinburgh in the following February had been to settle with her. Whatever the nature of the settlement it had not helped much. When in 1791 Jenny somehow communicated with Clarinda, the latter found the girl ill, destitute, and friendless, in a miserable lodging. Clarinda's discovery of the means whereby Sylvander had managed to keep his courtship on so lofty a plane must have been humiliating and disillusioning, but she was woman enough to turn her discovery to account. Her letter to Burns described Jenny's condition briefly and effectively and suggested that there was a striking contrast between his practice and the high principles of generosity and humanity which he professed. She meant her letter to sting, and it did. Burns begged her to relieve Jenny's immediate needs and promised personal action at the first opportunity. At this point Jenny vanishes from the record. What Burns did, whether Jenny lived or died, whether her son lived or died, if he lived what became of him—all these are questions without answers.

Meanwhile Clarinda had been attempting to re-establish her own life. Her husband had sought a reconciliation, and she was planning to join him in Jamaica. When Burns made his last visit to Edinburgh in November, 1791, her departure was already arranged. She was fully reconciled to Sylvander now, and for the first time their relationship revealed simple and genuine emotion. The Arcadian names vanished in the correspondence; she became 'my dearest Nancy' instead of Clarinda, and when Burns returned to Dumfries, fully convinced that he had said farewell forever, he produced the one really first-rate lyric Clarinda ever inspired—'Ae Fond Kiss, and Then We Sever'.

The sequel was the last of the anti-climaxes which marked the affair. Clarinda reached Jamaica to find James M'Lehose's disposition not sweetened by time, and a brood of mulatto children proved that he had not suffered by her absence. She returned to Scotland on the same ship which took her out. For some time after her return she did not communicate with Burns. When she did so it was in terms of cautious esteem which inspired him to so bombastic a reply that he shortly afterwards tried to disguise its date by describing a transcript of it as 'the fustian rant of enthusiastic youth'. The first part of the description is accurate. For Burns the episode was closed, and closed, as it had opened, in posturing affectation of emotion. But Clarinda lived on it for the rest of her long life, exhibiting his letters to her friends after his death until some of them were worn to tatters. Her caution, however, equalled her vanity. After some of the letters had been surreptitiously transcribed and published in 1802 she went over the manuscripts, destroying the addresses, scoring out or clipping away proper names and erasing some of the more ardent love-making, and being reduced at last in senile old-age to selling some of them for a few shillings each. Sylvander's was the happier fate after all.

Meanwhile, whatever bombast or adoration her husband was addressing to Clarinda, the 'certain woman' was lavishing on Burns the devotion he had wished for at his first meeting. Various stories are told of how and when he acknowledged Jean as his wife. The probability is that he never did so, in the sense of going through a formal marriage service. On April 28th he confided to James Smith that 'Mrs. Burns' was Jean's 'private designation'; a month later, in a letter to Ainslie, he avowed the title 'to the World'. By Scots law, avowal in the presence of witnesses constituted a legal, though irregular, marriage; a peculiar letter to Smith at the end of June suggests that Burns even evaded this legal requirement:

'I have waited on Mr. Auld about my Marriage affair, & stated that I was legally fined for an irregular marriage by a Justice of the Peace.—He says if I bring an attestation of this by the two witnesses, there shall be no more litigation about it.—As soon as this comes to hand, please write me in the way of familiar Epistle that, "Such things are." '

In other words, he was asking Smith—who had not lived in Mauchline for two years—to testify, but not on oath, that Burns had acknowledged the marriage in his presence. Armed with Smith's letter, and another, he then presented himself again before the minister, who overlooked the doubtful legality of the evidence as two years before he had allowed Burns's doubtful status as a bachelor. On August 5th Burns and Jean made their formal appearance before the Kirk Session, avowed their marriage as of 1786, and were readmitted to the communion after

'Mr. Burns gave a Guinea note for the behoof of the Poor.'

All this time Burns was alternating between Mauchline and Ellisland, to the detriment of his interests in each place. A man absent from his farm every other fortnight could scarcely expect work to go forward quickly, but there were no living accommodations for Jean and young Robert until in October a neighbour, moving into Dumfries for the winter, offered Burns the use of his house. But the periods of absence roused Burns once more to lyric fervour for Jean, and the man who six months earlier had pledged undying devotion to Clarinda composed 'Of a' the airts' in tribute to his wife.

But it was the last song that can with complete certainty be connected with Jean. She sank before long to the status of a hard-working, child-bearing domestic fixture, losing her good looks—at first sight of her in 1790 John Syme concluded that Burns's lyrics in her praise were poetic licence—but keeping her equable temper and her devotion to her husband. Of all the women who had loved Burns more or less, and whom he, more or less, had loved, she alone had to live with him. And yet she continued to love him, not weighing his merits, but pardoning his offences. She had things to pardon, though when he married her Burns thought he had shaken himself 'loose of a very bad failing.' Eighteen months after this announcement of reformation, Jean went home to Ayrshire for a visit, and her husband strayed into the arms of Anne Park at the Globe Inn. When the

blonde barmaid in due course bore him a child, and
died in doing it, Jean took in the little girl and reared
her with 'no distinction shown between that and the
rest of their children.' Maria Riddell, whose words
are just quoted, added that Burns told her the story
'with much sensibility'.

Burns could not take Jean into the society to
which he was himself admitted, so she remained un-
noticed at home, tending the children and keeping
the house in slatternly Scots fashion, but with a sober Scots thrift which probably accounted for her
husband's living within his income and at last dying
with little more than the debts incurred during his
final illness. Burns seldom spoke of her in his last
years, but when he did so it was 'with a high tribute
of respect and esteem'. Maria Riddell—perhaps a
prejudiced witness—states that 'he did not love her,
but he was far from insensible to the indulgence and
patience, "the meekness with which she bore her faculties" on many occasions very trying to the tempers
of most individuals of our sex.' One suspects, sometimes, that Burns would never have continued to
love any woman after he had won her; that no matter who she was, he might still have summed up his
marriage as he did to John Beugo:

'Depend upon it, if you do not make some damned foolish
choice, [marriage] will be a very great improvement on
the Dish of Life.—I can speak from Experience, tho' God
knows my choice was random as Blind-man's buff. I like
the idea of an honest country Rake of my acquaintance,
who, like myself, married lately.—Speaking to me of his

late step, "L—d, man," says he, "a body's baith cheaper
and better sair't!" '—

Maria Riddell may have been one reason for
Burns's abrupt closure of the correspondence with
Clarinda in 1793. After Clarinda had refused to continue it as an emotional communion he no longer
needed it as an intellectual one. He had found a
woman friend who surpassed Clarinda as much in
intellect as she did in social position, and the only
occasion on which he reopened communications
with Agnes M'Lehose was during his subsequent estrangement from Mrs. Riddell—when he used the
opportunity to send Clarinda copies of the crude
lampoons he had composed upon Maria.

Walter Riddell, younger brother of Burns's friend
at Friars Carse, had compressed a good deal of experience into the first twenty-eight years of his life.
After a short period in the army he had married an
heiress who within a year made him a widower and
the owner of an estate in Antigua. In 1790 he met at
St. Kitts Maria Banks Woodley, youngest daughter
of the governor of the Leeward Islands, and after a
brief courtship married her when she still lacked two
months of being eighteen. Though Maria's mother
was a native of St. Kitts, the girl had been born and
educated in England and soon after their marriage
the young couple returned there.

According to one interpretation of a letter from
Francis Grose to Burns in January, 1791, they must
have proceeded at once to an autumn visit at Friars

Carse, where Grose was also a guest. Grose told
Burns that 'after the Scene between Mrs. Riddell
Junr and your humble Servant, to which you was
witness, it is impossible I can ever come under her
Roof again.' The letter also refers to the Governor—
'a spoilt Child with a Number of good Qualities'—
whom its editor identifies as Walter Riddell,
Mrs. Riddell Junior being Maria. But there was
also an extremely senior Mrs. Riddell at Friars
Carse, for Robert's grandmother lived with him.
Hence the Junior may equally well have been
Mrs. Robert Riddell, and inasmuch as Maria had
no roof of her own in Scotland until 1792, it is
hard to see how any misconduct of hers could have
shut Friars Carse to Grose.

If this was really Maria's first meeting with Burns
it was an inauspicious start. But the early stages of
the friendship are obscure. The extant correspondence does not begin until February, 1792, and by
that time Maria's life was so truly invaluable to
Burns that to lose her would leave a vacuum in his
enjoyments that nothing could fill up. By this time,
too, she was the mother of a daughter, born in England in August, 1791. Her husband was again in
Dumfries, negotiating for an estate, and Maria had
gone to Edinburgh with the double purpose of seeking expert medical advice and finding a printer for
her narrative of her voyage to the West Indies. To
this latter end Burns introduced her to his old friend
Smellie in a letter which paid the highest compliments to her intellectual and literary accomplish-

ments—if it can be called a high compliment to say
that her verses 'always correct, and often elegant',
were 'very much beyond the common run of Lady
Poetesses of the day'. The introduction resulted in a
friendship between Smellie and Maria of which the
written records, being more decorous than Burns's
own letters to the printer, were published by the latter's biographer. Maria liked to collect curios, and
her interest in Smellie might perhaps be thus explained. But the gruff and erudite printer's continued interest in Maria is further evidence that she
had brains as well as charm, though her letters are
evidence enough.

In the spring of 1792 Walter Riddell purchased
the estate of Goldielea near Dumfries, renamed it
Woodley Park in Maria's honour, and set up as a
country gentleman. More accurately, he paid a
small deposit on the purchase price without knowing how he would raise the main sum. Burns visited
frequently at Woodley Park, though its master bored
him. Walter Riddell apparently shared his brother's
convivial habits without his brother's modicum of
literary and intellectual interests, and the poet's attitude towards him is more clearly shown by the
almost total absence of Walter's name from his letters to Walter's wife than even by the crude epitaph
which described the man as empty-headed and
poisonous-hearted.

In letter-writing at least the friendship with
Maria reached perihelion in the autumn of 1793.
Walter was then in the West Indies, trying to raise

money on his estate there, and Maria was living alone at Woodley Park with her books, her music, and two baby daughters. By this time Burns was ponderously flirtatious. Maria was the first and fairest of critics, the most amiable and most accomplished of her sex, and it was the final proof of his unhappy lot that when he was in love 'Impossibility presents an impervious barrier to the proudest daring of Presumption, & poor I dare much sooner peep into the focus of Hell, than meet the eye of the goddess of my soul!' At least one impassioned lyric which originally began 'The last time I cam o'er the moor And passed Maria's dwelling' had been composed and submitted to the lady's criticism accompanied by a postscript which transparently disclaimed personal application. In Walter's absence, many of their meetings during this autumn were at the homes of mutual friends or at the little receptions which Maria held between the acts in her box at the theatre. These latter, however, were sometimes subject to interruptions. On at least one occasion Burns found an army officer—'a lobster-coated puppy'—already in possession, and withdrew without even announcing himself. Maria chided him for his failure to appear and invited him formally to share her box at the next performance; he kept her supplied with all his latest lyrics, including those addressed to Clarinda.

It would be a mistake to take Burns's impassioned avowals too seriously. Maria was a young and fascinating woman of the type which pleases men

better than it does members of her own sex, and Burns
thoroughly enjoyed her conversation. To the pleasures of intellectual intercourse her company added
a subdued erotic stimulation which he expressed
in the only language he knew. The very frankness of
his remarks and Maria's calm acceptance of them is
proof that they were neither meant nor taken literally.

And then came the breach seemingly inevitable in
Burns's relations with every woman of higher station. Its details are still obscure. Even its exact date
cannot be determined, though it must have been in
Christmas week of 1793. The traditional story is that
Burns was dining at Woodley Park and that the
men's talk over their wine somehow got round to the
Rape of the Sabines. It was drunkenly agreed that
on returning to the drawing-room the men should
stage a burlesque of the espisode. They did, and
Burns, singling out his hostess as his prey, put too
much ardour into the game. Mrs. Carswell inter-
prets the thing as a deliberate rag on the part of the
other men to get Burns to make a fool of himself.
Such at any rate was the result. After a stormy scene
during which some of the other ladies present tried
to intercede for the poet he was ignominiously expelled. The next day he grovelled in contrition before the offended lady in the painfully humiliating
'letter from Hell'. She refused to be placated and
after two more abortive efforts on Burns's part the
breach between them was complete.

This accepted story leaves unexplained several

important details. Foremost among them is the fact that in his apology Burns blames his host for constraining him to drink more than he wished to. Maria had told Smellie in November that Walter Riddell was in the West Indies and was not expected back until spring. On January 12th, when the breach with Burns had already occurred, she again mentioned her husband's absence. If these letters were correctly printed by Smellie's biographer, Walter Riddell could not have been the host; therefore the scene could not have occurred at Woodley Park. The alternative explanation is that it really happened at Friars Carse, with Robert and Elizabeth Riddell in the roles usually assigned to Walter and Maria. In this case Maria, hearing of Burns's conduct, must have undertaken to discipline him.

Whatever the circumstances, Burns's subsequent conduct was inexcusable. During the early spring of 1794 he wrote several epigrams on Maria which are utterly caddish, lacking alike in wit and decent feeling. One of them he even offered to a London newspaper, the editor of which had sense enough to reject it. He also wrote the long, dull, and vulgar parody of Pope which bears the title 'Esopus to Maria' and which attacks everything about Mrs. Riddell from her hair to her morals. This last was meant for the 'quite private' delectation of John Syme and one or two other intimates, but even if Burns had published it his conduct could not have appeared in much worse light. The epigrams and the 'Monody on a Lady Famed for Her Caprice' are enough in themselves to put it beyond condoning.

While Burns was thus exhibiting the worst side of his nature, his victims' circumstances were changing. Walter Riddell had returned from the Indies without the money he had gone to raise, and in the course of the spring Woodley Park was repossessed by its former owner, Walter forfeiting his £1000 deposit on the purchase price as well as all that he had laid out in improvements. On April 21st Robert Riddell died, and Friars Carse was put on the market, the relations between the two families being so uncordial that Elizabeth Riddell refused any settlement which would leave her brother-in-law in possession of the estate. Walter and Maria attempted the usual expedient of impoverished gentry—a prolonged stay on the Continent—but found their way barred by the armies of the French Revolution. Accordingly after a few months in England they returned to the neighbourhood of Dumfries to resume life on a much reduced scale. They settled at Tinwald House, a tumble-down estate near Lochmaben, or rather Maria settled, for her husband was absent most of the time. In May, 1795, they moved again, this time to Halleaths, between Lochmaben and Lockerbie, where they remained until they left Scotland forever in 1797. How much Maria had heard of Burns's conduct towards her no one but herself knew, and she never told. When Currie published some of the letters referring to the quarrel she affected complete ignorance of their relation to her-

self, though it is hard to believe that some kind friend
had not shown them to her.

If Burns showed the worst side of his nature in the
quarrel, Maria showed the best of hers in the reconciliation. Early in 1795 she made the first move by
sending him a book she had heard he wished to read.
He replied in a formal note in the third person which
nevertheless welcomed the overture and opened the
way for further intercourse. By the beginning of May
he was writing in his old vein of flirtatious gaiety and
even confiding to Maria about the mysterious Reid
miniature of himself—mysterious because no one
knows for whom he had it painted, nor why. The
woman who quarrelled with Burns in 1794 may
have been capricious, and have pushed her rigour
further than was wise in dealing with a man of
Burns's temperament. After all, twenty-one is not in-
fallible even when feminine and married. But the
woman who reinstated Burns in her good graces in
1795, after his caddish attacks upon her, was certainly not petty.

The renewed friendship had not long to live.
Shadows of another sort soon began to fall across it,
for Burns's health was breaking. A note written at
the end of May to accompany the loan of the Reid
miniature mentioned that he was so ill as scarcely to
be able to hold pen to paper; a month later he feared
that his health was gone forever. The autumn
brought further affliction in the death of his little
daughter, and it was to Maria that he uttered the
only existing record of his grief: 'That you, my

friend, may never experience such a loss as mine, sincerely prays R B.'

And so, through bereavement, illness, and despair, the passionate, irritable poet and the vivacious young woman of the world drew towards their last meeting. The bleak little watering-place, the Brow Well on the Solway, was the scene. Maria's health also was bad, and she evidently, like Burns, lacked the funds to take her to a better resort. On the 5th of July, 1796, she sent her carriage for Burns: not until she saw him did she realize how serious his condition was.

He was dying, and knew it. His overdriven heart, which had never wholly recovered from the strain of doing a man's work on insufficient food at the age of fourteen, was giving out, and he was hastening his end according to the best medical advice in Dumfries. A doctor who thought that angina was 'flying gout' had ordered sea bathing, and the dying poet was plunging himself daily in the chilly waters of the Solway, as he had earlier in life sought to cure fainting-fits in a tub of cold water at his bedside. Maria was startled by the visible stamp of death on the features of the emaciated man who tottered from her carriage, and her concern was increased by his almost total inability to eat. But the presence of a young and attractive woman could still, as always, rouse Burns to his best efforts, and his talk might even have been gay—after his preliminary, 'Well, Madam, have you any messages for the other world?'—had Maria been able to forget his haggard countenance long enough to reply in kind.

As it was, they had 'a long and serious conversation about his present situation, and the approaching termination of all his earthly prospects.' The man who had never lied about himself, to himself or others, now frankly faced the fact that he was dying. And the presence of a sympathetic and intelligent listener urged him on to speech about the matters nearest his heart. Two things perturbed him on the brink of the grave—anxiety for his family, and anxiety for his fame. His eldest son was not yet ten; there were three younger, and Jean was hourly expecting a fifth; at least two others needed a father's help to lighten the stigma of illegitimacy. And as for his literary reputation—

'He said he was well aware that his death would occasion some noise, and that every scrap of his writing would be revived against him to the injury of his future reputation: that letters and verses written with unguarded and improper freedom, and which he earnestly wished to have buried in oblivion, would be handed about by idle vanity or malevolence when no dread of his resentment would restrain them or prevent the censures of shrill-tongued malice or the insidious sarcasms of envy from pouring forth all their venom to blast his fame.'

Could Burns have looked into the future, the prospect would have deepened the pain in his harassed soul. His anxiety for his family would have been allayed, to be sure, but not even in his darkest hour could he have visualized the future of his personal

and literary fame. He foresaw attacks of his enemies; he did not foresee the cowardice or treachery
of his friends. He need not have worried about his
trivial or unguarded writings, for time automatically washes away the sand and leaves the gold, if
gold there be, and the publication of trifling letters
cannot harm their writer if the pattern of his soul
itself is not trifling. That spiritual descendants of
Holy Willie should deplore his best and strongest
work and shake their heads over passions of which
their impotent pulses were incapable, that enemies
eager for revenge and underlings eager for drink
should lie about their relations with him—these
things were to be expected. But that Bob Ainslie,
turned pious, should exemplify his own piety by
preserving and circulating Burns's worst letters, that
George Thomson should not only ignore his dying
wishes but even, before his corpse was in the grave,
rush into print with a distorted and melodramatic
version of his last years which would set the tone
of biographies for a century to come, that Gilbert
should lack the courage to deny stories which he
knew to be false—all this, and much more, was mer-
cifully hidden from him. But it would have warmed
his heart to know that the one intimate friend who
would come before the world with a truthful account of his character, extenuating nothing, and
setting nothing down in malice, was Maria Riddell,
on whom he had made unforgivable attacks, and
who nevertheless had forgiven him. The woman
with whom the dying poet talked that day until the

distant bulk of Criffel turned dark against the sunset, and the chill tide in which he had been ordered to bathe ebbed away from the dismal flats of the Solway, was to prove herself the most devoted friend of her sex he had ever had, Jean Armour always excepted.

V

LIVELIHOOD

To Burns in the vigour of his early manhood the question of livelihood seemed easily answered. He was a good enough ploughman to be assured of the porridge and the few shillings a week which a skilled labourer could earn on a Scottish farm. There was no degradation in such service. The labourers, like the hired help on New England farms, ate with the family and took whatever share in the conversation they were capable of. Moreover, anyone, whatever his rank, who was capable of 'a sensible crack' was sure of welcome in households which had either to provide their own entertainment or go without. Not even the prospect of dependent old age held any terrors. The tradition of the blue-gowns, or licensed beggars, still persisted in rural Scotland. An old man past work who could talk interestingly could count on a meal and a place by the fire at almost any farmer's ingle. Burns seriously thought of this as a possible end of his own life. The expression of the idea in several poems might be dismissed as rhetoric had he not repeated it in the sober prose of his letters. He actually pictured himself as spending his manhood in labour, love-making, and poetry and his old age as a sort of Edie Ochiltree.

Such a vision of course was adolescent. To fulfil it

a man must have no dependents. Burns seems to have imagined at first that if he could help to keep the home together until his brothers and sisters were able to establish themselves his responsibilities would end. The liberation of his poetic talent entailed among other things a shrinking from the burdens of marriage on narrow means. His rejected proposal to Alison Begbie had come before his realization of his poetic calling; his rejected offer to Jean Armour in 1786 was the result of sympathy for her condition and not of a desire to settle down. But he soon learned that he could not so simply escape responsibility. His children must be provided for somehow even if he did not marry their mothers. Despite the casualness with which he incurred paternity his parental feelings were strong. '*Vive l'amour et vive la bagatelle*' sounded well as a motto until it was confronted by the actual problem of helpless lives which owed their existence to him. As a Man of Feeling he could not, even had he wished to, turn his back on them with Don Juan-like callousness. Besides, the law might have something to say in the matter—as Burns learned in the course of four suits or threatened suits by four different women within two years. Unless he chose to flee the country and repudiate his obligations he had to provide himself with settled livelihood.

For a man of his rank and education the possible choices open in 1786 were limited. He could continue as a farmer; he could attempt to support himself by writing, or he could seek a salaried position at

home or in the colonies. Each alternative had its
drawbacks. By the beginning of 1786 his reputation
in the community was such that he could scarcely
continue the partnership at Mossgiel, but he lacked
the capital necessary for setting up independently
elsewhere. The hope of any large financial returns
from his poetry seemed too fantastic for consideration; he lacked the training for journalism or hack-
work when Grub Street was crowded with penniless
university men. There remained the chance of some
salaried position. Yet even if he had been tempera-
mentally fitted for a commercial job he was by this
time too old. Merchants' clerks began their apprenticeship as boys in their teens. Burns was twenty-
seven. A post in the Excise Service might be feasible
but was not easy to get. All government jobs went
by favour, and despite the unpopularity of the service among the people at large the number of aspir-
ants so far exceeded the available places that the
endorsement of some influential person was almost
essential. The same thing was true of India, where
the East India Company's monopoly gave patronage as large a part as it had in the government services. The United States, not yet united, were in
economic chaos; Canada was undeveloped. There
remained the West Indies, then at the height of a
prosperity built on slave labour, where independent
planters with Scottish connexions were numerous
enough to make it possible for a Scotsman with the
necessary introductions to secure some sort of work.
The story of Burns's struggle for livelihood is the

story of his efforts in each of the four possibilities open to him.

The West Indian venture was the only one which never came to actual trial. The documents are lost which would settle the date at which Burns began seriously to consider emigration, but his mind was made up at the very beginning of 1786. Through friends in Ayrshire he obtained the offer of a position at thirty pounds a year as clerk and overseer on a Jamaica plantation. The story is still repeated that he published the Kilmarnock *Poems* to pay his passage-money, but his own contemporary account of the matter is sufficient refutation. He had already arranged to go to Jamaica, his employer to pay his fare and deduct the sum from his first year's salary, before he decided to print the poems. For Burns emigration was not only flight but almost a death sentence. He had some justification for his feeling. The West Indian climate helped to insure the financial success of a small minority of white immigrants by killing off most of their rivals. He published his poems because he wished, before saying farewell forever to Scotland, to leave behind some tangible memorial. When the publication proved so unexpectedly successful it immediately cancelled his flight.

Burns's first extant reference to Jamaica is in a letter to John Arnot of Dalquhatswood, which was written in April, 1786, when the subscription for the *Poems* was well under way. Negotiations were then almost complete: by June 12th Burns was able to announce that the ship was on her way home that was to take him out; on August 14th he explained that he was entering the employ of Charles Douglas of Port Antonio and all that remained to settle was the route by which he was to travel. In view of the time required for exchange of letters between Scotland and the West Indies it is certain that the correspondence with Douglas must have begun in the winter, before the Kilmarnock volume was planned and while a considerable part of it was still unwritten. As the troubles with the Armours thickened during the summer so did Burns's references to his impending emigration. During July and the first part of August he was announcing that he had booked passage from Greenock to Savannah-la-Mar in the *Nancy*, sailing about September 1. Then returned Jamaicans advised him that the route was too roundabout, and when the captain of the *Nancy* notified him that the ship was about to sail, Burns decided that the notice was too abrupt. The *Nancy* sailed without him, and he transferred his booking to the *Bell*, which was to sail direct to Port Antonio at the end of September.

The truth was that he was already wavering. The enthusiastic reception of his poems, the interest which influential gentlemen began to take in his welfare, were changing his opinion of himself and his prospects in Scotland. Moreover, the Armours were calming down; friends had promised to help him should Jean's father renew the effort to execute his warrant. Nevertheless he did not immediately

abandon the Jamaica plan. Though the *Bell* in her
turn sailed without him, he still watched the ship-
ping news as he collected his subscriptions and set
his affairs in order. Jean's twins, born on September 3rd, increased the need for settled livelihood, but
increased also his reluctance to leave Scotland.

Most of his letters of the autumn of 1786 have
perished. As late as October he was still talking of
emigration, though he had again postponed it after
actually packing his trunk and starting for Greenock
at the end of September. He still feared, he told
Robert Aiken, that 'the consequences of his follies'
might banish him; in other words, Betty Paton was
threatening to sue him. The Armour affair had already been compromised by dividing the responsibility for the care of the twins between the two families. When the extant correspondence resumes a
month later, Jamaica had been discarded. By
November 1st the poet had decided to try his luck
in Edinburgh. For this reversal the Kilmarnock
volume was directly responsible.

When Burns had begun in April to solicit subscriptions for a volume of his poems he had had no
idea of making it a commercial success. The book
was intended as a memento of himself—a souvenir
for his friends and a final and unanswerable fling at
his enemies. He probably hoped for no more material return than would cover the expenses of publication. Its success therefore was all the more intoxicat-
ing. Six hundred and twelve copies were printed, of
which about half were subscribed for in advance,

thanks mainly to Robert Aiken. When the book came out at the beginning of August it furnished the first literary sensation Ayrshire had ever known. The subscribers' copies were passed from reader to reader, creating such a demand that the entire edition was sold within three months. When Mrs. Dunlop ordered six copies in mid-November only five were left. At the end of July Burns had been a fugitive with a warrant out against him, to escape which he was shifting from one friend's house to another. Two weeks later he was a celebrity. His journeys through the country as he collected his subscriptions became a sort of royal progress. The fact that he was making a profit out of the book meant far less to him than the applause of all sorts and conditions of men. People of influence assured him that something could be done for him at home, though they were vague as to precisely what. After the printer's bills were paid the volume showed a profit of more than £ 50, though forfeited deposits on passage money and a substantial payment to Betty Paton reduced his net gain to about twenty. But Burns still had no wish to write poetry for money. He considered that 'downright Sodomy of Soul'. Poetry was his calling, but he refused to think of it as his livelihood.

Another man for other reasons doubted the commercial prospects of poetry. In spite of the handsome balance-sheet of the first edition, John Wilson, the Kilmarnock printer, declined to undertake a second without advance payment for all labour and materials. He felt that the first had glutted the market.

His timidity helped to transform Burns from a local celebrity into a national figure. When friends in Mauchline and Ayr suggested republishing the poems in Edinburgh Burns thought it an attractive but impractical dream. But when copies of the book reached people of influence in the capital and they repeated the suggestion it wore a different look. By October the hope of a favourable reception in the city had come to Burns from at least three different sources. His friend, the Rev. George Lawrie of Loudoun, had sent a copy of the book to Thomas Blacklock, the blind poet; Blacklock had commended it warmly and had even promised—not so warmly— to bring it to the attention of Hugh Blair. The famous professor of rhetoric, Blacklock thought, was too refined in his taste to relish it. Another eminent professor was not so finicky. Dugald Stewart, whose country home was at Catrine a few miles from Mauchline, read and enjoyed the poems, invited the poet to dinner, and added his personal encouragement to the Edinburgh venture. Finally the book reached even the peerage.

On November 1st Alexander Dalziel, steward of the Earl of Glencairn's estates, wrote that he had showed the poems to the Earl and that the Earl had expressed his pleasure in them and his desire to befriend their author. This approbation was heartening as Blacklock's and even Dugald Stewart's could not be. The Earl had a reputation for generosity and for keeping his word; he was one of the most popular and influential peers in Scotland and his endorsement would have weight with the people of wealth and fashion on whom the success of a subscription would have to depend. But the Earl had nothing to do with the abandonment of Jamaica. The same letter which brought the news of the Earl's interest also brought Dalziel's congratulations on Burns's giving up his plans for leaving the country. What Glencairn really did was to confirm the poet in his determination to offer his poems to a larger audience.

Undoubtedly Burns realized before he went to Edinburgh that he was setting out on the old and painful quest of patronage—a quest which had broken the hearts of more poets than it had ever freed from penury. But it was still fame more than money that he looked for from his poems. He continued to hope for some means of modest livelihood independent of his writing; if his subscription brought a little capital to help him on his way, so much the better. When he reached Edinburgh he made no effort to appear more than he was; he even sought deliberately to appear less. He dressed as a plain young farmer, and finding that the metropolitan critics were praising his work as that of an unlettered ploughman who wrote from pure inspiration he did his best to act the part. When Robert Anderson pointed out in private conversation some evidence of extensive knowledge of other poets Burns readily admitted his indebtedness, but in public he would not permit his claims to pure inspiration to be challenged. If an unlettered bard was what his

patrons wanted he would do his best to be one.
Many times, however, his role was trying, especially
when stupider people than himself condescended,
and gave him good advice.

Undoubtedly there were matters in which he
needed good advice, but he did not get it even from
the patrons who did not condescend. Among all his
new friends there was no one to take his part as Sir
Walter Scott later took Southey's in seeing that he
got a fair contract with his publisher. Glencairn had
been as good as his word in securing fashionable
subscriptions. The Countess of Eglinton made the
Earl subscribe ten guineas; the entire membership
of the aristocratic Caledonian Hunt put down their
names, but altered the first proposal that they give
two guineas each to a mere subscription at the regular price. But Glencairn knew nothing about the
business end of publishing. In introducing Burns to
William Creech, his brother's former tutor and the
best-known publisher in the city, Glencairn no
doubt felt that he had done his best. He had, up to
that point, but at that point a good contract lawyer
was needed. Unfortunately Henry Mackenzie and
the other men of letters in the city still adhered to
the convention of the writing gentleman who was
supposed to disdain pecuniary rewards. A few years
earlier, when David Hume was alive, Burns might
have been secured better terms; a few years later
under the leadership of Scott he would certainly
have secured them. Burns's perverse pride would not
allow him to haggle over a contract which in any

case offered more ready money than he had handled in all his previous life. What he needed and did not have was a hard-boiled business friend to do his haggling for him.

As it was, Creech made an agreement which left Burns to bear all the immediate risks and perhaps to receive a modest immediate profit, but which reserved the long-term earnings for the publisher alone. As was often the case with books published by subscription, the man whose name appeared on the title-page was not the publisher in the modern sense, but merely the author's agent. He provided the facilities for collecting the subscriptions and distributing the books, but took none of the financial responsibility. The author received the entire payment for the subscribers' copies, but out of these receipts had to pay the printer, the bookbinder, and also, presumably, the transportation charges on copies delivered out-of-town. Furthermore, the agents who distributed the books naturally expected to be paid. Hence Burns, wherever possible, enlisted his friends for this service—Alexander Pattison at Paisley, for instance, and Robert Muir at Kilmarnock—and when that was not feasible still sought to avoid the regular booksellers because they took 'no less than the unconscionable, Jewish tax of 25 pr Cent. by way of agency'.

The price to subscribers was set at the modest sum of five shillings, and close to three thousand subscriptions were obtained. Burns objected to printing the names of the subscribers—quite naturally, for the thirty-eight pages meant money out of his pocket merely to gratify the vanity of people yearning to see their names in print as patrons of literature—but was overborne by some friends whom he did not 'chuse to thwart'. Professor Snyder calculates Burns's utmost possible gross receipts from the subscription at £750. But after all charges were paid the net profit cannot have been more than half that sum. He told Mrs. Dunlop that he cleared about £540, but there, as in a similar statement to John Moore, he was reckoning in Creech's payment of 100 guineas for the copyright.

That was the sum agreed on when, just as his book was ready for delivery, Burns decided, 'by advice of friends' to dispose of his copyright. Once more he had sought the advice of others, and once more they told him the wrong thing. In this instance, the person most at fault was Henry Mackenzie, to whom Burns and Creech referred the question. Mackenzie was a lawyer, and ought to have warned Burns against the absolute sale of his rights in a potentially valuable piece of property. Instead Mackenzie contented himself with naming one hundred guineas as his idea of a fair price. That was on April 17. Creech delayed his acceptance until the 23rd, on the pretence of waiting to hear if Cadell and Davies would buy a share for their London trade, but finally consented to 'take the whole matter upon himself, that Mr. Burns might be at no uncertainty in the matter.' Thereupon Creech left town, without either paying the money or giving his note for it. A few days later Burns himself started on his Border tour, still without any legal contract with Creech, but with his hands full for the time being with the task of arranging deliveries, collecting subscriptions, and paying the printer and the binder. Had not Peter Hill, then Creech's chief clerk, taken a good part of the burden on himself, Burns would have been swamped under the worry of larger transactions than he had known in all his life before.

In August Burns returned to Edinburgh, but Creech was either again absent or again coy. Not until October 23 did the publisher at last set his hand to a note promising to pay the sum 'on demand'. How soon Burns began to ask for payment is uncertain, but by January Creech had delayed and evaded so often that Burns 'broke measures with [him], and . . . wrote him a frosty keen letter. He replied in forms of chastisement', promised payment on a set date—and broke his promise. To add to the poet's anxiety, rumours were afloat. It was hinted that Creech was on the verge of bankruptcy; it was also hinted that he had cheated Burns by secretly printing additional copies of the *Poems*, which he sold for his own profit. Burns bewailed his own fate as a 'poor, d–mned, incautious, duped, unfortunate fool'; two months later 'that arch-rascal Creech' was still making promises, and still reneguing. Not until May 30, more than seven months after he had agreed to pay 'on demand', did Creech at last part with his hundred guineas. And even then Burns's troubles were not over. Still another visit to

Edinburgh, at the end of February, 1789, was necessary before Creech paid over the final sums due the poet for subscription copies, so that at last he could report to Jean: 'I have settled matters greatly to my satisfaction with Mr. Creech.—He is certainly not what he should be nor has he given me what I should have, but I am better than I expected.'

The estimate of Creech was temperate enough; indeed, it erred, like Burns's statement to John Moore that Creech had 'been amicable and fair' with him, on the side of charity. It is easy to condone Mackenzie's blunder and Creech's sharp bargain on the ground that neither of them could guess the future value of the copyright, but it is impossible to excuse Creech's postponements of the day of reckoning. Prompt settlement of accounts after the book was published would have sent Burns back to the country with his pockets comfortably lined and with some of the glowing enthusiasm of his first season in Edinburgh still undimmed. By his paltry delays Creech kept the poet in the city until the interest of his fashionable 'patrons' had waned, until all the pleasure of publication and fame had evaporated in bitterness and disgust, and until the mere necessities of living must have made considerable inroads on his irreplaceable capital.

Indeed one of the extraordinary facts about Burns's life in Edinburgh is that he emerged from it without greater depletion of his capital. Contemporary report calls him dissipated. Yet somehow Burns managed to spend nearly a year and a half either in residence in Edinburgh or in journeying to and fro, and still came out with about four hundred and fifty pounds. So far as is known he had no income from July, 1786, when he assigned his rights in Mossgiel to Gilbert, until he reaped his harvest, such as it was, at Ellisland in the autumn of 1788. Even then he netted little, for the outgoing tenant exacted a price of £72 for the standing crops. However great his experience in the distracting 'task of the superlatively Damn'd—making one guinea do the business of three'—his twenty pounds from the Kilmarnock volume cannot have lasted long, and if there were any gifts except the Earl of Eglinton's ten guineas and the same sum from Patrick Miller he nowhere mentions them. If Burns dissipated heavily he managed somehow to do it without heavy expenditure, an art few people have ever learned.

The possibility that he received funds from Gilbert even after the deed of assignment must be ruled out. The flow of funds in fact was the other way. The supposedly careful and efficient Gilbert was in constant difficulties at Mossgiel. Robert sent him ten pounds from Edinburgh in the spring of 1787; during the following winter he authorized John Ballantine to pay over to Gilbert about thirty pounds of subscription money then in Ballantine's hands. And this was only the beginning. The letter to Gavin Hamilton already quoted indicates that Gilbert was so far in arrears with his rent in March, 1788, that Hamilton wanted Burns to sign some sort of a note for him. This Burns refused to do, because he had already lent Gilbert £ 200—nearly half his receipts from the Edinburgh edition. Whether the previous payments were counted as part of this loan or not is uncertain; probably they were not, for after the poet's death John Syme declared that Gilbert owed £ 300, though the legal accounting sets the figure at £ 200. It seems likely therefore that Gilbert regarded the earlier payments as gifts, and that the sum which Gilbert at last repaid to his brother's family represented the final loan in 1788. As part of the interest on the loan Burns arranged that Gilbert should pay his mother an annuity of £ 5 a year and should continue to care for Betty Paton's daughter. The result was that Gilbert made no cash payment during Burns's life, and never was able to pay off the principal until he undertook to re-edit the *Poems* in 1820. Burns had given most substantial proof of his loyalty to his family and in doing so had destroyed his only hope of success in his own venture at Ellisland.

Gilbert and his mother and sisters were not the whole of Burns's responsibilities. His younger brother William was approaching manhood and turned naturally for support to the celebrity of the family. He appears to have been an amiable but ineffective youth. He had served at least part of an apprenticeship as a saddler, and in the autumn of 1787 Burns made some fruitless efforts to find him a job in Edinburgh. A year or so later William set out to look for employment and held jobs briefly in

Longtown, in Newcastle, and finally in London, where he died of typhus and where his funeral was arranged by John Murdoch and paid for by Burns. Burns's letters to this brother during his year of wandering consist in about equal proportion of exhortations to brace up and be a man and of enumerations of gifts—shoes and shirts and waistcoats and above all money. Burns's position as family capitalist was no sinecure.

While he was struggling with Creech and trying to keep Mossgiel afloat, Burns was constantly harried by the problem of his own future. The only two possibilities he could see were a farm of his own or a post in the Excise, and for a long time there seemed little chance of achieving either. He had no intention of trying again for public aid through his writing. One subscription might be regarded as a public tribute; a repetition would look like begging. Besides, his common sense told him that a second subscription would have little hope of success unless it came at a long interval after the first and for work of a different character. He had not exhausted his talents, but he had exhausted his novelty. For the rest of his life he steadfastly refused to accept payment for anything he wrote and actually gave away poems which make up two-thirds of the bulk of his collected works. His sole payment for 'Tam o' Shanter' was a dozen copies of the proof-sheets; his payment for Creech's second edition in 1793—which included 'Tam' and a score of other new poems —was twenty presentation copies grudgingly allowed him. His fondness for making gestures of gallant but unwise generosity can hardly be better illustrated than by his dealings with Creech over this edition. The publisher wrote to him in 1791, proposing a reissue of the work and asking Burns to contribute some new poems to it, but without suggesting payment for them. Burns told Cunningham that he had taken a damned revenge of Creech by ignoring his letter. Yet a few months later he relented, and after reminding Creech that the new poems were his own absolute property, turned them over to him without asking any payment except the twenty gift copies. Such a gesture might have shamed some publishers, but Creech merely accepted it as his right. In the same spirit Burns hotly resented George Thomson's payment of £5 for his contributions to the first number of the *Select Scotish Airs*, and Thomson, like Creech, felt no compunction at accepting the poet's quixotic generosity.

On at least two occasions, moreover, Burns was offered pay for journalistic writing in party newspapers. The origin, extent, and duration of his relations with Peter Stuart of the London *Star* are all obscure, but it is plain that Stuart as a zealous Whig tried to get Burns as a regular contributor. The poet refused. When he struck off a satirical skit he was willing to give it to Stuart, but the only pay he accepted was a free subscription to the paper. Thus he managed to acquire the reputation, injurious to his hopes in government employ, of being a partisan writer without any reward except notoriety. Again

in 1794 Patrick Miller, Jr., his landlord's son who
had been put into Parliament at the age of twenty-
one, persuaded James Perry of the London *Chronicle*
to offer Burns what for those days was a fair salary
if he would come to London and devote his talents to the press. Again Burns refused. He realized
well enough that the prosperity of a newspaper was
often short-lived and he feared to jeopardize his
children's future by exchanging an assured though
meagre income for the chances of the journalistic
profession. Besides, the writer in a partisan paper in
1794 was risking jail as well as economic insecurity,
as the sedition trials then in progress had proclaimed
to all the kingdom.

But if he was not to support himself by writing
how was he to support himself? That question ham-
mered in his mind from the time he abandoned the
Jamaica project until the early spring of 1788. Even
before he went to Edinburgh he had thought of the
Excise. But he found his Edinburgh patrons cold to
all hints. These gentlemen reasoned simply. Burns
was the ploughman poet: ergo, he should continue
to plough. The only definite gesture made towards
getting him government work was Mrs. Dunlop's.
She offered an introduction to Adam Smith in the
hope that Smith might help him to a job in the customs, but the philosopher had left for London the
day before Burns presented his letter. Moreover
Smith no longer took an interest in much except his
own health, and if Burns sought later to renew his
application nothing came of it. His most favourable

opportunity to cultivate the acquaintance of high officials was lost when he allowed William Nicol to drag him away from Blair Athole, where Robert Graham of Fintry, Commissioner of Excise, was one of the guests, and where Henry Dundas was shortly to appear.

Meanwhile an offer of another sort was being pressed upon him. He had been in Edinburgh only a few weeks when the prosperous and enthusiastic Patrick Miller sought his acquaintance. Miller, after a varied career, at sea and as a banker, had retired from business with a comfortable fortune and was devoting himself to miscellaneous experiments. He was the sort of capitalist who is a godsend to struggling inventors, for his enthusiastic imagination enabled him both to visualize the inventor's aims and to overlook all the practical details and delays which intervene between a project and its fulfilment. His strongest enthusiasm at the moment was the improvement of navigation, but his interests also included agriculture. Not long before Burns came to Edinburgh Miller had bought the run-down estate of Dalswinton near Dumfries, and it was Ellisland, one of the farms on this estate, which he urged upon Burns.

The poet was afraid of it from the start, and for good reason. Miller, he said, was no judge of land, and what Miller thought was an advantageous offer might ruin his tenant. Had Burns been gifted with second-sight he could not have prophesied more accurately. Yet the difficulty he always found in saying 'No' to people whose intentions were friendly combined with his own inclinations to keep him from refusing Miller's offer outright. Farming was the business he knew best, and a farmer's life he held was the best of lives—if one could live by it—but Mount Oliphant, Lochlie, and Mossgiel had been a triple lesson on the fate of the tenant who undertook a lease without capital enough to stock a farm profitably. Even if the Dalswinton farm were all that Miller thought it, Burns doubted if his literary profits would suffice to give him a start. However, he agreed to look at Ellisland when he reached Dumfries at the end of his Border tour. When he did so he could scarcely have been in the mood for a really critical examination. The savage hospitality he had experienced for the past three weeks had left him jaded and depressed, and the annoyance of being greeted at Dumfries by Meg Cameron's letter would not sharpen his critical faculties. Even so he could see at a glance that the soil was exhausted and would require long and careful nursing. In fact the only thing to be said for Miller's offer was that, recognizing the run-down condition of the property, he was offering it at a low rental for the first three years. Fifty pounds per annum for a farm of more than a hundred acres contrasted favourably with the prices in East Lothian, where landlords were asking as much as thirty shillings an acre. Burns went home to Mossgiel without having made up his mind; if discussion with the cautious Gilbert contributed to any decision it was a negative one. Ellisland was too big a risk. He returned to Edinburgh in the fall with his mind made up. He would renew his efforts to secure an Excise commission and would bank the profits of his poems as a reserve fund for the education and security of his children.

But Miller was not easily discouraged. He had evidently decided that the poet as a tenant would be an asset to Dalswinton. Accordingly he urged Burns to go down again and have a more critical look at the place. A severe cold which confined him to the house enabled Burns again to evade committing himself and not long afterwards came the injury to his knee which laid him up for weeks and involved him in the Clarinda affair. But meanwhile his endeavours for an Excise commission were not prospering. Glencairn disapproved; Mrs. Dunlop disapproved; apparently everyone who might have exerted the necessary influence disapproved. In January Miss Nimmo sent him to a Mrs. Stewart who was supposed to have influence with the commissioners. The interview was not a success. Burns came away from it boiling with helpless rage. He had been questioned like a child about his most private affairs and Mrs. Stewart had further improved the occasion by rebuking him for the Jacobite sentiments he had scratched on the window of the inn at Stirling. If the quest for an Excise job was to expose him to this sort of thing Burns was ready to throw up the whole project.

Just when the matter appeared most hopeless his chance came from an unexpected quarter. The surgeon who had treated his injured knee was Alexander Wood, better known to his fellow-citizens as Lang Sandy Wood, who after a wild youth had become one of the most respectable characters, in both senses of that word, in Edinburgh. Wood learned of his patient's desire and offered to do what Glencairn and the others had refused or evaded— to bring Burns's case directly and personally before the Board. The result was that before he left Edinburgh Burns found himself, 'without any mortifying solicitation' on his own part, equipped with the official order for the six-weeks' course of special instructions which would entitle him to an Excise commission. It came none too soon. One of the rules of the service was that no man could enter it who was in debt, who was more than thirty years old, or who had more than three children. Burns's time for meeting these two latter qualifications was getting very short indeed.

But now that he saw an open road into the Excise Burns's mind veered round. Farming after all was a more poetical occupation than 'searching auld wives' barrels'. Miller was still urging Ellisland upon him, and the possibility of failure there did not look so black when he knew that if he did fail he had the Excise to turn to. He agreed to revisit the farm. No doubt he told himself, as he told Clarinda, that he did so only out of courtesy to Miller, knowing that the Excise must be his lot. His judgement warned him that the farm would not do; his emotions swayed him in its favour. In an effort to strengthen his judgement he invited his old friend, John Tennant of Glenconner, to join the tour of inspection. Glenconner's mind would not be biased by any poetic considerations. It did not occur to Burns that even the most experienced of farmers, looking at soil different from that he was accustomed to, could scarcely gauge its productivity rightly at the end of February. The rule-of-thumb farming which Glenconner and most of his contemporaries practised required the sight of growing crops for correct judgement. Tennant looked the place over and told Burns it was a bargain at Miller's price. The opinion astonished the poet, but he failed to realize that it was merely a guess less accurate than the opinion he himself had formed on seeing the place the previous June. Burns frequently made mistakes, but his worst ones were made when he relied on other people's judgement. In March he signed Miller's lease and committed himself to three years of struggle and discouragement which swallowed all the capital which had not already been poured into the bottomless morass of Mossgiel.

Legend has it that Burns was offered his choice of two farms on the Dalswinton estate and selected Ellisland because of its more attractive location— 'a poet's choice and not a farmer's'. In fact Miller offered no choice, and in drawing up the lease employed all the usual legal technicalities with one or two additions of his own. The rent was to be £ 50 a year for the first three years and £ 70 thereafter, and Miller's zeal for improvements was to have scope even while the tenant was in possession. The landlord reserved the right to take over the river-bank, a twenty-yard-wide belt along the Friars Carse boundary, and two acres of other land at his own choice to plant with trees. He agreed, however, to put money of his own into the place. It had not even a farmhouse when Burns signed the lease, and Miller undertook to provide adequate buildings. The contractor's delay in constructing these caused further needless anxiety and actual loss to Burns.

After the die was cast all Burns's earlier doubts about Ellisland and his own ability to handle it returned with redoubled force. His first move was to make sure of his Excise appointment by taking the necessary six weeks of special instructions from the officer at Mauchline, even though this delayed his settlement until mid-June. Inasmuch as these six weeks included also the emotional stress of the ending of the Clarinda romance and his acknowledge-ment of Jean as his wife, his nerves were over-wrought when he finally reached his farm. The prospect there might have discouraged a more phlegmatic man. The farmhouse was not even started, and his only shelter was a leaky and chim-neyless labourer's hovel. The sparse growth of the crops planted by his predecessor confirmed the ex-haustion of the soil, and he was confronted as never before with the need for executive skill. That aspect of his nature which led him to remark that some-how he could make himself pretty generally beloved yet never could get the art of commanding respect told heavily against him when he had both to keep his own labourers at work and to bully or cajole the contractor into finishing the farmhouse at the time agreed upon. When he was not present the farm-hands lay down on the job; when he was present they found it altogether too easy to engage him in talk while the work suffered. The friendship he formed with Thomas Boyd, the contractor, led among other things to an acquaintance with Thomas Telford, the great engineer, but it did not lead to the speedy completion of his house. As late as March, 1789, he was still pleading with Boyd to get at least the shell of it finished. Moreover he was too sympathetic with his workmen. The margin of profit on such a farm was too small to permit indulgence in humanitarian sentiments, but Burns knew too much of the lives of the lower classes to have the necessary hardness. Two letters to the owner of the neighbouring farm with whom Burns had co-operated in digging a drain do credit to his feelings if not to his business capacity. The labourer who undertook the job at seventeen pence a rood had underestimated the time. In order to give him a fair wage for his labour Burns added three-pence a rood to the contract price for his share and asked the neighbour to do the same—with what result is not recorded.

But there was a still deeper psychological hindrance to success at Ellisland. Even had the soil been productive, even had he secured a foreman who could have kept his hands at work, the Burns

who undertook Ellisland was not the Burns of
Lochlie or even of Mossgiel. Though by no means
setting up as a gentleman farmer, he had become
conscious of having a position to maintain. Gilbert,
he thought, might be able to take over Ellisland and
succeed with it; 'as he can with propriety do things
that I *now* cannot do.' Physical debility was also
to be reckoned with, for he must have got out of
training during almost two years of exemption from
regular labour, and his weakened heart would prevent his easily recovering his lost tone. But in fact
his mind was filled with other matters and metres.
That during his first summer he spent alternate
fortnights with Jean in Mauchline was a temporary
circumstance without relation to the success of the
farm thereafter, but that his work for Johnson's
Museum was filling his mind was a fact less easily
discounted. In the middle of his first summer he had
a fiddler with him for at least two days playing
over a collection of Highland music in quest of lyric
tunes for Johnson. It was a prelude to his greatest
period of lyric creativeness, but it was not an augury
of success in managing a poor farm on limited
capital.

The first season's harvest offered little encouragement. Wet weather and scanty labour made it difficult to salvage whatever thin crop the fields had
produced. Before his lease was six months old Burns
was confiding to his friends that he was uncertain
of his farm's doing well, but, as he told Ainslie, he
had his Excise commission in his pocket and did not

care three skips of a cur dog for the gambols of Fortune. The chance of obtaining the commission had made him willing to undertake the farm; possession added still another psychological handicap to its successful conduct. Embittered youthful memories of the humiliations of a tenant farmer had been reinforced by the development of his poetic vocation to clog whole-hearted effort. Now the existence of his commission held always open a door of escape from any threatened renewal of the old humiliation and thereby unconsciously slowed still further the endeavours which were his only safeguard. He was defeated at Ellisland before he began.

By the following spring he had begun to realize his defeat. The farm and his family, including William, were swallowing the remains of his capital so rapidly that it was doubtful if he could hold on without more income than the farm was likely to yield. It occurred to him that he might use his commission while he still held the farm. He had not thought of this at first. The usual procedure for a beginner was to be assigned to some district where a place was vacant, there to serve several months' apprenticeship without pay. When pay commenced, it had until recently been at the rate of £ 35 a year, but about the time Burns obtained his commission the initial stipend was raised to £ 50. Looking about his own neighbourhood, Burns learned that the officer in charge of the rural parishes to the north of Dumfries was a certain Leonard Smith, who had recently inherited money and was not distinguishing himself by activity in the service. Burns decided to play politics.

His commission had been obtained through Robert Graham of Fintry, one of the chief Commissioners for Scotland. Fintry had expressed personal interest in the poet's welfare in terms which must have soothed his bristling pride, for Burns had already addressed to him both a prose letter of thanks and a poetic epistle in imitation of Pope. Though Fintry never quite supplanted Lord Glencairn in Burns's esteem, he in fact became the poet's second patron and in the long run did more for him than even the Earl had done. Graham's first favour had been the commission itself; his second was the appointment to active duty. Before his first harvest was over Burns coolly suggested that Smith might be relieved from duty without serious loss to himself and perhaps with a gain to the Service. On his visit to Edinburgh in February, 1789, Burns pressed the matter further. Graham promised to do what he could, but pointed out that it was clean against regulations to start a new man at full pay without a probationary period. Nevertheless he undertook to investigate Smith's conduct and by midsummer had found cause for removing him, had given Burns the place, and had circumvented the rule against starting a new man at full duty and on full pay. For one who had always boasted his independence and had spoken scornfully of the political quest for favours, Burns had done a neat and successful job of wire-pulling.

Having once got his appointment, however, Burns had no intention of treating it as a sinecure. His district covered twelve sparsely-settled parishes and his tours of inspection required, to fulfil the letter of the law, that he ride two hundred miles a week in all weathers and all states of the uniformly bad roads. This meant that he could give little of his time and less of his strength to Ellisland. To provide for the farm he endeavoured to increase his dairy stock, which Jean could supervise in the intervals of having babies and managing her household. The cattle, too, might help in the slow task of rebuilding the worn-out acres.

But the strain of his new duties soon took physical toll. In the late fall of 1789, after less than two months of service, 'a malignant squinancy and low fever' laid him up for six weeks. His handwriting indicates that the illness was really serious; the letters written during convalescence are in a hand almost as weak and straggling as that of June and July, 1796. Nevertheless he had proved his qualifications for the job. An official report on various subordinate officers in the Excise bears after Burns's name the notation 'a poet—never tried—turns out well.' He had moreover established friendly relations with his immediate superiors, Alexander Findlater, the Supervisor, and John Mitchell, the Collector, of the Dumfries district. With the latter, indeed, he was already on terms approaching intimacy, sending him gifts of new-laid eggs from Ellisland and accompanying them at least once with a poetic epistle so broadly humorous that no editor has ever printed it all. Both men testified to Burns's fidelity by defending his character after his death and— what is far more significant—by reporting favourably on him during his life.

He was giving reason for favourable reports. His predecessor had been so slack that Burns was able to appear, at the first session of court after he began duty, with an impressive array of cases of tax evasion. In handling these he again displayed political astuteness. The minor offenders, mostly poor men who could ill afford a fine, he begged off with warnings or suspended sentences. This almost compelled the magistrates to fine the larger offenders for whom he refused to intercede, and inasmuch as Excise officers then, like American customs inspectors today, received a percentage of these penalties, Burns found his procedure remunerative in cash as well as in official credit. He soon discovered, though, that zeal had its drawbacks. Gentlemen of position, including some of the magistrates themselves, had their favourite smugglers or home-brewers, and when Burns caught one of these he started all the machinery of influence and political pressure so familiar to Americans during the prohibition era. Once he told Collector Mitchell, after a hard day's riding in rounding up witnesses in a case, that he expected for his pains to be clapped in jail for annoying the friends of half the gentlemen in the county. The grosser temptations of bribery, however, did not touch him. The various legends, de-

riving from highly unreliable oral tradition, of his
leniency with small offenders mean no more, even
if literally true, than that Burns had learned the
common sense of his profession. A customs in-
spector knows that his job is not to penalize every
tourist who has failed to declare a dozen handker-
chiefs but to catch the large-scale smuggler. The
same was true of the laws Burns had to enforce,
which imposed taxes on everything from whisky to
candles. Not but what he made ordinary human
distinctions between his public and his private capacities. William Lorimer, father of 'Chloris', was
one of the poet's intimate friends. He was also a
bootlegger whose ways were, 'like the grace of G—,
past all comprehension'. Seemingly Lorimer maintained a moderate legal stock for inspection purposes, but once when he was absent and his wife
drunk something slipped in the working of the
gentlemen's agreement, and Burns had to explain
to Supervisor Findlater. Another time he helped,
as revenue officer, in a series of raids on Dumfries
haberdashers who had been selling smuggled French
gloves. A few days later, as private citizen, he supplied Maria Riddell with similar gloves from a still
unraided dealer's stock. The problems and conditions of law enforcement are among the few immu-
tables in human history.

After two years' experience Burns reaffirmed that
the Excise was after all the business for him. He
added, 'I find no difficulty in being an honest man
in it; the work of itself, is easy; and it is a devilish

different affair, managing money matters where I care not a damn whether the money is paid or not; from the long faces made to a haughty Laird or still more haughty Factor, when rents are demanded, and money, alas, not to be had!' His position as tenant farmer was no longer an irritation; it was an obsession. Ellisland, he told Gilbert, had undone his enjoyment of himself. He looked forward with the same desperate hope as his father's at Mount Oliphant to the 'freedom in his lease'. The three-year period of the £ 50 rental ended in 1791. After that, if he chose to stay, Ellisland would cost £ 70 a year. Naturally, his discouragement and defeat on the farm had affected his relations with his landlord. Miller's kindness, he said, had been just such another thing as Creech's, and the fact that Mrs. Miller had failed to appreciate one of his poorer contributions to Johnson's *Museum* did not heighten his esteem for the family. He wanted no more to do with landlords or anything that belonged to them.

His only good luck at Ellisland came at the end. The surrender of the lease did not annoy Miller as Burns had expected, for a purchaser was in the market, and Miller was glad enough to dispose of the farm which the Nith separated from the rest of his estate. After sending Jean and the children to Mauchline, Burns held an auction of his standing crops and provided the lavish drinks expected by auction-goers. One result was that the exhilarated bidders ran up the prices nearly a guinea an acre beyond the market rates; another was that house and stable-yard were strewn with helplessly drunk and retching neighbours. The sale brought ready cash for the first time in two years, and Burns used some of it to clear up a variety of small debts, including the four pounds he owed his namesake, Robert Burn of Edinburgh, for erecting Fergusson's tombstone. He also celebrated his manumission by a brief visit to Edinburgh to say farewell to Clarinda and to try to do something for sick and penniless Jenny Clow.

While things had been going so badly on the farm his position in the Excise had been improving. After less than a year and a half in his laborious rural division he had wangled a transfer to a vacant 'footwalk', the '3d, or Tobacco, Division', in Dumfries. This meant lighter work, and enabled him to dispense with his horse—not too soon, for his poor worn-out mare had given him several nasty falls on the bad roads, bruising him severely and once breaking his arm. In town, though, he had small opportunity for increasing his income through fines and penalties as he had done in the rural division. When at the end of 1791 he moved his family into Dumfries the best quarters he could afford were a crowded and uncomfortable half-of-a-house in the Stinking Vennel, near the river. He was still receiving only the minimum salary of £ 50 a year, and though Jean said long afterwards that they did not come empty-handed into Dumfries not much cash can have remained after he had discharged his debts. As early as March, 1790, he had estimated that he would be lucky if he did not lose more than £ 100 out of an investment of little more than £ 200. Such anticipatory estimates are oftener under the mark than over it; one suspects that if Burns recovered as much as £ 50 of the money he had put into Ellisland, he was lucky.

By comparison, his prospects in the Excise were roseate. The Port Division in Dumfries, best paid of the subordinate posts, was vacant, and Burns lobbied for it with William Corbet, general supervisor of Excise, as he had done with Graham of Fintry for his first appointment. Corbet was an old friend of Mrs. Dunlop's, and her intercession was effectively supplemented by a warm recommendation from Findlater, the local supervisor. Burns got the job early in 1792. The salary was £ 70 a year with various perquisites worth another £ 20. It scarcely represented luxurious living, but it was a better income than most Scottish schoolmasters or even ministers received in the eighteenth century, and though 'Robin's temper was not cold and frugal' he managed to be fairly comfortable. After a year in the Stinking Vennel he moved to a better house in what was then called Mill Street and is now Burns Street—the last of his numerous abodes.

Even before he left Ellisland Burns's name had been placed on the list of those eligible for promotion to the rank of Supervisor. This was the most laborious of the Excise posts, for the supervisors did most of the real work of collection and administration. They received salaries of from £ 200 to £ 400 a year, but their duties filled most of their waking hours. So long as he was merely Port Officer Burns had time and energy for reading and song-writing. He knew, however, that when in the course of seniority he became a supervisor most of this would cease. But he was already looking beyond. The next rank above Supervisor was Collector, and the collectors held well-paid sinecures. In theory at least supervisors were appointed by merit, but collectorships admittedly went by favour, and Burns began to cultivate political friendships which might in the future secure him the necessary influence.

Not that he had any intention of soldiering on his job and trusting to influence to lift him to a better one. He was taking an intelligent interest in his work and sought the attention of his superiors by his understanding of their business. Thus he had not been long in his Port Division before he wrote to Provost Staig of Dumfries pointing out that the town was losing revenue through failure to assess a tax on imported ale, and backed his statement with an estimate of the sums involved and some shrewd advice as to the best method of getting his chiefs to enforce their collection. A year or so later he pointed out to Robert Graham that one of the Dumfries divisions could be abolished and its duties distributed among the other officers without overburdening them. There cannot be many instances on record of a government employee's informing his superiors that he was underworked. On this occasion

at least Burns took an unusual way of drawing attention to himself. He was also once more suggesting
his own advancement at the expense of another man,
but admitted the fact and coupled his recommendation with a plea that if the change were made the
present incumbent, burdened with an expensive
family, be provided for elsewhere.

He would have been the last to claim that these
suggestions were free of any ulterior motive beside
the general one of making himself known as a
thoughtful and efficient officer. He had other and
more immediate purposes. Not long after showing
Provost Staig the revenue possibilities of the 'twa
pennies' tax on ale he had a petition to make to the
Burgh Council. When he first visited Dumfries in
1787 he had been made an honorary burgess; he
now wanted that nominal citizenship converted into
a real one so far at least as concerned the local
schools. The sons of burgesses were entitled to free
tuition at Dumfries Academy, and the chance of
getting his boys into a first-rate school was not to be
neglected. His petition set forth in detail the help he
had given to the local revenues. This may not have
been the reason why the Council at once granted
his application, but it certainly did not hamper it.
Similarly his letters to Graham were frankly motivated by a desire to get a post as acting supervisor
at the earliest possible moment and thereby to secure
not only some small immediate increase in income but
the experience and reputation which would count
in his favour when a permanent position opened.

These were reasonable and legitimate efforts to gain prestige. He indulged in others more ticklish and, in the perspective of history, more futile. Burns lacked the right temperament for cultivating politicians, but he could not help trying. He was once introduced, for instance, to that very shady character, the Duke of Queensberry, whom previously he had rated with some justice as a complete scoundrel. At their meeting the Duke proved affable, and hearing that Burns had written a song about the notorious 'Whistle' drinking bout mentioned that he would like a copy. Burns sent it to him with a flattering letter, no doubt hoping that at some future date the Duke's influence might be useful. There was nothing particularly dangerous in this, for the Duke's rank made him a public character irrespective of what party was in power. But when Burns undertook to meddle in parliamentary contests he was playing with fire. He had of course no vote himself, but he wrote ballads in support of Whig candidates and continued to do so until a few months before his death. From the viewpoint of 1792 something might have been said for this as good strategy, regardless of the poet's actual sympathies. Except for the brief Rockingham ministry at the end of the American War the Tories had been in power for nearly a generation and a reversal was overdue. When and if the Whigs came in a man who had supported them in their time of adversity would be entitled to special favours. Neither Burns nor anyone else in Britain could foresee Napoleon and realize that Pitt's ministry, which had already been on the verge of disaster over the Regency Bill, would, thanks to the Frenchman, remain in office until after Burns and most of his parliamentary friends were in their graves. As things turned out, silence would have been the better part for Burns, but he had no gift for silence.

In the same year moreover in which Burns secured his Port Division the effects of the upheaval in France were stirring both Burns and Scotland. The cries of Liberty and Equality and Fraternity were echoed in the North and enlisted as in England a motley collection of supporters who ranged from poetic idealists, like Burns and Wordsworth, through professional agitators like Thomas Paine and Horne Tooke to unprincipled rabble. Burns's first public gesture of sympathy with the French Revolution came as a by-product of the most exciting episode in his career as an Excise officer. In the early spring of 1792 a smuggling schooner named the *Rosamond* was caught in the Solway. The ship was heavily armed and thanks to the active co-operation of the coastwise folks, who staved in all their rowboats to keep the Excise officers from using them, she landed her cargo. The *Rosamond*, however, remained aground on the tidal flats and when an armed force of dragoons and Excise officers—Burns among them—waded out to attack her the crew fled after scuttling the ship. Salvaged and towed into the Nith the *Rosamond* with all her gear was confiscated and sold at auction. Her armament included four carronades which Burns bought for £ 4 and dispatched as a gift to the French Convention. Such at least is the traditional story, and every detail of it, except the actual dispatch of the carronades, is corroborated by documents found among the Abbotsford papers. The tradition continues that the guns never reached France, being seized by the customs officials at Dover; but here again confirmation is lacking. Legally there was nothing wrong in Burns's action. France and England were still officially at peace, though their relations were steadily growing tenser. Nevertheless, from the practical viewpoint of a government employee with a dependent family it was a gesture of almost criminal recklessness. The government has never yet existed which looked benevolently upon manifestations of revolutionary sympathies among its servants, and before many months had passed Burns had good reason to be frightened.

The autumn of 1792 saw England ready to join the coalition against revolutionary France, though war was not declared until February 1, 1793. To the privileged classes in England the war had all the characteristics of a crusade except the obligation to take a personal share. The Revolution threatened the very foundations of the aristocratic social system, and the depth of the government's fear is measured by the violence alike of official denunciations of France and of the suppression of dissenting opinion at home. Charges of sedition were pressed not only against avowed revolutionary sympathizers but against almost anyone who had advocated the slightest modification of the existing order. It was not surprising that Burns, always unguarded in speech and action, should face investigation of his conduct. The details of the charges and their outcome belong in another chapter. For a time Burns thought that all his hopes of advancement were blasted, but the storm soon blew over, and even before he advertised his loyalty by enlisting in the Dumfries Volunteers he had good reason to anticipate that promotion would come in due course.

But though he escaped the storm of persecution he did not escape the economic consequences of the war. It had the usual and inevitable results of tight money and rising prices; a wave of bankruptcies swept over Scotland; the monthly lists of failures in the *Scots Magazine* increased from an average of half-a-dozen a month to forty-six in July, 1793, and among the victims was Burns's friend, Walter Auld the saddler. The poet himself was not exempt. The war cut off the greater part of the import trade and with it much of the income and perquisites of Dumfries Port Division. Burns had just begun to extend his expenditures in keeping with his increased income. The carronades and his better house were only part of the expansion. He had backed a friend's note and had to pay it when the friend defaulted; he had lent considerable sums to another friend, the schoolmaster at Moffat, who was engaged in a long-drawn-out wrangle with the Earl of Hopetoun, patron of the school; there were other smaller loans as well. Caught thus with ready cash exhausted, income reduced, and prices rising, Burns found himself once again in the grimly familiar position of being unable to pay his landlord. That the landlord was a gentleman and a personal friend who did not dun for his money made the situation more painful. In January, 1795, Burns had actually to borrow three guineas from his friend, William Stewart, in order to pay part of his rent. Nevertheless even in these hard times he managed occasional expenditures that came in the class of luxuries—a week's tour in Galloway with John Syme, the restoration of a Jacobite relic in form of Lord Balmerino's dirk, even a miniature portrait of himself. He and his family never lacked for the necessaries of life, and though he was somewhat in debt the accounting of his executors is proof that the amount never passed reasonable bounds.

As soon as the excitement over the sedition charges subsided his prospects in the Excise brightened steadily. Friends in Edinburgh were secretly trying to get him transferred to a more lucrative position, but even in Dumfries things looked hopeful. At the end of December, 1794, Supervisor Findlater fell ill, and Burns took over his duties. The work lasted three months or more, and though it is uncertain if Burns received any extra pay for his labour he at least gained valuable experience and competently handled his complex duties. The only adverse criticism of his conduct related to a technical irregularity in his final report, and this was the fault not of Burns himself but of one of his subordinates. The passage of each year brought him higher on the list of candidates for supervisor's posts. Had he lived another year or two he would automatically have been appointed even if his Edinburgh friends had failed in their efforts to hasten the process.

The prospect of promotion was becoming very real—so real that during the very months when he was acting as supervisor Burns devoted some of his scanty leisure to composing a group of political ballads. Patrick Heron of Heron—the same Heron whose bank failure had once ruined half Ayrshire— was the Whig candidate in a by-election at Kirkcudbright. In return for the support of Burns's pen Heron asked if he could do anything for the poet. Burns's reply showed his mind at its coldest level of realism. Nothing could be done, he said, for two or three years, until he reached the head of the supervisors' list. Then a political friend could be of service in getting him appointed in some agreeable part of the kingdom and of still more service in hastening his next step in rank. Collectorships went by favour, and the time he must spend in the drudgery of a supervisorship would therefore depend on the amount of influence his friends could exert. The letter is graphic proof of Burns's open-eyed acceptance of the system in which he worked; it is also proof of his irrepressible lack of discretion. From the viewpoint of mere self-interest he would have done better to hold aloof from all political contests and, when the time came, to base his appeal for influence upon his standing as a poet instead of identifying himself with any party. But such calm calculation was not in his nature.

In any case his hopes were vain. His disease was gaining on him; he experienced sharp twinges of pain which he and his doctors called rheumatism, but which were probably angina pectoris. In June and again in December, 1795, he had serious illnesses which left him weak and shaken. In the face of his increasing weakness he had taken on additional labour by enlisting in a volunteer company organized in Dumfries in the early spring. The manual of arms and frequent drills were dangerous medicine for a diseased heart, and to this physical labour Burns added active participation in all the business affairs of the corps. His final breakdown could not in any circumstances have been long delayed, but the Dumfries Volunteers undoubtedly hastened it.

The winter of 1795–6 was a time of famine. Crops had been bad; trade was dislocated by the war. Nearly one-fourth of the inhabitants of Edinburgh were being fed by charity, and flour was so scarce that even those who could afford it were asked to ration themselves to one loaf of bread per capita a week. Conditions in the smaller towns were as bad or worse; there were serious food riots in Dumfries in February and March. With his health steadily declining Burns was exposed to constant worry for the welfare of his family. Excise officers who were unable over long periods to perform their duties because of illness were reduced to half-pay, and as matters stood in the spring of 1796 half-pay would have meant almost starvation for his children. That things did not come to this pass for Burns was due to the generosity of Adam Stobbie, who handled his work for him and refused compensation for the service. This relieved some of his immediate anxiety, but did little to answer the main question of what would become of Jean and the children if he died.

The problem of livelihood, never long absent from his mind, occupied it during his last weeks almost to the exclusion of other thoughts. The only prescriptions the doctors could offer in his illness involved expenditures he could not afford, and his enlistment in the Volunteers now returned to plague him. The tailor who had made his uniform began to dun for payment, and to the poet's fevered imagination it seemed that his life was going to close as his father's had, under the shadow of a debtors' prison. He spent some of his last days of consciousness in writing frantic letters begging the friends to whom he had lent money to repay their loans and asking others like George Thomson and James Burness to advance him money. Thomson was the only one who gave grudgingly. The others willingly and promptly sent what he asked, but too late to lift the cloud from his dying mind. His last articulate words were an imprecation against the tailor who had threatened him, and he died without the comfort of knowing that his death would awaken the generosity he had never experienced in his life, and that the admirers of his poetry would make it possible for Jean to keep her home together and for his children to be decently educated and launched on respectable careers.

VI

SONG

BURNS never wrote a 'Prelude, or Growth of a Poet's Mind', and left only a few fragments of his projected satire on 'The Poet's Progress'. Yet his letters and journals, as well as the poems themselves, so definitely describe his moods and methods of composition that his poetic psychology can be studied almost as fully as Wordsworth's own.

Conscious pleasure in poetry read or heard first came to him in boyhood through one of Addison's hymns; mingled with martial and patriotic sentiment he found it also in 'The History of Sir William Wallace' and the Life of Hannibal. This latter, he said, 'gave my young ideas such a turn that I used to strut in raptures up & down after the recruiting drum and bagpipe, and wish myself tall enough to be a soldier, while the story of Wallace poured a Scotish prejudice in my veins which will boil along there till the flood-gates of life shut in eternal rest.' But this, like the similar thrills from all the odds and ends of English poetry and Scottish song which came his way, was commonplace boyish emotion. The need and desire to write poetry of his own did not awaken until his adolescent blood was warmed, in his 'fifteenth autumn', by the first consciousness of sexual attraction in the company of Nelly Kilpatrick.

'I never expressly told her that I loved her.—Indeed I did not well know myself, why I liked so much to loiter behind with her, when returning in the evening from our labors; why the tones of her voice made my heartstrings thrill like an Eolian harp; and particularly, why my pulse beat such a furious ratann when I looked and fingered over her hand, to pick out the nettle-stings and thistles.— Among her other love-inspiring qualifications, she sung sweetly, and 'twas her favorite reel to which I attempted giving an embodied vehicle in rhyme.—I was not so presumtive as to imagine that I could make verses like printed ones, composed by men who had Greek and Latin; but my girl sung a song which was said to be composed by a small country laird's son, on one of his father's maids, with whom he was in love; and I saw no reason why I might not rhyme as well as he, for . . . he had no more Scholarcraft than I had.'

'Thus', Burns summed up, with a juxtaposition of ideas never far separated in his mind, 'with me began Love and Poesy.' In all respects save one the episode was the commonest experience of calf-love. But that one difference was decisive. When a girl roused him to lyric fervour, Burns did not sit down and merely string his emotions together in rime. Another element went to make the song; an element that ultimately would mean more, poetically, to Burns than any girl—namely, a tune. His mind did not work from emotion directly to words; it worked from emotion to music, and the music brought the words which expressed its mood. Herein Burns was almost unique among modern poets. Fully to appreciate his lyrics one must hear them sung to the airs which evoked them. To read many of them in bare print is like reading the libretto of an opera. Even in his satires and epistles the process of composition was usually the same, though another man's poem, instead of music, fired the train. Acquaintance with his models is almost as illuminating as acquaintance with his tunes.

His first effort at song-writing led to a conscious study of the poet's craft. The elaborate criticism appended to 'Handsome Nell' when Burns copied the poem into his Commonplace Book is too obviously a bravura piece to merit consideration; more noteworthy is his account of how he studied his collection of English songs: 'I pored over them, verse by verse; carefully noting the true tender or sublime from affectation and fustian.—I am convinced I owe much to this for my critic-craft such as it is.' But these were *English* songs, and their effect on his early work shows mainly in such things as 'My father was a farmer' and 'Man was made to mourn', which latter in the Commonplace Book is entitled, 'A Song: Tune, Peggy Bawn'. Even his most doleful lines came to him in music.

But lugubrious notes were not the only ones. It was as inevitable that a young Scot should try his hand at metrical paraphrases of the Psalms as that a young Etonian of the same century should paraphrase Horace. The results in both cases are equally negligible. Youth has to repeat the stale patterns of its predecessors before it can find its own. It was

much more important that 'I murder hate by field
or flood' was written in the same way. This is an epigrammatic song in the Restoration manner, and as
English in language as in style. But it was written to
a Scottish air, 'Gillicrankie'. The innate Scottish culture of the poet was beginning, as early as 1781, to
assimilate and adapt the alien materials of Restoration England.

Though Burns failed to act on Richard Brown's
suggestion that he send some of his early verses to a
magazine, the idea stuck. The yeasty stirrings of a
still immature mind which had led him in 1780 to
plague his friends with pompous discourses on Pride
and Courage were slowly giving place to more personal thinking on topics which he better understood.
His customary chronological vagueness in referring
to his early manhood makes it uncertain whether he
began his Commonplace Book before he discovered
the poems of Robert Fergusson, or after. The internal evidence indicates the former. So does the elaborate title-page:

'Observations, Hints, Songs, Scraps of Poetry, &c., by
Robt. Burness; a man who had little art in making
money, and still less in keeping it; but was, however, a
man of some sense, a great deal of honesty, and un-
bounded good-will to every creature—rational or irra-
tional. As he was but little indebted to scholastic education, and bred at a plough-tail, his performances must be
strongly tinctured with his unpolished, rustic way of life;
but, as I believe they are really *his own*, it may be some
entertainment to a curious observer of human-nature to

see how a ploughman thinks and feels under the pressure
of Love, Ambition, Anxiety, Grief, with the like cares
and passions, which, however diversified by the modes
and manners of life, operate pretty much alike, I believe,
in all the Species.

> "There are numbers in the world who do not want
> "sense to make a figure, so much as an opinion of their
> "own abilities, to put them upon recording their ob-
> "servations, and allowing them the same importance
> "which they do to those which appear in print."—
> Shenstone.

> "Pleasing when youth is long expir'd to trace,
> "The forms our pencil, or our pen design'd.
> "Such was our youthful air, and shape, and face!
> "Such the soft image of our youthful mind."
> Ibidem.'

Burns was already conscious of something more in
himself than there was in the average young peasant; as an escape from worries over his own health
and the family's future he was undertaking to leave
a record of himself to edify some hypothetical future
reader. Whatever tinge of humility there might be
on his title-page was, like the pretence at third-per-
son reporting, assumed. He meant to prove that a
peasant youth shared the feelings of his betters and
could rime and moralize to as good effect as they.
But the title-page, the quotations from Shenstone,
and the opening paragraph about Love all announce a programme he soon abandoned. When he

began the book he was still thinking in the terms of his first letters about Pride and Courage; before he ended it he was thinking in poetry.

Though he might continue to assert that he rimed for fun, the fact was that from the day in April, 1783, when he commenced the Commonplace Book he was composing for publication, though not necessarily for print. His earliest verses were either the expression of a personal emotion, social *jeux d'esprit*, or conventional exercises in versification, with no purpose beyond the momentary and personal one; the 'Observations, Scraps of Song, &c.', were to be his legacy to the world. Not by chance did the Commonplace Book and its successor survive the general destruction of his private papers when he supposed himself on the eve of flight to Jamaica. Even though by that time the best of his verse had escaped the hazard of manuscript and was safely enshrined in the good black print of the Kilmarnock volume, he could not bring himself to destroy these records. It was well that he saved them. The Commonplace Book remains the sole record of what Burns was doing, intellectually and poetically, between April, 1783, and October, 1785. Commencing with self-conscious commentaries on life and on his own first efforts at writing, it reveals before its close his steady growth in artistic competence.

Not that it resembles the notebooks of Keats and Shelley, with their evidence of how poems grow in the poet's mind. Burns's poems stayed in his mind until they were mature. His poverty and his method of composing to music combined to prevent his committing half-formed ideas to paper. Paper was scarce and expensive; often in his early days he failed to write down his poems even when they were complete. Sometimes he forgot them entirely; sometimes he managed to reconstruct them long afterwards, as he did when he recalled 'The Mauchline Wedding' for Mrs. Dunlop's amusement. One of the few poems composed on paper is the disastrous 'Elegy on the Death of Sir James Hunter Blair', which Burns drafted in his Border journal. Here he was working with an English verse-form for which no melody existed. It took him three different sittings painfully to wring out the first seven stanzas. Again in 1791 he reported that he had 'these several months been hammering at an Elegy' on Miss Burnet of Monboddo, but found elegy 'so exhausted a subject that any new idea on the business is not to be expected'; the original manuscript of the 'Lament for James Earl of Glencairn' reveals similar struggles. When no tune sang itself in his head, composition was labour and the results were wooden. The 'Lament', with a more lyric stanza and with stronger personal feeling at its root, came nearer than the others to success, but even it cannot be ranked among the great elegies. Declining Cunningham's suggestion of a theme, he once said, 'I have two or three times in my life composed from the wish, rather than from the impulse, but I never succeeded to any purpose.' In commemorating Lord Glencairn, wish and impulse combined, yet even here he did not wholly succeed because the tune was lacking.

Poetic expression with Burns was not, as with Wordsworth, the fruit of emotion recollected in tranquillity; it was the fruit of emotion expressing itself to music. Though as he grew older the emotion no longer needed to be so strongly personal as when he wrote his earliest songs, the dependence on music became correspondingly greater. How he composed in his later years he told George Thomson in the autumn of 1793:

'Until I am compleat master of a tune, in my own singing (such as it is) I never can compose for it.—My way is: I consider the poetic Sentiment, correspondent to my idea of the musical expression; then chuse my theme; begin one stanza; when that is composed, which is generally the most difficult part of the business, I walk out, sit down now & then, look out for objects in Nature around me that are in unison or harmony with the cogitations of my fancy & workings of my bosom; humming every now & then the air with the verses I have framed: when I feel my Muse beginning to jade, I retire to the solitary fireside of my study, & there commit my effusions to paper; swinging, at intervals, on the hind-legs of my elbow-chair, by way of calling forth my own critical strictures, as my pen goes on.—

Seriously, this, at home, is almost invariably my way.—What damn'd Egotism!'

Though it would probably be impossible to overstress Robert Fergusson's influence on Burns's development, the elder poet's primary service was to clarify and confirm ideas already present but as yet inarticulate in Burns's mind. He knew what he liked, and what his own poetic impulses were; the discovery of Fergusson enabled him to define both his method and his objective. To realize how much he matured intellectually between the beginning of the Commonplace Book in 1783 and its conclusion in 1785, one need merely read the strutting, self-conscious, and essentially empty criticism of 'expletive phrases' of 'too serious sentiment', and 'flimsy strain' which he appended to 'Handsome Nell', or the pseudo-devotional passage about the grand end of human life being 'to cultivate an intercourse with that Being to whom we owe life'. These things of 1783 are juvenilia. The following, written in September, 1785, is adult:

'There is a certain irregularity in the Old Scotch Songs, a redundancy of syllables with respect to that exactness of accent and measure that the English Poetry requires, but which glides in, most melodiously with the respective tunes to which they are set. For instance, the fine old song of "The Mill Mill O," to give it a plain prosaic reading, it halts prodigiously out of measure; on the other hand, the song set to the same tune in Bremner's collection of Scotch Songs which begins "To Fanny fair could I impart," &c., it is most exact measure, and yet, let them both be sung before a real critic, one above the biasses of prejudice, but a thorough Judge of Nature, how flat and spiritless will the last appear, how trite, and lamely methodical, compared with the wild-warbling cadence, the heart-moving melody of the first. This par-

ticularly is the case with all those airs which end with a
hypermetrical syllable. There is a degree of wild irregularity in many of the compositions and fragments which
are daily sung to them by my compeers, the common
people—a certain happy arrangement of Old Scotch
syllables, and yet, very frequently, nothing, not even *like*
rhyme, or sameness of jingle at the ends of the lines. This
has made me sometimes imagine that perhaps, it might
be possible for a Scotch Poet, with a nice, judicious ear,
to set compositions to many of our most favorite airs . . .
independent of rhyme altogether. . . .'

With nothing except mother-wit and a sure ear to
guide him, Burns had reached conclusions regarding
poetic rhythm at complete variance with the critical
theories of his century and beyond the practice of
even nineteenth-century orthodoxy. He had recognized that the real charm of folk-poetry lies in the
fact that it is musical rather than regular. In an age
when the essence of poetry was thought to abide in
the accurately counted syllables of the heroic couplet such an opinion would have seemed not merely
heresy but sheer insanity. Compared with it, Cole-
ridge's supposed innovation of hypermetrical syllables in *Christabel* is timid conventionality. Blake
alone among Burns's contemporaries had bolder
theories of rhythm, and his work, which the Scotsman never saw, had to wait more than half a century for recognition. Burns later expended much
time and ink in trying to persuade George Thomson
that a song could be poetry even if all its lines did
not count up the same number of syllables, but he

was never optimistic enough to offer that silly body
a lyric which dispensed with rime.

So, too, in regard to the physiology and psychology of composition, Burns, before he ever published
a line, had reached closer to fundamentals than an
academician like Hugh Blair could ever go. Like
Milton he had recognized from his own experience
that there is in many poets a seasonal rhythm of
creativeness. In himself it usually began in August,
and continued for several months. That month, he
said in his autobiography, was always a carnival in
his bosom; in 1793 he told Thomson, 'Autumn is
my propitious season. I make more verses in it, than
all the year else,' and at the beginning of the next
summer he repeated the assertion: 'Now, & for six
or seven months *I shall be quite in song.*' In other
words, it took all the scanty sunshine of the Scottish
summer to bring him physically to that level of well-
being at which creation was possible.

The psychology of composition, moreover, which
he explained in prose in 1793 he had defined in poetry in the epistle to William Simpson of Ochiltree,
composed in May, 1785, and published in the Kilmarnock volume. It is surprisingly like A. E. Hous-
man's, who recorded that some of his best poems
came to him spontaneously while walking on Hamp-
stead Heath and thinking of nothing in particular,
after drinking a pint of beer at luncheon. Burns's
formula is precisely similar:

> The Muse, nae Poet ever fand her,
> Till by himself he learn'd to wander

Adown some trottin burn's meander,
An' no think lang.

In these circumstances, when his emotional pressure
was high enough, lines and stanzas would come un-
sought to his mind, and it was to this experience he
referred when he repeatedly called himself 'a Bard
of Nature's making'. Burns knew as well as Hous-
man did that this spontaneous birth was only the beginning and not the end of composition. Gilbert reported the process without realizing its significance:

'Robert often composed without any regular plan.
When anything made a strong impression on his mind,
so as to rouse it to any poetic exertion, he would give
way to the impulse, and embody the thought in rhyme.
If he hit on two or three stanzas to please him, he would
then think of proper introductory, connecting, and concluding stanzas; hence the middle of a poem was often
first produced.'

It suited with the role of inspired ploughman which
Burns assumed among the Edinburgh gentry to give
the impression that the finished poem also was spontaneous, but he knew better. His poetry was often
born under the open sky, with the physical rhythm
of his farm-work supplying the muscular accompaniment he later sought in strolls on the banks of Nith,
but it was matured and revised by concentrated
study of the implications of his theme. As the piper
has to walk his measure, so Burns's body moved to

the rhythm of the tune which was in his mind, and the rhythm brought the words which expressed his mood.

It was only Scots music that saved Burns in the end from complete subjection to the false elegance of his century. Though he was better read than most of his 'patrons' ever realized, he had the self-educated man's diffidence in the face of established reputations. His ear, so quick to distinguish 'the true tender or sublime' from 'affectation or fustian' in a lyric, failed him in the reading of more pretentious works. 'The Cotter's Saturday Night' is shot full of verbal echoes of English poets; what is worse, it echoes their sentiments, in such a passage as Stanza X, to an extent which divorces the thought from all the realities of peasant life. He never acquired the degree of sophistication which would have enabled him to use the current English conventions freely and originally, yet he was too sophisticated to use old folk conventions when they were not reinforced by music. Thus he never—with the possible exception of 'John Barleycorn'—wrote a serious ballad. His political verses, and above all such an uproarious parody as 'The Ballad of Grizzel Grimme', show that he had all the ballad conventions at his tongue's end; he had collected numerous old ballad texts, of which Dr. Currie named more than a dozen to Sir Walter Scott, though without thinking it worth while to preserve them; yet he could employ the ballad only in satire or burlesque. Thanks to music, he was able in all seriousness to sing a song in the old folk style, but he could not tell a story.

Even his Scottish vocabulary was more literary and derivative than his contemporaries realized. It was not so much a direct transcript of Ayrshire speech as it was a generalized vernacular pieced together from Allan Ramsay, Robert Fergusson, and the anonymous folk lyrists and ballad writers. He was genuinely interested in the variations of dialect—on his Border tour, for instance, he jotted down definitions of local words which were new to him—but his poetic use of it was chiefly due to its pithiness, its humour, and, above all, its flexibility. This was what he had in mind when he admitted to Robert Anderson 'the advantages he enjoyed . . . from the *copia verborum*, the command of phraseology, which the knowledge and use of the English and Scottish dialects afforded him'. He habitually alternated between Scottish and English spellings of the same word, as the exigencies of rime and measure required, thereby achieving a more flexible expression than was possible in either dialect by itself. His vernacular writing, in short, was nearer to Lowell's New England speech or Kipling's Cockney than it was to Gawain Douglas's or William Dunbar's single-minded expression in his native tongue. Even Robert Fergusson's dialect, with its strong infusion of Fifeshire elements, is closer than Burns's to being a direct transcript from life.

In one sense the poems in the Kilmarnock volume which were written under Robert Fergusson's influence are a divergence from Burns's deepest impulses, even though his method of composing them was fundamentally the same as in his song-writing. Instead of a tune to which he could set his own words Fergusson supplied a pattern or a theme to be adapted to his own experience. The parallels between 'The Plane-stanes and the Causey' and 'The Brigs of Ayr', between 'The Daft Days' and 'Hallowe'en' or 'The Holy Fair', between 'Caller Oysters' and 'Scotch Drink' or 'To a Haggis' are too obvious and have been too often mentioned to need reiteration. Burns borrowed, but he did not copy; even borrowed phraseology he made his own. His imitations almost invariably surpassed their originals both in poetic fire and in the epigrammatic quality essential for quotability. Yet in these forms of verse he showed no inventiveness. His own phrase that Fergusson had roused him to *emulating* vigour is literally true. That Fergusson's impetus failed to sweep Burns on to discover similar themes of his own reveals him as after all on foreign ground. Nevertheless, by demonstrating that poetry could still be written in the vernacular, Fergusson had done inestimable service. Beyond that his influence brought Burns to a dead end. The unhappy young lawyer's clerk had no music in his soul.

Allan Ramsay rather than Fergusson showed the way to the sort of poetry without musical setting in which Burns found his genuine freedom and inspiration. The imitations of Fergusson end with the lines 'To a Haggis', written in December, 1786; Ramsay supplied the models for the vernacular epistles which Burns never wholly ceased to write until a

few months before his death. And between the poetic
epistle as Burns wrote it and the dramatic monologue in which he also excelled there is little basic
difference. The writer of a poetic epistle is usually
dramatizing himself. Like the professional humor-
ist, he assumes a role which is a projection or exaggeration of one phase of his own temperament, but
which is not really himself as the workingday world
knows him. For Burns to pass from such self-drama-
tization as marks the epistles to Lapraik, Simpson,
Rankine, and Smith to the pure drama of 'The Auld
Farmer' or even 'Holy Willie's Prayer' involved
merely an extension of imaginative scope and not a
different technique.

To put it another way, Burns could either talk or
he could sing. When he was not writing to music he
was at his best only when he was speaking, either
for himself as personified bard or humorous spectator, or as he identified his own personality with another's. Nothing in the poems composed in 1786
more clearly shows his maturing artistic powers
than does the dramatic character of 'The Auld
Farmer' and 'Holy Willie' when contrasted with the
lyrics of 'The Jolly Beggars', composed the year before. In these last, magnificent as they are, the
reader can seldom forget that it is Burns who is
speaking through the mouths of the vagabonds. The
lyrics are only half dramatic, and perhaps it was
realization of this that made the poet in 1793 tell
George Thomson that none of the songs pleased
him except the last—in which Burns himself is

speaking as the 'Bard of no regard'. In 'Holy Willie' and 'The Auld Farmer', on the other hand, the poet has identified himself with the character whom he is portraying as completely as Browning ever did with Fra Lippo Lippi or the Duke of Ferrara.

Less than adequate notice has been taken of the fact that Burns had mastered the art of the dramatic lyric and the dramatic monologue more than half a century before Browning gave the forms their names. His own statement that all his early lyrics had a personal basis has both led biographers on wild-goose chases after autobiographical elements in songs which possess none, and has been used to give false emphasis to many poems really based on personal experience. Such interpretations ignore the very foundation of creative art. That the impulse to write a lyric comes from personal emotion does not mean that the finished poem is literal history. Keats's love for Fanny Brawne helped to make 'The Eve of St. Agnes' what it is, but not even Mr. Middleton Murry has been fatuous enough to call Madeline a portrait of Fanny. Rose Aylmer was not necessarily as perfect as Landor's elegy upon her; William Douglas may have had no real intention of laying him down and dying for Annie Laurie. Yet the whole Highland Mary legend, for instance, rests on precisely this sort of treatment of a handful of Burns's songs, in obstinate disregard of the plain fact that the woman who inspires a love-lyric no more needs to be herself a lyric woman than the model for the Victory of Samothrace needed to be a woman with wings. Everyone has recognized Burns's unsuccess in his effort to dramatize himself for Clarinda's benefit as the pure man of sentiment; his true achievement could be better understood by recognition of his success in dramatizing his real self in many of his best 'personal' poems. From the 'Mary Morison' of his youth to the 'O wert thou in the cauld blast' of his last illness, his best songs display not Burns himself but a dramatic projection of one aspect of his mind.

Commentators from Henry Mackenzie onward have regretted that Burns never carried out his plans for writing a drama. Yet his triumph in the dramatic monologue is the best reason for believing that the attempt would have failed. His numerous references to the drama and dramatic writing never so much as hint that Burns had grasped the elements of theatrical technique. For him a play was merely a vehicle for declamatory speeches and the expression of 'sentiments' which would make neat quotations; a cobbling together of purple patches and of scattered episodes supposed to depict 'originality of character'. If it ever occurred to him that a good play is a unified structure in which a single impression is built up through a series of artfully contrived climaxes, he never put the idea on paper. But even had he understood the technique he had not the right psychological approach for dramatic writing, any more than Browning had. The true dramatist stands apart from his characters and develops them from without; the writer of dramatic monologues identifies himself for the moment with another individual and develops the character from within. The two temperaments are seldom united in one man, and Burns in turning away even from the pastoral drama which Mackenzie had urged him to undertake was once again instinctively following the bent of his own genius. In the light of what he accomplished in his chosen forms, Mackenzie's suggestion was almost as inept as John Moore's proposal that he try something like Virgil's Eclogues.

Before he went to Edinburgh Burns had explored his own capacities, but had not yet realized more than half of them. Fergusson had shown him how to write satires and descriptions in the vernacular; Ramsay had revealed the possibilities of the poetic epistle. But his interest in the folk-songs of which the words and melodies haunted him, still seemed a rustic or even childish survival. So far as he knew, it was like taking nursery rimes seriously as poetry. Though he must have been aware that scholars of repute were beginning to collect old ballads, he had not yet discovered that they were turning also to the words and music of folk-songs. In this respect at least, his Edinburgh sojourn was of incalculable benefit. Apparently he never met David Herd, the greatest collector among his contemporaries, but he soon became acquainted with Herd's published work and learned that even some university professors esteemed such things. Sending a couple of songs, 'the composition of two Ayrshire Mechanics', to the Rev. William Greenfield a few weeks after arriving in the city, he hailed that eloquent but in-continent clergyman as 'Professor of the Belles lettres de la Nature'; in the following summer he told William Tytler that he had once a great many fragments of traditional literature, but as he had no idea that anybody cared for them, he had forgotten them. And his next remark showed that he already possessed the essential qualification of the collector: 'I invariably hold it sacriledge to add anything of my own to help out with the shatter'd wrecks of these venerable old compositions; but they have many various readings.' Yet not even then, not even though the singing of old melodies was one of the commonest amusements both in Edinburgh drawing rooms and at convivial meetings at taverns, did he realize immediately the task and the opportunity before him.

The convivial meetings at first meant much more to him than the drawing-rooms. The jolly gentle-men who made up the Crochallan Fencibles had probably as a group little interest in pure poetry, but they had a very lively interest in brisk songs. If the songs happened to be improper, that was no handicap among a club which included Charles Hay and William Smellie and Robert Cleghorn, and to whom Alexander Cunningham used to sing 'charmingly' one of the most indecent of Irish ditties. Burns's memory was already well stored with such gems, and in this congenial company he added to his stock, enriched old songs with new stanzas of his own, and occasionally composed original verses of the same type, as I e had often done at Mauchline. As a means of enhancing the pleasures of male company over a bowl of punch such song-writing amused him and delighted the Fencibles.

Not until after his Edinburgh *Poems* were off the press did it begin to dawn upon him that he might also win new fame in the drawing-room and—what meant much more to him—do a patriotic service to Scotland. In the last weeks of April, 1787, he made the acquaintance of an engraver named James Johnson, who was just bringing out the first volume of a work which he called *The Scots Musical Museum*. Johnson was known to Smellie, Dunbar, and others of Burns's friends, but he cannot have been in the inner circle of the Crochallans, or Burns would have met him sooner. He was almost illiterate—his picturesquely bad spelling is notable even for the eighteenth century—but he was an enthusiast for the collection and preservation of the traditional music and songs of his country. He had invented a process for printing music by stamping the notes on pewter plates instead of the steel or copper engraving then generally employed. Though the result was a mean and smudgy page, the process was much cheaper than the old one and encouraged Johnson to try his hand at publishing. His enthusiasm, however, far exceeded his knowledge. He had had difficulty in gathering the hundred songs which made up his first volume, and had even eked it out with a few English pieces. His meeting with Burns not only remade the *Museum*, but, poetically considered, was the most important event of the poet's life in the capital.

Writing to Johnson on the eve of his Border tour Burns regretted that they had not met sooner: 'I have met with few people whose company & conversation gave me more pleasure, because I have met with few whose sentiments are so congenial to my own.' But though he contributed a song or two to the collection, the idea that he might take an active part in the work was still far from his mind. The fantastic Earl of Buchan, as early as February, had advised Burns to 'fire [his] Muse at Scottish story and Scottish scene.' Burns had replied, in language even more inflated than the Earl's: 'I wish for nothing more than to make a leisurely Pilgrimage through my native country; to sit & muse on those once hard-contended fields where Caledonia, rejoicing, saw her bloody lion borne through broken ranks to victory and fame; and catching the inspiration to pour the deathless Names in Song.' Unfortunately, added the poet, he had instead to go back to working for his living. Nevertheless, the Border tour offered a chance to fulfil part of the Earl's suggestion—according to Burns's real tastes, if not the Earl's. His greatest pleasures on the journey were not the civic receptions and the elaborate hospitality of the gentry, but the sight of Gala Water, Leader Haughs and Yarrow, the Bush aboon Traquair, Elibanks and Elibraes, and other spots celebrated in song. It made no difference whether the song was singable before ladies or before Crochallans, so long as it was Scottish, and old.

The Highland tours added so effectively to his stock that in 1793 he was able to say that he had made pilgrimages to every spot commemorated in Scottish song except Lochaber and the Braes of Ballenden. Presumably on his passages through Edinburgh in August and September he talked with Johnson, but not until late October, after his return from Ochtertyre, did he really begin to put his energies into the work. Johnson obviously had solicited his help, and the poet's first move was to write to all his friends who possessed words or music which might be usable. Nor did he confine himself to his own circle of acquaintance. Learning to his chagrin that he had unwittingly passed near the home of the Rev. John Skinner without calling to pay his respects to the author of 'Tullochgorum' and 'John o' Badenyon', he seized the opportunity given by receipt of a poetic epistle from Skinner to beg the venerable clergyman's support for Johnson's enterprise. He soon started also to fit words of his own to fine melodies which either lacked them or had unsuitable ones—at first with a personal motive, in order to publish the complimentary verses he had written to Margaret Chalmers and Charlotte Hamilton, but soon with no purpose except that of supplying his favourite music with words which could be sung. Moreover, he commenced to gather all available publications of Scottish songs and song music. How thoroughly he went into this search is revealed by his quiet remark to George Thomson five years later: 'Let me have a list of your airs, with the first line of the verses you intend for them. . . . I say, the first line of the verses, because if they are verses that have appeared in any of our Collections of songs, I know them & can have recourse to them.' He had in fact ranged so widely in the old song books that even yet his editors have been unable to identify the originals of some of the songs he altered and adapted for the *Museum*, and later on for Thomson's *Select Collection*. But though in 1787 he realized better than Johnson did the magnitude of the task and the opportunity before them, he was still unaware of its true scope. He conjectured that there would be three volumes of a hundred songs each. The completed work filled six.

From October, 1787, onwards Burns was in fact though not in name the chief editor of the *Museum*. He collected words and music, wrote prefaces for the successive volumes, and helped to enlist the aid of a competent musician, Stephen Clarke, organist of the Episcopal chapel in Edinburgh, in harmonizing the airs. Johnson willingly submitted to the poet's leadership, which he needed. The surviving correspondence shows Burns carrying on a struggle which nothing except his enthusiasm for the work could at times have made endurable. Johnson required constant supervision even in such elementary matters as spelling; Clarke's carelessness and indolence were maddening. The work sold slowly and Johnson, under the pressure of other affairs, inclined to procrastinate. 'Why,' Burns asked in 1793, and the passage is typical of many, 'did you not send me

those tunes & verses that Clarke & you cannot
make out? Let me have them as soon as possible,
that, while he is at hand, I may settle the matter
with him.' Clarke, 'with his usual indolence', was
worse. More than once he mislaid or lost whole
sheafs of songs which had been entrusted to him.
' "The Lochmaben harper" ', said the poet in 1795,
'I fear I shall never recover; & it is a famous old
song.—The rest are, I doubt, irrecoverable.—I
think it hard that, after so much trouble in gathering these tunes, they should be lost in this trifling
way.—Clarke has been shamefully careless.' Yet
Burns's enthusiasm kept him going, however negli-
gent or incompetent the partners on whom he had
to depend. The time-table of the work is sufficient
proof of his influence. Volume II, prepared while
he was in Edinburgh, was ready six months after
Volume I; the next two volumes, for which the
poet's contributions had to be made by correspondence, took two years each. Volume V was prepared
while Burns was working also for George Thomson;
it was four years on the stocks. The final volume,
prepared by Johnson's unaided efforts, took six
years, even though he had still on hand a considerable quantity of Burns's verse for which space had
been lacking in the earlier numbers.

Burns's preface to the second volume, published
in February, 1788, in the very midst of the Clarinda
imbroglio, shows how completely, in the fifteen
months since his first arrival in Edinburgh, the poet
had awakened to the literary importance of folk-

song. 'Ignorance and Prejudice', he wrote, 'may perhaps affect to sneer at the simplicity of the poetry or music of some of these pieces; but their having been for ages the favourites of Nature's Judges—the Common People, was to the Editor a sufficient test of their merit. . . .' He was no longer apologetic for his interest in popular literature. If the highbrows could not appreciate it, so much the worse for the highbrows. He was determined, moreover, that no poet of the people should lack recognition if it were possible to give it. 'Wherever the old words could be recovered, they have been preserved; both as generally suiting better the genius of the tunes, and to preserve the productions of those earlier Sons of the Scottish Muses, some of whose names deserved a better fate than has befallen them—"Buried 'mong the wreck of things which were." Of our more modern Songs, the Editor has inserted the Authors' names as far as he could ascertain them.' The passage is almost a direct transcript, even to the hackneyed quotation from Blair's *Grave*, of what Burns had written in the Commonplace Book two and a half years before, when he added that it had given him 'many a heart-ake' to reflect that the names of such glorious old Bards were clean forgotten. No more of them should be forgotten if he could do anything to prevent it. The 'communal' theory of ballad-composition still slumbered in Cloud-Cuckoo-Land; Burns was sure that somewhere at the source of every old song was an individual poet of like passions with himself, and such as he himself might still be but for the accident of print.

His one exception to the rule of publishing authors' names was his own contributions. He told Mrs. Dunlop that the songs signed 'R', 'B', or 'X' were his own, and those signed 'Z' were old songs he had altered or enlarged. But no one can go through the volumes with this simple key and identify all of Burns's contributions. His own negligence and Johnson's omitted his initials from numerous songs unquestionably his own, and the verses signed 'Z' have puzzled the ingenuity of editors ever since. Burns admitted that 'of a good many of them, little more than the Chorus is ancient; tho' there is no reason for telling every body this piece of intelligence.' Sometimes his own annotations or the survival of earlier texts show the extent of his contributions, ranging from eking out a too-brief song with an extra stanza of his own to composing a whole lyric to fit a fragment of traditional chorus. Public opinion unanimously credits Burns with 'Auld Lang Syne', yet he never claimed it. He declared that it 'had never been in print, nor even in manuscript', until he took it down from an old man's singing. Three different times, for people as unlike as Mrs. Dunlop, Robert Riddell, and George Thomson, he wrote out the words without even an indirect claim to their authorship. Nevertheless, no trace of the song in anything like Burns's form has ever been found in earlier records, and the public has refused to believe that a poem of such appeal could have been current without being noticed. On the other hand, every stanza of 'A Red Red Rose' has been traced to some older poem; yet Burns's skill in selecting the one good image in a mass of commonplace and weaving his cento of borrowings into a single compact and vivid lyric makes the song his own, as *Macbeth* is Shakespeare's and not Holinshed's.

In such lyrics as these and scores of others Burns had achieved a sort of dramatic impersonation which far surpassed even the best of his earlier monologues and dramatic lyrics. Guided always by the spirit of the music, he had so identified himself with the thoughts and feelings of the anonymous and half-articulate folk poets whose songs he was rescuing from oblivion that the most critical eye cannot be certain where their work ends and Burns's begins. Again and again he took fragments of old work and not only reunited them into coherent wholes but gave the restored poem the lyric elevation its original author had felt but could not express. Emerson said that an institution was the lengthened shadow of a single man: Scottish song as the world knows it today is the lengthened shadow of Robert Burns. What he did not actually write is so coloured by his influence that it could not exist without him. With the exception of Lady Nairne's, his was the last poetry written in the old folk tradition. The romantic sentimentality which tinges Burns's songs at their weakest, overspreads many of Lady Nairne's; Scott's masterpiece, 'Bonnie Dun-

dee', is glorious, but it is not a folk-song. Most of
what has been written since 1800 is merely imitation Burns.

The *Museum* was Burns's opportunity to combine
his poetic inclinations with his fervent patriotism.
But it was more than that. By enlisting the poet's
help in his enterprise, Johnson unwittingly furnished
him the means of sustaining his creative life amid his
toil as farmer and Exciseman. After 1788 extended
composition was probably impossible for Burns. He
could scarcely hope to be revisited by the almost
continuous excitement under which he wrote the
greater part of his first volume, and without emotional excitement he could not create. He had
plenty of leisure for writing during his Edinburgh
days, but the urge was lacking. His whole sojourn
there produced less poetry than a single month at
the beginning of 1786. Removal to Ellisland, with
all the strain of its 'uncouth cares and anxieties',
brought his creativeness to a still lower ebb. Repeatedly he complained that the Muses had deserted
him; during his first two years on the farm the
'Lines in Friars Carse Hermitage' were almost his
only serious attempt at non-musical composition,
and in the revision of the poem he wavered between versions in a manner wholly unlike the vigour
of 1786. The frequency, indeed, with which he circulated both versions among his friends suggests at
times a bankrupt's clinging to the last relic of his
prosperity. But thanks to the *Museum* he had work
to do which could be shaped to music as he followed

his business, and be committed to paper in his snatches of free time.

Meanwhile, under Burns's leadership, the whole plan of the *Museum* had been altered. The original scheme had been merely to collect the existing songs. For this task—at least for all the songs that were printable—Johnson's first estimate of two volumes was not a serious understatement. Burns, ransacking the collections of instrumental music, and stealing time from his farm work to listen to a fiddler playing over the pieces that had interested him, discovered, however, that Scottish music was teeming with good tunes to which no words had ever been set. The reels and strathspeys which fiddlers and pipers played as dance tunes had just as much lilting charm as the airs of traditional songs. His plan now was nothing more nor less than supplying words to every cottage melody which was capable of vocal interpretation. He was also making musical experiments in tempo, finding that gay tunes played in slow time might be transformed into 'the very language of pathos'. The name 'Museum' was growing steadily more inappropriate; the work was becoming an experimental laboratory in both poetry and music. Probably Burns never fully defined, even to himself, the scope of the ambitious project he did not live to achieve, but the more than three hundred songs he left are evidence that if anyone could have achieved it, he could.

Not that all these songs are masterpieces. Burns had no illusions on that score. His contention was always that the music was the important thing, and that a good air might better have mediocre words than none at all. Nevertheless when he was composing Scottish words to tunes of his own choice the percentage of the commonplace was small and the range of themes extraordinarily large. The critics who read autobiography into every love poem pass lightly over the fact that in some of the best love lyrics, such as 'Tam Glen', 'An' O for ane-and-twenty, Tam', and 'Whistle and I'll come to you, my lad', the speaker is a woman, and that such wholly dramatic lyrics as 'M'Pherson's Farewell' and 'John Anderson' have a more sustained intensity of emotion than the admittedly autobiographic 'Ae fond kiss'. When Burns's lyrics were commonplace it was usually because he was composing them to tunes not of his own choice; above all when such assigned composition demanded English words. Music which worked downward from the intellectual to the emotional centres could never give the same creative release as when the engagement of the emotions came first. Such was the case with the last of his major poetic projects—supplying lyrics for George Thomson's *Select Collection of Scotish Airs*— but before turning to that work something must be said of the last and finest of the poems which he did not write to music.

'Tam o' Shanter' is not only Burns's greatest single poem but one of the finest short poetic narratives in all literature. It is the only one of Burns's works of which it may truly be asserted that he opened a new

field wherein he never had the chance to reveal the
full range of his powers. In the satire and the epistle,
as in the lyric, he had abundantly displayed both his
strength and his limitations. In the versified folk-
tale 'Tam' stands alone; it is, as he said, his 'standard performance in the Poetical line'. Though he
was doubtless right in concluding that it showed 'a
force of genius & a finishing polish that I despair of
ever excelling', he might in happier circumstances
have equalled it. But here, as in the satires and epistles, his inspiration came from without, and the
stimulus was never repeated.

The story of its composition is too familiar to need
rehearsing in detail. In 1789 Francis Grose the antiquary arrived at Friars Carse in the course of a collecting tour. He had successfully published an elaborately illustrated work on the antiquities of England and Wales, and was now gathering material for
a companion volume on Scotland. The fat and jo-
vial captain, whose encyclopædic knowledge ranged
from ancient arms and armour, costume, and ecclesiastical and military architecture, to the ribald
slang of his day, was as unlike Sir Walter Scott's
bookish Jonathan Oldbuck as any man could well
be. Beside his vast erudition and ardent spirit the
amateurish antiquarianism of Robert Riddell faded
away. Grose was one of the most stimulating men
Burns ever met, and the friendship which sprang up
between them had the double basis of community
of interest and congeniality of spirit. Burns saw in
Grose's projected book an opportunity to glorify

his own birthplace, and suggested that the ruins of
Alloway Kirk were a good subject for an illustra-
tion. Grose, no doubt mentally comparing the
scrubby little church with the glories of Melrose and
Arbroath, hesitated. Alloway had neither grandeur
of architecture nor richness of historical association.
The latter, however, might be supplied. Burns had
been telling some of the tales of the supernatural
which he had heard in his boyhood, and Grose
agreed to include the picture of Alloway if Burns
would furnish a witch-legend to accompany it. Thus
casually his greatest poem was born.

Burns's qualifications for writing this tale of witchcraft were analogous to his qualifications for writing
folk-songs. In each instance he belonged by education to a world where such things were no longer
alive. But his childhood and youth had been spent
among people to whom they were still real. Intellectually he had no more belief in witchcraft than
Benjamin Franklin had, but he knew the minds of
the people who did believe. Hence the blend of
broad humour and real terror which makes the
poem unique. To an Elizabethan audience there
was nothing humorous about the witches in *Macbeth*; they were real beings inspiring fear and hatred.
To Washington Irving or Charles Dickens a tale of
the supernatural was purely an excursion into the
Land of Make-Believe. It is only when a belief is
fading but not yet dead that it can be handled with
the mixture of humour and conviction which Burns
used. Ghost stories suffered the same fate about a

century later, as scepticism regarding personal immortality became more widely prevalent. And 'Tam
o' Shanter' is as perfect in structure as it is unique in
tone. Custom cannot stale it. To read it or hear it
read for the hundredth time is still to be swept along
by the rush of the narrative and to realize more
clearly the artistry which balances each increasingly
wild episode with its introductory paragraph of humorous philosophizing. A few of its early readers,
Mrs. Dunlop among them, thought the poem scan-
dalously indecent; to the rest it was an artless effu-
sion of the Heaven-taught ploughman. If any early
reader realized that besides being a merry tale it was
a consummate work of art the opinion was not committed to print. In 1791 literary art still connoted
eighteenth-century 'elegance'.

Could Burns have had more of the society of a man
like Grose, had even young Walter Scott of Edinburgh, who in the intervals of his legal studies was
already steeping himself in the ballads and legends
of the Border, thought it worth while occasionally to
ride as far as Dumfries to visit the man whom he had
once seen in an Edinburgh drawing-room, the
world might have more poems like 'Tam o' Shanter'. But there was no one in Dumfries to provide
the necessary stimulus. Robert Riddell took much
but had little to give; his sister-in-law Maria belonged too much to the world of fashion to have any
enthusiasm for folk-tales; John Syme's taste ran
more to satirical epigrams than to narrative poetry.
And these three represented the best intellectual

companionship Dumfries had to offer. As for Edinburgh, the influences dominating the literary life of
Scotland at the end of the century were better represented by George Thomson than by Francis Grose.

In September, 1792, Burns received a letter from
a friend of Alexander Cunningham's, asking aid in
a poetical and musical venture. George Thomson,
clerk to the Board of Trustees in Edinburgh, was
two years the poet's senior and possessed all the elegance of taste which Burns's education had pro-
tected him from. Thomson enjoyed Scottish music
in his ultra-refined way, but was irked by the crudity
of the traditional songs. Baldly stated, his proposal
was to collect a hundred of the best Scottish melodies, to get a professional musician to dress them in
all the frills necessary for concert performance, and
to provide them with tidy English lyrics which
would disguise their provincial origin. In writing to
Burns, however, he did not express himself so
bluntly. After explaining that Ignaz Joseph Pleyel,
'the most agreeable composer living', had been engaged to arrange the music, he continued:

'To render this work perfect, we are desirous to have
the poetry improved wherever it seems unworthy of the
music; and that it is so, in many instances, is allowed by
everyone conversant with our musical collections. The
editors of these seem in general to have depended on the
music proving an excuse for the verses; and hence some
charming melodies are united to mere nonsense and dog-
gerel, while others are accompanied with rhymes so loose
and indelicate as cannot be sung in decent company. To

remove this reproach would be an easy task to the author of "The Cotter's Saturday Night". . . . It is superfluous to assure you that I have no intention to displace any of the sterling old Songs: those only will be removed which appear quite silly or absolutely indecent. . . .'

The publication, in short, was to be a sort of Golden Treasury of Scots music, and Burns's share in the work was to be 'writing twenty or twenty-five songs, suitable to the particular melodies' which Thomson selected. The editor said nothing, in this first letter, about his preference for English words.

No literary salesman ever received more enthusiastic response than Thomson got from Burns. The poet promised whole-hearted co-operation, but he had detected enough of Thomson's temperament to make certain reservations. In order of importance they were these. His share in the work was to be a patriotic labour of love, and he would accept no compensation. For the time being at least his participation was to be anonymous—perhaps because he did not wish his official superiors to think he was neglecting his Excise duties; perhaps because he feared that Johnson might conclude that he was deserting the *Museum*. He was not to be asked to compose unless he could do so spontaneously, and Thomson was to have free editorial authority to take or reject his contributions. Finally, 'If you are for *English* verses, there is, on my part, an end of the matter.—Whether in the simplicity of *the Ballad*, or the pathos of *the Song*, I can only hope to please myself in being allowed at least a sprinkling of our native tongue.' English verses were precisely what Thomson *was* for, 'because the English becomes every year more and more the language of Scotland,' but he hastened to disavow any wish to confine the poet to English—preferring to wait and argue it out later, poem by poem.

Greater enthusiasm, knowledge, and art were never enlisted under more incompetent leadership than in Burns's alliance with Thomson. It did not take the poet long to discover that the elaborate plan which Thomson had outlined in his first letters was really as vague as an Edinburgh fog. The editor had not yet decided on the list of airs he intended to include; he had not succeeded in getting the co-operation of the English poetaster, John Wolcot ('Peter Pindar'), to write English songs; Pleyel, who was supposed to be handling the music, soon departed on a visit to Germany and found his return route to Britain closed by the armies of the French and the Allies. James Beattie was to have been asked to furnish an introductory essay on Scottish song, but Beattie was old and ill and not really interested in the subject. In consequence of all this, Burns, who had begun on the understanding that he was to furnish only a few lyrics, shortly found himself saddled with the entire burden of the literary end of the work. Even so his position, though laborious, would not have been difficult had Thomson been merely muddle-headed. But as soon as the editor had furnished the list of the twenty-five airs he meant to include in the first number of his collection, and Burns had sent in his first group of lyrics, Thomson revealed himself as a literary tinker. He was constantly proposing amendments in phraseology—which always meant substituting banal English expressions for racy Scots ones. At times his niggling criticism was too much even for Burns's enthusiasm and good nature. One letter, for instance, began with the abrupt outburst, 'That unlucky song "O poortith cauld," &c. must stand as it stands—I won't put my hand to it again.' In later years Thomson, to sustain his pose as whole-hearted admirer of all Burns's work, carefully inked over that sentence in the manuscript. But he was guilty of worse than that. Burns, as always, was steeping himself in the rhythms of the airs to which he was composing; Thomson had to display his own musical knowledge by suggesting that the proffered song be set to another tune. The fact that to Burns the words and the tune were always inseparable never penetrated his mind.

Occasionally Burns came forward with a lyric written to an air not on Thomson's list, and at such times the editor's taste and tact were most fully displayed. For instance, Lady Elizabeth Heron, wife of Patrick Heron, from whom Burns hoped for political favours, had composed a little tune called 'Banks of Cree' and asked Burns to supply it with words. Burns told the lady he would like her permission to publish the song, and sent the words to Thomson, saying that 'the air I fear is not worth your while,' but evidently hoping that Thomson would ask for it. Thomson instead proposed setting the words to an air on his own list, 'Young Jockey was the blithest lad'. Burns replied sharply: 'My English song, "Here is the glen & here the bower" cannot go to this air; it was written on purpose for an original air composed by Mrs. Heron of Heron.' But after the poet's death Thomson erased the vetoing phrase and published the words to the tune, 'The Flowers of Edinburgh', thereby leaving Burns under the imputation of having lied to Lady Elizabeth in promising to publish her music.

Another time Burns found himself haunted by the old lilt of 'Hey tutti taitie', which a wholly unreliable tradition declared to have been Bruce's march to Bannockburn. At the end of August, 1793, his impotent fury over the Edinburgh sedition trials, combined with his enthusiasm at the news of the French levy *en masse* for the repulse of the Allied invasion, found an outlet in composing 'Scots wha hae' to this air. Historically the song is an anachronism. The ideas underlying it are those of Rousseau and Thomas Jefferson and not of the feudal Middle Ages; its very language is Scoticized English rather than the true vernacular—Sir James Murray pointed out, for instance, that in real Scots the opening phrase would be 'Scots that has'. The song owes its enduring popularity largely to the perfect union of the words with the music they were composed to. But when Burns sent it to Thomson, that worthy thought the music vulgar, and suggested that lengthening the fourth line of each stanza would fit the words to another tune, 'Lewis Gordon', which

he liked better. This time Burns yielded, accepted
the silly changes, and thereafter circulated the song
always in the weakened version. Thomson published
it in this form after the poet's death, but the appearance of the original version in Currie's edition
showed the music-loving public the immense superiority of Burns's first thought. Thomson bowed to
public opinion, and consigned his 'improvements' to
the oblivion they deserved.

In most instances, however, the public had no
chance of checking up on Thomson's disregard of
Burns's wishes, and by destroying his own end of the
correspondence, after furnishing Dr. Currie with
some carefully edited extracts from it, the editor
sought to cover up the extent of his nagging criticisms. Inasmuch as his vandalism stopped short of
destroying Burns's letters the ultimate publication
of their complete texts exposed the nature of his
fault-finding almost as clearly as if he had preserved
his own originals. He nevertheless inked out a number of passages in which Burns was too outspoken in
comment on his taste, or seemed to deny his claim
to the copyright of the poet's contributions. Thomson was intensely jealous of Johnson's *Museum*, dis-
liked Johnson personally, and resented Burns's continuing to help the rival work. Again and again in
the letters Burns would say that if a song did not
suit, Thomson was to return it, and Burns would
send it to the *Museum*. To keep the material out of
Johnson's hands, Thomson never definitely rejected
anything. He carefully docketed the letter in which

Burns said that he had given Johnson no permanent copyright in his songs, but inked over passages which indicated that Burns was contributing to the *Select Collection* on precisely the same terms as to the *Museum*.

When Burns's health was failing in the spring of 1796 Thomson sought to frighten him by a report that a pirated edition of the songs was being planned, and enclosed for the poet's signature a legal document assigning him the whole copyright. Burns, ill though he was, and careless as he had always been of his literary property, refused to sign, and sent instead 'a Certificate, which, though a little different from Mr McKnight's model, I suppose will amply answer the purpose,' adding that 'when your Publication is finished, I intend publishing a Collection, on a cheap plan, of all the songs I have written for you, the Museum, &c.—at least of all the songs of which I wish to be called the Author.' This was tantamount to telling Thomson that he had a claim on the first serial rights only, and though Thomson later published two different texts of what he alleged was Burns's deed of assignment, he never produced the original holograph, and it was not preserved among his papers. In after years Thomson tried the same trick on Sir Walter Scott and Sir Alexander Boswell. He had succeeded in making Burns's executors believe that he owned the copyrights and was generously waiving them for the benefit of the subscription edition, but Scott and Boswell were lawyers and saw to it that where their own

work was concerned he got no more than the serial
rights.

Burns ought to have treated Thomson as Beetho-
ven did in 1813, when the editor demanded changes
in the airs which the great musician had undertaken
to harmonize:

'I regret that I am unable to oblige you. I am not accustomed to tinker my compositions. I have never done
so, being convinced that every partial modification alters
the whole character of the composition. I am grieved
that you are out of pocket through this, but you cannot
lay the blame on me, for it was your business to make
me more fully acquainted with the taste of your country
and the meagre abilities of your performers.'

But such blunt truth-telling was more than Burns
was ever capable of to a man who claimed taste and
education. He said what he thought about his songs,
but said it gently and deferentially, and left them in
Thomson's hand to be mangled or misapplied.

To go into such detail of Thomson's misdoings
would be pointless had he been merely a thick-
headed and thick-skinned editor who failed to appreciate what Burns was doing for him. But Thomson was much more than that. He represented the
whole Anglicizing tendency of the Scottish gentry
and bourgeoisie who were seeking to destroy the
language and individuality of their country. 'Now
let me declare off from your taste.—"Toddlin hame"
is a song that to my taste is an exquisite production
of genius.—That very Stanza you dislike

"My kimmer & I lay down to sleep"

is to me a piece of charming native humour.—What pleases me, as simple & naive, disgusts you as ludicrous & low.—' So said Burns in one of the passages which Thomson tried to obliterate. But Thomson's opinions were shared by most of his educated countrymen, including some of Burns's most intimate friends. Where earlier criticism of the poet's vernacular work had failed to break down his Scotticism by the very absurdity of such suggestions as imitating Virgil, Thomson tried to accomplish it by the more insidious means of minor verbal changes which individually seemed to amount to little but which in their cumulative effect would emasculate the poetry. It is generally recognized that Burns's contributions to the *Select Collection* include a much larger percentage of the conventional and the commonplace than does his work for the *Museum*; the marvel is that in the circumstances he achieved so much that was not second-rate. He was composing to order, frequently sending off by return of post the lines to a particular tune which Thomson had asked for, and his efforts were constantly hampered by his consciousness that certain themes and methods would never please the silly editor's taste. It was no wonder that many times he had to induce a synthetic emotional thrill in himself—either by putting himself through a course of admiration for a handsome woman, or by the help of a bowl of punch—in order to be able to compose at all.

His power of poetic response to music and emotion nevertheless did not fail with his failing health.

A few weeks before his death he asked Jessie Lewars, sister of one of his best friends among the Excise officers of Dumfries, to play him her favourite tune. She responded with the roguish little air, 'The robin cam to the wren's nest, and keekit in, and keekit in'. Burns, humming the tune to himself and altering the tempo, produced almost extemporaneously the beautiful 'O wert thou in the cauld blast'. From his earliest lyric to his latest, music was the catalyst which transformed emotion into poetry. Yet for more than a century after his death the dominating influence of music on his art went almost unrecognized; and George Thomson, the man who of all others among Burns's contemporaries had had the best opportunity to realize the nature and the power of his lyric expression, wrote an obituary which, besides inaugurating the legend of mental and moral deterioration in the last years at Dumfries, summed up its author's appreciation of the wit, critical acumen, and real erudition of Burns's letters by saying that probably the poet 'was not qualified to fill a superior station' to the humble one he held in the Excise. Of all the Holy Willies who eyed Burns askance during his life and after his death, he would probably, had he realized his true character, have despised Thomson most. The others were merely trying to blacken Burns's own character. Thomson was trying to destroy the vitality of Scottish song.

VII

THE SCOT

NOT merely in his struggle for livelihood and in the poetic art which immortalized him was Burns a Scot of the Scots. He was equally so in his religion, his politics, and, above all, his patriotism. Only in this last was he untypical of his generation. Yet such statements are misleadingly simple. All they can safely mean is that Burns, like all men in all ages, was influenced in thought and conduct by the environment in which he lived. Nevertheless, in a nation so small and self-contained as Scotland in the eighteenth century the pressure of environment was felt to a degree unrealized in larger and more cosmopolitan communities. In England during Burns's manhood the social and literary worlds of Burke and Sheridan and Horace Walpole, of Cowper, of John Wesley, of Godwin, of Blake, touched each other only lightly and tangentially; in the rising generation of Wordsworth, Jane Austen, Lamb, and Byron the separations would be even wider. Scotland by comparison was all of a piece. Even her greatest philosophers, Adam Smith and David Hume, even the much-travelled and Anglophile Boswell, retained their national stamp.

Though in their final form Burns's religious ideas differed little, if at all, from the sentimental 'com-

mon sense' deism of England and France, the
process by which he reached them was Scottish.
The rigidity of the doctrines to which he was sub-
jected in his youth determined the vigour of his reaction from them. As David Hume would scarcely
have been so militantly sceptical if he had been
reared in a milder faith, so Burns might have been
less sentimental. His earliest teachings, it is true,
did not stress the more rigorous themes in Scottish
Calvinism. The preaching of Dr. William Dalrymple of Ayr, whose church the Burnes family attended during the years at Alloway and Mount
Oliphant, was notably mild and gentle; William
Burnes's own little 'Manual of Religious Belief',
though it gave a reasonably orthodox definition of
the Fall of Man, was silent on such doctrinal points
as predestination and the Four-Fold State. Undoubtedly, therefore, the Old Light tenets of Daddy
Auld of Mauchline made a deeper impression on
Burns's eighteen-year-old mind than they would
have done had he been exposed to them from in-
fancy. Yet Burns had encountered *The Man of Feeling* before he left Mount Oliphant; the doctrines of
sentiment and deism were in the air he breathed;
his emotional nature would have brought him to
them sooner or later, regardless of other stimuli.
The most that can be attributed to Auld is a little
hastening and intensifying of the process of revolt.

Despite his constant citing of Young's exhorta-
tion, 'On Reason build Resolve', Burns's approach
to life and ideas was always emotional and not

intellectual. When he described himself in 1786 as having little of divinity 'except a pretty large portion of honour and an enthusiastic, incoherent Benevolence,' his self-analysis had his customary accuracy. To him, as to the New England Unitarians and to a man like Mark Twain, escape from the orthodoxy of his youth had come as a relief and not as a loss. Calvinism had erected a system of thought as rigidly deductive as the science of geometry. Starting from certain 'self-evident' axioms like the omnipotence and omniscience of God, the fall of man, and the literal authority of the Scriptures, it had created a religious philosophy from which all emotion except fear had been removed. Through the sin of Adam all men had earned damnation, but the inscrutable mercy or caprice of God would choose a remnant minority for salvation—for His merit, not theirs. Human faith and human righteousness were filthy rags.

This cold determinism outraged Burns's sense of fairness and justice, as it outraged Channing's and Emerson's and Holmes's. It seemed to him that the New Lights were 'squaring Religion by the rules of Common Sense, and attempting to give a decent character to Almighty God and a rational account of his proceedings with the Sons of Men.' But in investing their deity with human benevolence and loving-kindness, the New Lights were also, again like the New England Unitarians, more or less unwittingly surrendering the supernatural sanctions of religion and assimilating their ideas to those of the Deists. God was the 'Great First Cause, least understood'; Christ tended to sink from Godhead to merely an inspired human teacher; personal immortality became a pious hope instead of a divine promise. If man were indeed immortal, the surest passport to salvation was righteous living rather than adherence to a particular creed. And the guide to righteous living was the still small voice of conscience, the Moral Sense which Francis Hutcheson had taught was an innate human faculty.

In his attitude towards these doctrines, Burns was a man of his century and a Scot of his century. The rigidity of the Kirk, so unlike the comfortable looseness of Anglican theology, left him no place within its pale, even though he never openly severed his connexion. As a youth he had, along with most of his countrymen, read popular works of divinity like Boston's *Four-Fold State*, Fisher's *Marrow of Modern Divinity*, and Cole *On God's Sovereignty*. In 1791, when his rural neighbours of the Monkland Friendly Society insisted on adding these and other books to their co-operative library, Burns obediently ordered them from Peter Hill, and lumped them all together as 'damned trash'. Though he told James Candlish in 1787 that after having 'in the pride of despising old women's stories, ventured in "the daring path Spinoza trod"; . . . experience of the weakness, not the strength, of human powers, made me glad to grasp at revealed religion,' it was not the revelation of the Kirk. Not even his infatuation for Clarinda, though it made him momentarily qualify his admiration for Milton's Satan, could compel him to bow the knee to Calvin. 'Mine', he told her when she undertook to preach orthodoxy to him, 'is the Religion of the bosom.—I hate the very idea of controversial divinity; as I firmly believe, that every honest, upright man, of whatever sect, will be accepted of the Deity.—If your verses, as you seem to hint, contain censure, except you want an occasion to break with me, don't send them. . . . "Reverence thyself" is a sacred maxim, and I wish to cherish it.'

His fullest statement approximating to orthodoxy was written to Mrs. Dunlop in 1789:

'I have just heard Mr Kirkpatrick preach a sermon. He is a man famous for his benevolence, and I revere him; but from such ideas of my Creator, good Lord, deliver me! Religion . . . is surely a simple business, as it equally concerns the ignorant and the learned, the poor and the rich. That there is an incomprehensible Great Being, to whom I owe my existence; and that He must be intimately acquainted with the operations and progress of the internal machinery, and consequent outward deportment, of this creature which He has made; these are, I think self-evident propositions. That there is a real and eternal distinction between virtue and vice, and, consequently, that I am an accountable creature; that from the seeming nature of the human mind, as well as from the evident imperfection, nay, positive injustice, in the administration of affairs both in the natural and moral worlds, there must be a retributive scene of justice beyond the grave; must, I think, be allowed by every one who will give himself a moment's reflection. I will go farther, and affirm, that from the sublimity, excellence, and purity of His doctrine and precepts, unparalleled by all the aggregated wisdom and learning of many preceding ages, though, *to appearance*, He Himself was the obscurest and most illiterate of our species—therefore Jesus Christ was from God. . . .'

Another time he told the same lady, 'We can no more live without Religion, than we can live without air; but give me the Religion of Sentiment & Reason.—You know John Hildebroad's famous epitaph—

> "Here lies poor old John Hildebroad,
> Have mercy on his soul, Lord God,
> As he would do, were he Lord God,
> And thou wert poor John Hildebroad."—

This speaks more to my heart, & has more of the genuine spirit of Religion in it, than is to be found in whole wagon-loads of Divinity.' This was the same mood in which he had told Clarinda, 'My creed is pretty nearly expressed in the last clause of Jamie Deans's grace, an honest weaver in Ayrshire; "Lord, grant that we may lead a gude life! for a gude life maks a gude end; at least it helps weel!" ' Reason and Sentiment, but with the sentiment much more powerful than the reason, these were the dominant forces in Burns's religious attitude.

Nevertheless Burns was more courageous than many of his contemporaries in accepting the logical consequences of belief in universal benevolence. No

man knew more clearly the warfare between flesh
and spirit, but he was convinced that both were the
gifts of God. The lines which so shocked Wordsworth,

> 'But yet the light that led astray
> Was light from Heaven',

are his frankest summary of his experience. Whatever sufferings his passions had brought upon him,
the passions in themselves were noble. Asceticism
had no appeal for him. He took life as God made
it, and saw that it was good.

Taken by themselves, his utterances to Clarinda
and Mrs. Dunlop might not be above suspicion.
Burns had every motive for wishing favourably to
impress both women, and might have feigned an
interest which he did not feel, or at least have overstated his belief and understated his doubts. But
here, as in his feelings towards his children, what
he said when he may have been on dress-parade is
confirmed by his letters to his intimates. In 1788
he wrote to Robert Muir, then dying of tuberculosis:

'. . . An honest man has nothing to fear.—If we lie
down in the grave, the whole man a piece of broken machinery, to moulder with the clods of the valley—be it so;
at least there is an end of pain, care, woes and wants: if
that part of us called Mind, does survive the apparent
destruction of the man—away with old-wife prejudices
and tales! . . . . A man, conscious of having acted an
honest part among his fellow-creatures; even granting
that he may have been the sport, at times, of passions

and instincts; he goes to a great unknown Being who could have no other end in giving him existence but to make him happy; who gave him those passions and instincts, and well knows their force.'

In the same tone he said six years later to Alexander Cunningham that the two great pillars which bear us up, 'amid the wreck of misfortune and misery', are the 'certain noble, stubborn something . . . known by the names of courage, fortitude, magnanimity' and 'those feelings and sentiments which, however the sceptic may deny them or the enthusiast disfigure them, are yet, I am convinced, original and component parts of the human soul; those *senses of the mind* . . . which connect us with, and link us to, those awful obscure realities—an all-powerful and equally beneficient God, and a world to come, beyond death and the grave.'

The countryman of Francis Hutcheson could scarcely have indicated more clearly his obligations to the Glasgow philosopher. Burns's 'senses of the mind' are merely Hutcheson's Moral Sense a little expanded. Like Channing and Emerson, having rejected the authority of the church, and with it the supernatural sanctions of Christian doctrine, Burns fell back on the authority of intuition to support concepts which he was unwilling to abandon. The idea of the deity, and His relations with mankind, which is embodied in these passages, he never deviated from; what seemed to many of his readers shocking irreverence was aimed at intolerance and hypocrisy, and not at religion. But he was not able in all moods to convince himself of personal immortality.

At times he tried to argue himself into belief:

'The most cordial believers in a Future State have ever been the Unfortunate.—This of itself; if God is Good, which is, I think, the most intuitive truth in Nature, . . . is a very strong proof of the reality of its existence. . . .'

and he went on to reason that since the ideas of 'OUGHT, and OUGHT NOT' are 'first principles or component parts of the Human Mind' and are synonymous in our thinking with virtue and vice, the soul *must* be immortal because, 'except our Existence *here*, have a reference to an Existence *hereafter*, Virtue & Vice are words without meaning.' Thus he argued to Mrs. Dunlop, who had just told him that her daughter, Mrs. Henri, was widowed after a few months of marriage. But not long before he had said to Cunningham,

'All my fears & cares are of this world: if there is another, an honest man has nothing to fear from it.—I hate a man that wishes to be a Deist, but I fear, every fair, unprejudiced Enquirer must in some degree be a Sceptic.— It is not that there are any very staggering arguments against the Immortality of Man; but, that like Electricity, Phlogiston, &c. the subject is so involved in darkness that we want Data to go upon.—One thing frightens me much: that we are to live forever, seems too good news to be true . . .'

An emotional man deprived of any authority except emotion on which he could rely, Burns's religious views are of a piece with his politics and his patriotism. To get at the underlying emotions is to explain what appear to be glaring contradictions in thought. John Ramsay of Ochtertyre found Burns's politics 'abundantly motley', for the poet managed to combine strong sympathy for the exiled House of Stuart with liberal if not republican views on contemporary affairs. To Ramsay this seemed like being simultaneously Catholic and Protestant, whereas it was only putting into words the unexpressed philosophy that had swayed the popular mind of Scotland for close on a century. Burns admired Lord Balmerino, noblest of the victims of the '45; he also admired John Wilkes. Between a devoted Jacobite like Balmerino and a radical Whig like Wilkes, there was only one point in common: both were anti-Hanoverian. That one point reconciles Burns's divergent opinions. The Stuarts embodied the ideal of Scotland as an independent nation; even though from the accession of James to the death of Anne they had governed Scotland from London they still commanded the loyalty of their old kingdom. But the Georges were, as Burns said, 'an obscure, beef-witted, insolent race of foreigners whom a mere conjuncture of circumstances kickt up into prominence and power.' His phrase summarizes in vigorous prose the spirit of the ribald satirical songs by which Scotland had avenged herself for the humiliations following the rebellions of 1715 and 1745.

Burns was far from maintaining that the Stuarts were perfect, or that the Revolution of 1688 lacked justification; what he did maintain was that the Hanoverian system was not perfect either.

On the Fifth of November, 1788, Burns attended a special service of thanksgiving held at Dunscore Kirk to celebrate the centenary of the Revolution. The Rev. Mr. Kirkpatrick's remarks about 'the bloody and tyrannical House of Stuart' sent the poet home to write an open letter to his friend David Ramsay, editor of the Edinburgh *Evening Courant*, in which he mingled unveiled satire with a sense of historical perspective hardly to be looked for in an 'unlettered ploughman'. He went to church, he said, to give thanks for 'the consequent blessings of the Glorious Revolution. To that auspicious event we owe no less than our liberties religious and civil—to it we are likewise indebted for the present Royal Family, the ruling features of whose administration have ever been, mildness to the subject, and tenderness of his rights.' But, he continues, cannot we give thanks for our present blessings 'without, at the same time, cursing a few ruined powerless exiles, who only harboured ideas, and made attempts, that most of us would have done, had we been in their situation?' 'Were the royal contemporaries of the Stuarts more mildly attentive to the rights of man? Might not the epithets of "bloody and tyrannical" be with at least equal justice, applied to the house of Tudor, of York, or any other of their predecessors?' In short, the Stuarts were only fighting for prerogatives which former monarchs of England and contemporary monarchs of France enjoyed unchallenged, and the poet disclaims ability to determine whether their overthrow 'was owing to the wisdom of leading individuals, or to the justling of party.' And then comes the sting:

'Man, Mr. Printer, is a strange, weak inconsistent being.—Who would believe, Sir, that in this our Augustan age of liberality and refinement, . . . a certain people, under our national protection, should complain, not against a Monarch and a few favourite advisers, but against our whole legislative body, of the very same imposition and oppression, the Romish religion not excepted, and almost in the very same terms as our forefathers did against the family of Stuart! I will not, I cannot, enter into the merits of the cause; but I dare say, the American Congress, in 1776, will be allowed to have been as able and enlightened, and, a whole empire will say, as honest, as the English Convention in 1688; and that the fourth of July will be as sacred to their posterity as the fifth of November is to us.'

The concluding sentence of that peroration is paraphrased from a speech John Wilkes had delivered in the House of Commons ten years before. Manifestly Burns followed, closely and sympathetically, the utterances of the English radicals and reformers; it is well known that 'A Man's a Man' is 'two or three pretty good prose thoughts inverted into rhyme' from the writings of a former Excise

officer named Thomas Paine. Like most European
liberals, Burns admired the leaders of the American
Revolution—one of the toasts which gave offence in
Dumfries is said to have been his proposal of the
health of George Washington as 'a better man' than
William Pitt—and his admiration would be intensified by obvious parallels between the grievances of
the Americans and the Scots. His Jacobite sympathies were wholly emotional, and in part condi-
tioned by the fact that the Jacobites had written
all the good songs. One suspects that he would just
as readily have taken the Catholic view of the
Reformation if Scottish Catholics had embalmed
their lost cause in poetry. When he looked at current affairs, his reason backed his feelings. Politically, Scotland had almost as much to complain of
as the American colonies had had. In some respects,
indeed, she had more. American towns had been
free to manage their local affairs by a system of
representative government; in Scotland the muni-
cipalities, like the country's representation in Parliament, were self-perpetuating oligarchies. Burns,
in common with thousands of men of higher rank,
had no vote even in the government of his own
burgh. Yet his dislike of the system and his contempt
for most of its leaders would probably have expressed itself only in occasional satires had it not
been for the outbreak of the French Revolution.

A movement for reform of both burgh and parliamentary government was under way in Scotland.
George Dempster, one of the few men of indepen-

dent mind among the Scottish representatives at
Westminster, advocated such measures of reform as
would allow 'the industrious farmer and manufac-
turer [to] share at least in a privilege now engrossed
by the great lord, the drunken laird, and the drunk-
ener baillie.' Country gentlemen of unimpeachable
character took up the agitation, and Burns's letters
to men like William Robertson of Lude, John
Francis Erskine of Mar, and Richard Oswald of
Auchencruive, show that he looked to such leadership as the hope of the country. When his conduct
was under inquiry Burns declared that he had, as a
government employee, taken no active part, either
personally or as an author, in the movement for reform, but that as a man he 'would say that there
existed a system of corruption between the Executive Power & the Representative part of the Legis-
lature, which boded no good to our glorious Constitution; & which every patriotic Briton must wish
to see amended.'

The early stages of the French Revolution roused
the enthusiasm of the more liberal-minded men of
all classes in Scotland. A dinner in Edinburgh to
celebrate the second anniversary of the fall of the
Bastille was attended by a group of university stu-
dents which included John Allen, stepson of the
poet's friend Robert Cleghorn, by numerous country gentlemen like his friend Robert Riddell and
his acquaintance Alexander Fergusson of Craigdarroch, and by Lord Daer. It seemed to men like
Craigdarroch and Daer that the popular interest

in the principles of the Revolution might be harnessed for the benefit of Scotland in speeding measures for burgh and parliamentary reform. Actually the brief alliance with French sympathizers delayed reform for forty years. All the vested interests of Great Britain rallied to support Burke's condemnation of the revolutionary principles, and the counterattack swept away every attempt to alter in the slightest degree the existing scheme of things.

The full weight of the counter-attack was not felt at once. Indeed, it was a Scotsman, James Mackintosh, who published the fullest and best-reasoned of the numerous replies to Burke. Besides seeking to confute Burke, Mackintosh tried to rally his countrymen to the cause of reform by citing their medieval reputation as lovers of liberty who would die rather than surrender their freedom. Certain passages in Mackintosh were probably as directly responsible for the composition of 'Scots wha hae' as *The Rights of Man* was for 'A Man's a Man'. But as the Revolution swept on with increasing bloodshed to the execution of Louis XVI and as mobs in various parts of Scotland, including Edinburgh itself, celebrated King George's birthday by burning Henry Dundas in effigy, the authorities became panicky. Scotland felt the heaviest force of their fright. Long latent memories of the '45 revived at Whitehall, and to the dread of Scotland as a focal point for rebellion was added the practical detail that repressive measures could be better organized there than in England. England had a few constituencies, like London and Westminster, in which enough people were enfranchised to give a really popular vote, and a few members of Parliament whom neither fear nor bribes could silence. Scotland had neither. Hence the counter-revolutionary reign of terror struck first and hardest at Scotland.

Early in 1793 several leaders of the Friends of the People, a society organized to agitate for parliamentary reform, were arrested on charges of treason. Lord Daer was a member of the society, too, but the authorities, doubtless afraid that not even a packed jury could be trusted to convict the son of a popular earl, made no move to seize him. They contented themselves with lesser, but still conspicuous, victims, and before the series of trials—conducted with such disregard of justice as in Henry Cockburn's opinion had not been seen in Britain since Jeffreys's Bloody Assizes—was over Thomas Muir, Thomas Palmer, and several other reform leaders had been condemned to long terms of penal transportation. All opposition was crushed in Scotland for a generation. Henry Erskine, the one man who dared to raise his voice in defence of justice and common sense, paid for his temerity by being voted out of his office as Dean of the Faculty of Advocates. One of the last of Burns's satirical ballads commemorates the event, in which a young man just admitted to the bar, Walter Scott by name, voted with the majority to punish Erskine for having the courage of his convictions.

Such was the background against which Burns

undertook to display himself as a Friend of the People. He never, so far as can be learned, actually joined any of the reforming organizations, but it was not in Burns's nature to conceal his opinions. From the time when he appeared in Edinburgh drawing-rooms wearing a waistcoat of Foxite blue and buff, and inscribed on a window-pane at Stirling verses about the successors to the Stuarts being 'an idiot race, to honor lost', he was marked as a character who would bear watching. The wonder is not so much that he came near to losing his job in the Excise as that he ever succeeded in getting it. If William Corbet and Graham of Fintry had not been the generous and friendly souls they were, the poet's service career would have ended in 1793, and he might even have shared the fate of Muir and Palmer.

To note some of Burns's words and deeds during 1791 and 1792, and realize that for every reckless phrase that reached paper there were doubtless a score uttered over the punchbowl, is to marvel at the poet's escape. His phrase about the House of Hanover, already quoted, was written in the privacy of Robert Riddell's library, but it is hard to believe that he did not say equally sharp things in more public places. His most intimate friends in Dumfries were avowed sympathizers with the Revolution. Dr. James Maxwell had witnessed the execution of the king, cherished the handkerchief he had dipped in the royal blood, and was well enough known to the authorities to have his revolutionary connexions violently denounced by Burke on the floor of the House of Commons. John Lewars was tainted with 'D–m–cratic heresy'; Syme, after enrolling, like Burns, in the Dumfries Volunteers, became heartily disgusted with the whole wretched business; Maria Riddell was a parlour revolutionist who on her visits to London associated 'with a very pleasant set of Sans-culottes'. Throughout 1792 Burns had let slip few opportunities of proclaiming his own sympathies. In the spring he bought the *Rosamond's* carronades and dispatched them as a present to the French Convention; in the autumn, when Maria Riddell asked him to suggest a programme for a benefit night in Dumfries theatre, he chose from the repertory of the local company Mrs. Centlivre's *The Wonder: A Woman Keeps a Secret* because it contained some platitudinous lines about British liberty which could be given political significance by well-timed applause. Either on this occasion or another the crowd carried the matter further than Burns had anticipated.

When 'God Save the King' was called for, a group in the pit which included some of Burns's friends shouted for 'Ça Ira' instead. The ensuing clamour came to the verge of a free-for-all fight. In his defence Burns avowed that he never opened his lips 'to hiss, or huzza, that, or any other Political tune whatever' because he looked on himself 'as far too obscure a man to have any weight in quelling a Riot; at the same time as a character of higher respectability, than to yell in the howlings of a rabble.'

In other words, by sitting still and not applauding the national anthem he made himself just as conspicuous as if he had joined in the call for 'Ça Ira'. He was anything but the obscure individual he claimed to be, and it was apparently his public conduct on this occasion that led to his being reported to his superiors as a disaffected person.

Seemingly the idea that his opinions might get him into trouble had never occurred to Burns. The threat of an official investigation threw him into a humiliating panic, and must also have alarmed his friends in the higher ranks of the Excise. It is difficult otherwise to account for Supervisor Corbet's coming in person to Dumfries to look into the charges. An accusation brought against a minor officer in the service was scarcely in ordinary routine a serious enough affair to call in one of the highest officials; the inference is that Corbet was rightly fearful of the results if Burns were investigated by an unfriendly agent. Accordingly the Supervisor examined the poet across a dinner-table in company with Findlater and Syme, and in that mellow atmosphere found no ground for the charges 'save some witty sayings'. But even so, Corbet, in the name of the Board, had to admonish Burns—so the poet reported to Erskine of Mar—'that *my* business was to *act*, not to think; & that whatever might be Men or Measures, it was for me to be silent and obedient.'

The hair-splitting particularity of Burns's defence of his conduct is in itself proof of the real basis of the charges against him. He revered the King, he declared, in his public capacity as 'the sacred Key-stone of our Royal Arch Constitution', but George's 'private worth, it is altogether impossible that such a man as I can appreciate.' (On the report of the King's first admitted insanity in 1788 he had said, 'I am not sure whether he is not a gainer, by how much a Madman is a more respectable character than a Fool.') He had joined no party for revolution or reform; his contributions to the radical *Edinburgh Gazetteer* had been only a couple of non-political verses. But he did not mention that in subscribing to the *Gazetteer* he had urged its editor, William Johnston, to 'lay bare, with undaunted heart & steady hand, that horrid mass of corruption called Politics & State-Craft!' and to 'dare to draw in their native colours these "Calm, thinking Villains whom no faith can fix"—whatever be the Shibboleth of their pretended Party.' Oddly enough, the *Rosamond's* carronades had not been brought up against him. Hence he naturally did not mention them, but he took occasion to avow that though he had been an enthusiastic votary of France at the beginning, he had changed his sentiments since the Revolution had embarked on a career of bloodshed and military aggression.

Here Burns was making a Galileo recantation. On the same day on which he thus denied to Robert Graham that he any longer supported the Revolution he was using French in a letter to Mrs. Dunlop and adding that he hoped it was correct, for 'much would it go against my soul, to mar anything be-

longing to that gallant people: though my real sentiments of them shall be confined alone to my letters
to you.' Despite her repeated warnings to drop the
subject, he continued to talk about his devotion to
Liberty, his friendship with Dr. Maxwell, and his
approval of 'the delivering over a perjured Blockhead & an unprincipled Prostitute to the hands of
the hangman' until the offended lady broke off the
correspondence. Seething, as he had said of his feeling in 1788, with the impotent 'madness of an en-
raged Scorpion shut up in a thumb-phial', Burns
had to express himself to someone. He had lied
about his sentiments, and though the lie was to save
his family rather than himself, its taste was bitter in
his mouth. Nor was he helped by the realization
that all Scotland was equally cowed and that if he
had not made his recantation he would have shared
the fate of four other citizens of Dumfries who were
imprisoned for drinking seditious toasts. Once before
he had challenged authority in the shape of the tem-
poral power of the Kirk, and had come off not un-
scathed but undefeated. Now he had challenged
much less openly the State, and had learned the difference in strength between a vital institution and a
moribund one. The realization of defeat shook his
self-confidence as nothing else had ever done, and
helped to drive him to such unmanly conduct as
that which followed his quarrel with Maria Riddell.
He who had refused to sell his songs for money
had sold his independence for bread. That it was
his children's bread and not his own might salve

his conscience, but it could not heal his pride.

The Man of Feeling had bruised himself against a harsher reality than anything Harley had found in London or Bedlam; the idealist in politics had learned the substance of which politicians are made. Brimming with New Light theories about the Moral Sense, convinced by primitivists like Rousseau that 'mankind are by nature benevolent creatures' whom mere stress of hunger and poverty makes selfish, Burns had come naked to battle against the forces of alarmed conservatism and privilege. Like thousands of others he had taken seriously the slogans of 'Liberty' and 'the Rights of Man', and had seen in the French Revolution the signs that the world's great age was beginning anew. His disillusionment went deeper than mere realization of his own unsafe position as a government employee. He was watching the ancient forces of selfishness and aggression capture the movement from which he had hoped so much. His enlistment in the Dumfries Volunteers was not wholly from dread of further jeopardizing his livelihood by holding aloof. He still believed in the principles of the Revolution, but that belief did not commit him to endorsement of its practices, and so, like many another pacifist, he found himself, still hating war, nevertheless engaged in supporting it.

Though he dared no longer give direct utterance to revolutionary sympathies, he could, and did, express his detestation of war in a song like 'Logan Braes', and couple the ideas of his generation with the patriotic tradition of medieval Scotland. The low estate of contemporary Scottish liberty threw into more glorious relief the traditions of Bannock-burn and the lost cause of the Stuarts. His patriot-ism accepted without question the legend that 'Hey tutti taitie' had been Bruce's battle-march, as it accepted the romantic interpretation of Mary Queen of Scots. Burns might call himself an un-prejudiced inquirer and a sceptic, but his nature had no kinship with the cool remorseless scepticism of a man like David Hume. Hume's was the keenest Scottish mind of his century; Burns, at least in the height of his rebellion against the Kirk, might have been expected to find the philosopher congenial. But Burns could endure destructive criticism only of things he hated. Hume did not confine his scepti-cism to religion, and when he brought his devastat-ing intellect to bear on the romantic traditions of his country Burns turned away in anger. He might endorse Hume's demolition of the supernatural sanctions of the church, but he was disquieted by the application of the same scepticism to the belief in immortality, and infuriated when it was turned upon Queen Mary. Hume was mentally akin to Voltaire and Samuel Butler; Burns to Rousseau and Dickens.

In repudiating Hume's treatment of Mary, Burns was unconsciously illustrating the force of Johnson's ruthless dictum, which even the loyal Sir Walter Scott could not wholly deny, that 'a Scotchman must be a very sturdy moralist who does not love

Scotland better than truth: He will always love it better than inquiry; and if falsehood flatters his vanity, will not be very diligent to detect it.' Few men have lived more honest than Burns. He would not willingly lie, nor endorse a lie; but if offered choice between a romantic story which appealed to his patriotism and an unromantic one which did not, his choice was never in doubt. His own followers, in their hostility to anything like dispassionate investigation of the picturesque legends surrounding him, continue to illustrate the same attitude. Nor, indeed, have the Burnsians monopolized this aversion to inquiry. It remained for an Irishman and an American to set forth the true details of the life of Allan Ramsay, and for another American to write the only complete and scholarly study of Henry Mackenzie and his times.

Many Scotsmen besides Burns shared his passionate defence of Queen Mary; not so many shared his general patriotism. Here Burns, very Scot of very Scot, belonged to a generation which had passed, though he prepared the way for one to come. He had much in common with Claverhouse, Lochiel, or Fletcher of Saltoun; nothing in common with Bute, Wedderburn, or Henry Dundas. In so far as the patriotism of Sir John Sinclair sought the improvement of his country by collecting and tabulating her resources, Burns was with him, but when Sinclair tried to eradicate the national speech he struck at something Burns held precious. True, Burns was like his contemporaries in snatching at everything that seemed like proof that the Scots could equal or surpass the English at their own games. He applauded the *Mirror* and the *Lounger* because they looked like successful rivals of the *Tatler* and *Spectator*; he admired Thomson and Beattie and Blair the more because even the English had to admit that these men wrote well in the southern tongue. But he deeply resented the willingness of his countrymen to sink their national identity in the Union.

'Alas! have I often said to myself,' he wrote to Mrs. Dunlop in 1790, 'what are all the boasted advantages which my country reaps from the union, that can counterbalance the annihilation of her Independance, and even her very name! I often repeat that couplet of my favorite poet, Goldsmith—

"——States of native liberty possest,
Tho' very poor, may yet be very blest."

Nothing can reconcile me to the common terms, "English ambassador, English court," &c. And I am out of all patience to see that equivocal character, Hastings, impeached by "the Commons of England." Tell me, my friend, is this weak prejudice?'

Men like Boswell and Sinclair would have answered without hesitation that it was. The Union had admitted Scotland to as much share as she could grasp of the wealth of the British Empire; commerce and industry were increasing year by year; the poor relation was beginning to live like the prosperous branch of the family. For such profits, the change of name from 'Scotland' to 'North Britain' seemed a small price. To those who shared in the new prosperity, the suggestion of a nationalist movement would have seemed rank folly or even downright treason. So long as the prosperity continued, indeed, the 'practical men' had the overwhelming majority of their countrymen with them. The emergence of Scottish nationalism as a political force to be reckoned with had to await the collapse of Scottish industry which followed the World War. With the loss of material prosperity, the Scots have begun to question the value of the system which transfers to Westminster the control of their local affairs. Scottish poverty and Scottish pride are seemingly interdependent. Removal of the one will make the nation more willing to swallow the other.

Even if Burns had shared the material prosperity resulting from the Union, instead of helping, as tenant of rack-rented land, to pay for it, his feelings would have been the same. In every fibre of his being he shared the spirit of those Scots who, in contradiction of every proverbial association of pawky caution with their race, have been among the greatest soldiers, explorers, and idealists of modern history. Montrose and Livingstone, Admiral Duncan and Mungo Park, expressed in action the national traits which he expressed in song. His calling, consciously accepted, was that of national poet; his other activities merely the 'sweat, that the base machine might have its oil'. He refused payment for his songs, because the task of supplying words to national melodies was a patriotic service, embalming and treasuring up these relics of his country's spirit to a life beyond life.

Without Burns's share in the work of gathering old Jacobite songs, for instance, and composing new ones, it may be questioned if such a halo of romance would have surrounded, in the next generation, the Rebellions of 1715 and 1745; without that halo, Sir Walter Scott would have been less readily attracted to them; without Sir Walter, the romantic vision of Scottish history would never have conquered the world. No Scottish writer of the eighteenth century, except Burns, passed on the torch of national pride. Without him, the fact that Hume and Boswell were Scotsmen, that Thomson was born on Tweed instead of Thames, would mean no more to the ordinary reader than does the fact that Swift was born in Ireland or Wordsworth in Cumberland. Without him, Ramsay and Fergusson would be forgotten minor poets who wrote in a difficult and obsolete dialect. He gathered together in his own work all that was vital in the work of his predecessors, infused it with the fire of his own personality, and sent it out again to keep Scotland alive.

Burns came at the last moment when a national poet could succeed in his task. A few decades later, and the vernacular would have sunk too low for preservation. Even as it was, he could only embalm it and not renew it as poetic speech. Except for

Lady Nairne's, scarcely any vernacular poetry written in Scotland since 1800 deserves higher ranking than the *Barrack-Room Ballads*. As a poetic influence, Burns's work was weak. As a national influence, its force is not yet spent. He revealed the richness and colour of Scottish life, and in revealing it gave direction and vitality to the long and noble line of novelists which began with Sir Walter Scott and John Galt, and continued through Stevenson to John Buchan and the late Neil Munro. Through these men the Scotland which was no longer, politically, a nation became more enduring than anything which depends on rulers and boundaries—a nation of the mind and heart, a home of lost causes, of impossible loyalties, of high romance and simple faith. It is not Scott's kings and ladies and nobles who keep his books alive; it is people like Edie Ochiltree, Jeanie Deans, Meg Dods, and Dandie Dinmont—in other words, the characters who are part and parcel of the world which Burns depicted and glorified. Steenie Steenson, like Thrawn Janet and Tod Lapraik, carries on the great tradition of Tam o' Shanter. Without Burns the Scottish novel as we know it would never have been; without the Scottish novel, the literature of the nineteenth and twentieth centuries would be as much the poorer as seventeenth-century poetry would be without the Cavaliers.

In tracing the continuing tradition of sentiment from Henry Mackenzie through Burns himself to 'Ian Maclaren' and Sir James Barrie, Professor Thompson made perforce a grave omission. The difference between the dynamic romanticism of England at the beginning of the last century—the romanticism of the young Wordsworth and of Shelley —and the insipid prettiness of the same movement in America at the same time, lies in the invigorating power of the French Revolution. By giving a fighting edge to romance, the Revolution raised it above mere fancifulness and sentimentality. His patriotism did the same thing for the influence of Burns. Without it he might today be only a minor Man of Feeling. Even as it is, he is neglected and misunderstood. The strength, the humour, the fighting edge are there, but few people care to find them.

He saved Scotland; himself he could not save. Five years after his death a group of admirers in Greenock organized a Burns Club, and Paisley and Kilmarnock quickly followed suit. The fashion spread through Scotland, and among Scotsmen in the rest of the English-speaking world, bringing in its train the erection of more, and worse, statues and monuments than have been reared to the memory of any other British individual with the possible exception of Albert, Prince Consort. Soon the movement acquired the characteristics of a minor religious cult, complete with ritual meals and a thriving traffic in relics, genuine or spurious, of its hero.

In itself this establishment as hero of a national cult might be harmless. After all, if any writer was to fill the role, Burns was the inevitable candidate, for he alone of the great Scottish writers was truly a man of the people. Not the existence of the cult, but the direction it took, is the tragedy of Burns. The sentimentality which lies, like the soft core of an over-ripe pear, at the heart of writers like 'Ian Maclaren', Sir James Barrie, and A. A. Milne, is widespread in Scotland. In the Burns cult this softness yearns to the answering softness of 'The Cotter's Saturday Night', 'To a Mouse', and 'To a Mountain Daisy', extols its hero as the Bard of Humanity and Democracy, and rejoices in the bathos of Clarinda and Highland Mary. Meanwhile the ribald magnificence of 'Holy Willie' and 'The Jolly Beggars' is neglected, the homely realism of satires, epistles, and dramatic monologues goes unread. Worst of all, the splendid treasury of more than three hundred songs, Burns's most truly patriotic work, lies almost untouched on the shelves. Radio and concert stage alike ignore them. And choice of the few that are known to the public at large runs true to the same form as with the longer poems. Probably a hundred people know 'Sweet Afton' for one who knows 'M'Pherson's Farewell' or 'Rantin' Rovin' Robin'.

The flattery of being a national hero would delight Burns. If his followers were only mealymouthed where he was outspoken, they would merely amuse him. He would not mind if they slobbered over his sins, for the unco guid were old acquaintance of his. But at the thought of his worshippers exalting his weakest work and ignoring his best, his very soul would scunner. The real Burns was not the dropper of tears over ploughed-under weeds but the man who brought in the neighbours for a kirn-night and kissed the lasses after every dance; the man who sat by farmers' ingles and on ale-house benches listening to the racy earthy talk of his people and storing his mind with folk sayings and old songs. He was not ashamed of being a Scottish peasant, the heir of all the picturesque and frequently bawdy tradition of Scots folk literature. Neither was the man who wrote, 'But yet the light that led astray Was light from Heaven', ashamed of his human nature. But his worshippers are ashamed of the best part of his nature and his work. And nobody else reads him at all.

INDEX